GABE OPPENHEIM

New York City Love Triangle, 1931
A Tale of Three Families

First published by Solicitude 2024

Copyright © 2024 by Gabe Oppenheim

All rights reserved. No part of this publication may be reproduced, stored or transmitted in any form or by any means, electronic, mechanical, photocopying, recording, scanning, or otherwise without written permission from the publisher. It is illegal to copy this book, post it to a website, or distribute it by any other means without permission.

Cover photo: "East River Waterfront and Manhattan, 1931" By the Library of Congress, from the Corbis Historical Collection, managed by Getty Images.

First edition

This book was professionally typeset on Reedsy.
Find out more at reedsy.com

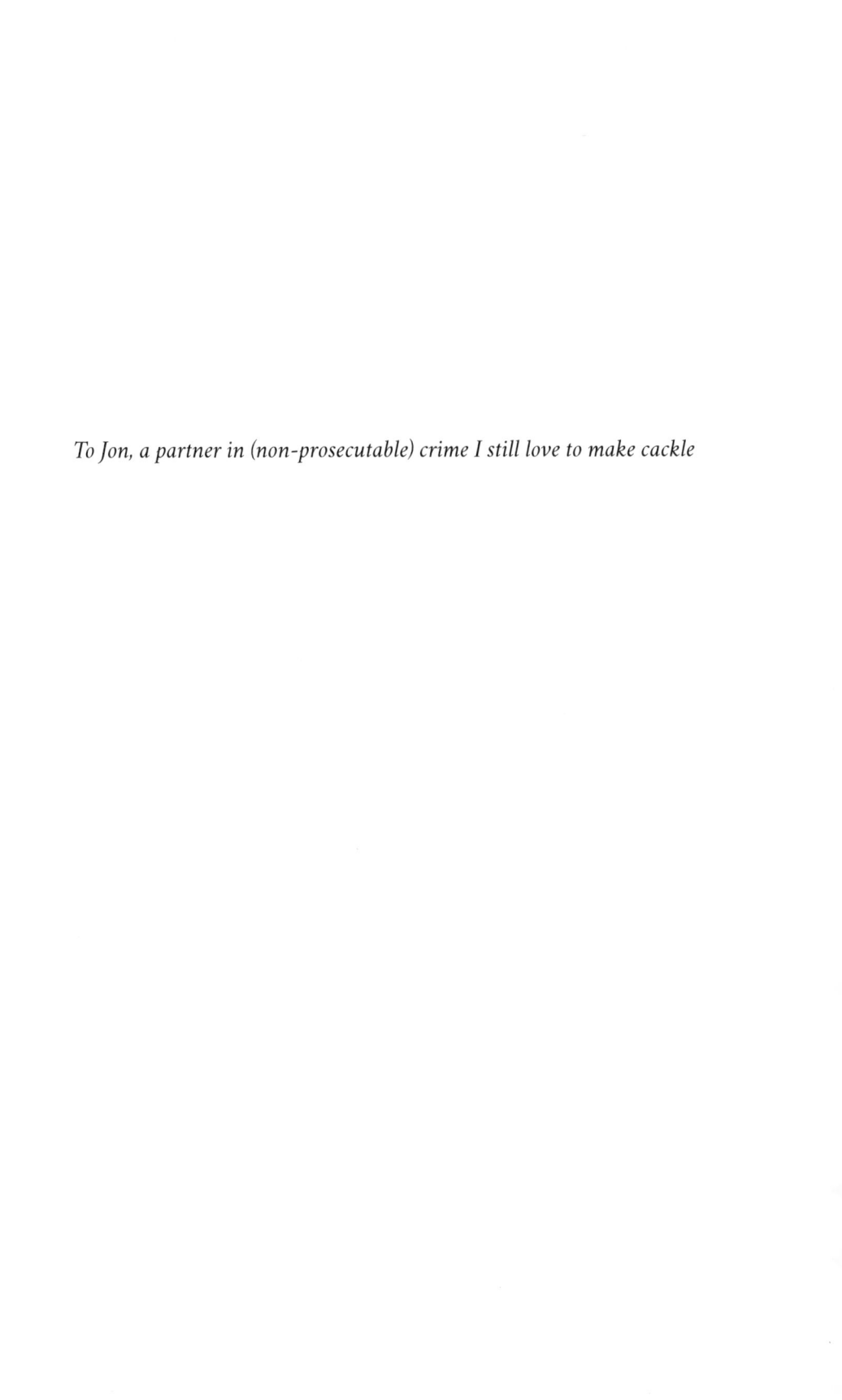

To Jon, a partner in (non-prosecutable) crime I still love to make cackle

Contents

I   Antecedents

Introduction	3
Chapter 1: Birdseye	14
Chapter 1A: 1931	38
Chapter 2: Thomashefsky	40
Chapter 2A: 1931	55
Chapter 3: Bernstein	57
Chapter 3A: 1931	89
Chapter 4: Thomashefsky	92
Chapter 5: Birdseye	95
Chapter 6: Thomashefsky	103
Chapter 7: Bernstein	118
Chapter 8: Birdseye-Thomashefsky-Bernstein	137

II   Descendants

Chapter 9: Smith	175
Chapter 9A: 1931	200
Chapter 10: Smith	205
Chapter 10A: 1931	226
Chapter 11: Thomashefsky-Bernstein-Bachelors	241
Chapter 12: Elegy for a Generation	263
Chapter 12A: 1931	281
Chapter 13: Inheritance	288

Acknowledgments	319
Notes	325
About the Author	336

I

Antecedents

"Every book is a quotation; and every house is a quotation out of all forests and mines and stone-quarries; and every man is a quotation from all his ancestors."
Ralph Waldo Emerson

Introduction

It's the most sensational and profound love story New York has ever forgotten.

* * *

A million tales have been written about Romeos and Juliets, about such violent delights having violent ends. It rings true – wild affections – raw and primal – existing adjacent to other atavistic outbursts, carnality abutting convulsive violence.

But what if we ignore the narrative crutch of the Montagues and Capulets never having gotten along – that easy star-crossedness – what about lovers' families who were never set against each other, who must navigate the surreal afterlife of lethal loves to which they're all by some relation connected?

Neither Sharks nor Jets, they all experience the outward ripples of the thing, even if one lover, by his or her passions overruled, is clearly more responsible for the awful conclusion.

What happens after "violent ends"? Also, didn't Romeo turn down a girl named Rosaline so as to be with Juliet? Presumably she survived. How did the rest of her life proceed?

* * *

A city like New York, whose substantial history of boom and bust, of slumminess and gentrification, means it has endured its fair share of grimy eras, can draw you in as much for those darker periods as those in which it has ostensibly thrived. There is in decay and absence something very palpable.

Toward the back end of the pandemic, my partner (now wife) and I had abandoned our individual apartments to move in together – to cohabitate in a beautiful co-op on Manhattan's Upper West Side.

Less than two years later, we received an email. Apparently, our building was in the 99th year of its existence, and the board president was seeking residents who might be interested in researching the structure's history for a centennial celebration the following year (and a possible Web site full of the fruits of such archival digging).

Only a handful of folks in the 45-unit, 15-floor building volunteered to undertake this work, and among them, I was easily the most avid (whether that reflects well on me I'm not really sure). So late at night in the fall of 2023, I began pouring over countless census forms, newspaper articles, draft cards.

Ultimately, I decided to post my findings not on the Web but in the lobby, as a kind of rotating museum exhibit so people would be forced to see them, whenever they left the building, upon their every return.

I'd discovered, for instance, that an unbeatable college tennis player of the 1920s, a major athlete in his day, had once occupied a top floor (Julius Seligson – his high school doubles' partner was Frank Shields, grandfather to Brooke). So had a chemist who'd fled Nazi Germany and held patents on a process for making kombucha as well as a gas mask for those with preexisting breathing difficulties (Siegwart Hermann).

I found that my own unit, the one my girlfriend and I watched reality television inside nightly to our great shared shame, had been home in 1942 to a dentist who'd helped the NYPD identify a washed-up, decomposed corpse on Coney Island by way of its teeth.[1]

But I withheld from the rotating displays – from mention in the meetings of the building's four-person centennial committee – a single incident that felt worthy of an exposition far greater than our exhibit might provide.

INTRODUCTION

In August of 1931, a 25-year-old woman living in the building – a painter trained in Paris, who'd already had her first solo show on West 57th Street, whose work had already appeared in the New York Times – Norma Jeanne Bernstein – had been driven back to Manhattan by her Tammany Hall-backed politician father, a former state assemblyman and future judge, from the summer camp she had been supervising in the Adirondacks to submit to a police interrogation. About the following.

* * *

Wednesday, Aug. 12:

It's a cool 65 degrees in New York City this summer evening. Inside the ground-floor office of a luxurious high-rise in Brooklyn, a debonair doctor has solved an enigmatic and grotesque crime of which he was the victim. And he's ready to confront the perpetrator.

Two nights earlier, someone snuck into his apartment and anesthetized him in his own bed – probably by chloroform. When he awoke the next morning, still groggy, he felt his skin split-open like paper cuts in the area of his genitals.

He'd been slashed all about his crotch – as if someone had wanted to scalpel away his member but had settled on lacerating its surroundings as if to suggest just how vulnerable he'd been. Or had been interrupted before he or she could really dig into the procedure. Stranger yet, the doctor noticed, the gashes were somewhat bandaged – not perfectly but not unprofessionally either.

How much more painful might it have been – morning air lightly kissing the raw skin exposed by these slits – had he not still been lightheaded.

Now, a day and a half later, the doctor stands resolute in his office. Furious. He knows precisely who accosted him – and she's standing feet away.

Dr. Milton Thomashefsky – who also happens to be the son of the most famous Yiddish actor in the world – turns on his assistant, Agnes Birdseye, who has been in his employ for a half-decade. Her father is Milton's former boss at a hospital and a major figure in Republican politics (former secretary to the chief of police, chief clerk to the Brooklyn District Attorney for a decade; he's also a direct descendant of the Englishmen who first settled Connecticut in the 1600s and those who fought in the Revolutionary War a century later and the cousin of the inventor of frozen foods, Clarence Birdseye).

You drugged and assaulted me, Milton says. You went through the mail. You read *her* letters.

Perhaps Agnes attempts to speak but nothing comes out.

We will never marry, Milton says. And you will never work here again.

Agnes, 5'2", 125 pounds, drops to her knees. Begs.

Yes, I've read the letters, she says. But only because I love you – and always have. And because we should marry – we still can. Everything is before us. Forgive me – please just forgive me.

The doctor has no such intention.

Please, she begs, do not tell my father about the slashes.

Bzzzz.

The doorbell to the office sounds. The doctor moves instinctively to get the door. But Agnes mulls the anonymity of the person on the other side: It could be any number of people whose knowledge of her situation would render her so embarrassed she'd rather be dead. And what does she really have left now anyway, having been led this far astray?

Agnes pulls a .38 caliber revolver from her desk drawer with her left hand, and as the doctor shifts his body weight toward the door, she fires once – *bang* – straight into his back. He crumples, but she pays that collapse no heed. Instead, she positions the gun against her own belly and fires.

And then she raises the firearm a final time – to her head.

Bang.

On WOR, 710 on the radio dial, Ozzie Nelson and his Orchestra play. Their big current hit is "Dream a Little Dream of Me."

* * *

After the two ambulances ferried away the doctor and his nurse, the police

INTRODUCTION

found in Agnes' purse certain items only an engaged couple would possess. They also found a passionate love letter— though one penned by a third party.

Naturally, the police had questions for its author, Norma Jeanne Bernstein, driven down from the Adirondacks, a resident of the building in which I live now.

What was Agnes' relationship to Dr. Milton (besides employee)? And what precisely was hers? How had she met the doctor – what had they been planning jointly?

And was there anything in the history of the Thomashefskys, in the history of the Birdseyes, to suggest such violence possible? Was there a precedent here of which they should be aware?

* * *

The interrogation of Norma Jeanne Bernstein was but a small point in a saga generations in the making (one that would echo well into the future). But it was my point of entry — for had she not been called into Brooklyn police headquarters for the inquiry, she would not have repaired from a camp she was running to the Manhattan apartment building in which I now live.

Her having returned amidst such a scandalous shooting was *itself* news in August 1931 — reporters even included her address in articles — that's how big the episode of the famed acting scion, the pedigreed nurse, and the alluring painter had become (and how I first found those articles — by searching my own address for a co-op centennial party committee).

The full story was a frenzied narrative of romance and betrayal, political power and social striving – involving preeminent families whom one would never imagine crossing paths and yet seemed to do so almost by odd destiny.

A quintessentially New York love story — in terms of how characters Old World and New had unexpectedly "met cute" and commingled — but also in the way the hasty action of one generation appeared to undermine the industriousness of those prior (as the city evolved from inchoate wooden

7

clusters into a gridded and gleaming metallic-concrete whole).

What's a legacy for, if not to be squandered?

What we have striven for and then frittered away — that, too, is New York.

(Or maybe, somewhat secretly, the parents were never alright; patterns of viciousness were already in place; the descendants had no choice but to make those mistakes already committed by their forebears — precisely the obscene actions they'd abjured.)

A story of convergence and cataclysm and recurrence.

And then, there was the painter whose portraits were so evocative and soulful they should have transcended the whole tawdry mess. A story of an artist with potential unlimited having to live in the wake of tragedy, whose downfall would wind up being another force entirely — the very rules of society.

Or were those rules the very reason the shooter felt she had no choice but to resort to violence?

All of it made for a book that had to be written. For a look at the tiny majesties achieved by family members, the little kingdoms they build together. An almost pedantic picture of all the details that can never be seen in the same light again — after the event.

**

New York City has seen its fair share of political scandals, entertainment industry blow-ups, lovers' quarrels. And it treats them all the same, really: it dives into their tawdriest aspects without pausing to consider all the generational events whose domino-topplings, one after another, brought all the figures into the picture. The papers cannot afford the pause such a consideration requires: After all, another edition must go to press daily.

And yet maybe there's something rather valid about the technique the press uses instead to plumb its city's crevices and depths, its vicious nightly doings: Shouting loudly — blaring like a police car siren — may seem artless as nonfiction exploration. But it calls attention to details in ways slower and subtler unfoldings certainly might not in a city of 8 million people whose every sordid doing may be buried by another soon.

Hey — pay attention to this — now!

The cheap glow of a neon sign brightens a dark corner all the same. This is the essence of film noir — not just the darkness in our midst, but the redeeming quality of even its most meretricious illumination.

Maybe that particular kind of radiance distorts matter. But it begins to facilitate some seeing, even if not all turns out how it first appears.

And in that manner the press goes to work in the wake of Agnes Birdseye, daughter of big shot Republican, plugging Dr. Milton Thomashefsky, son of the most famous Yiddish actor worldwide, for having a summertime, lakeside fling with Norma Jeanne Bernstein, a painter who has studied in Paris and was already rewarded with a one-woman show in a 57th Street Gallery (and whose father is a Tammany Hall insider).

The Daily Mirror writes of Agnes: "She was a stunning figure and drove her own car," calling Norma "the girl whose…charm Agnes feared most."

The Mirror, with great alliteration, discusses the newly-revealed attempted mutilation of the doctor's genitals by his nurse — part of her rage-filled revenge when she found out the doctor was wooing Norma Jeanne:

The headline: "Girl, Spurned by Doctor, Used Scalpel Before Gun."

"She used the knife to prevent him from caring for any other woman. But she bungled the job…So she shot him…And then killed herself…

"As a consequence of the shooting, the man who didn't care is lying in Jewish Hospital, Brooklyn, doomed to death or lifelong invalidism…

"The girl who couldn't have him, and wouldn't let another have him, is dead, a suicide."

The Herald Tribune says Agnes has powder burns on her body from firing the shots and that within minutes of her three squeezes of the trigger "a crowd gathered in front of the apartment house, blocking the sidewalk and extending out on the pavement. An emergency squad was sent to control the throng."

The Daily News claims Agnes fired the gun not so much to prevent the doctor from loving anyone else but because she was already so ashamed of her "ghastly" mutilation attempt and "he threatened to tell her politically prominent father how she had used her surgical knowledge in a peculiarly atrocious manner."

And yet, for as much as the Daily News claimed to know, it conceded: "The story of the love tragedy as told by the doctor brought forth a violent denial from the girl's father…and left glaring inconsistencies in the stories of the varied cast of characters that marched across the scene."

INTRODUCTION

Dr. Thomashefsky being carried out of his office by interns of the Jewish Hospital. The Evening Graphic was a New York City newspaper that existed only from 1924-1932 but in that time gave both Ed Sullivan and Walter Winchell their starts as columnists (the former was a sportswriter). It was published by Bernarr Macfadden, a vegetarian bodybuilder and proponent of "physical culture" who became a prominent magazine publisher. Family Trees below:

NEW YORK CITY LOVE TRIANGLE, 1931

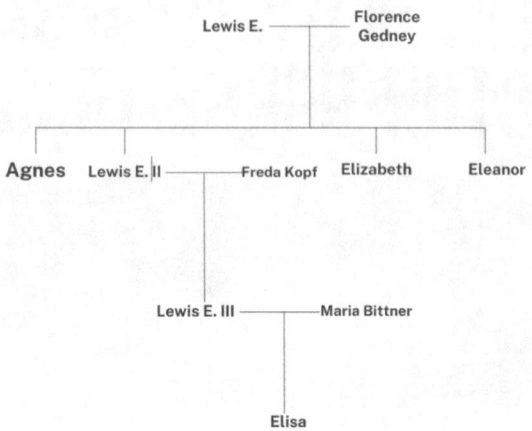

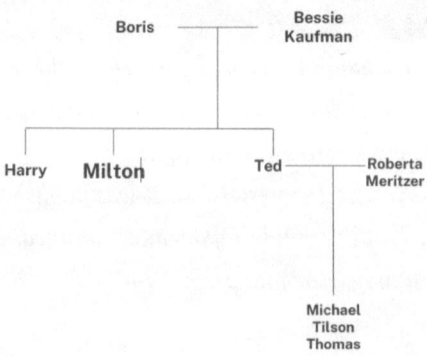

INTRODUCTION

Bernstein

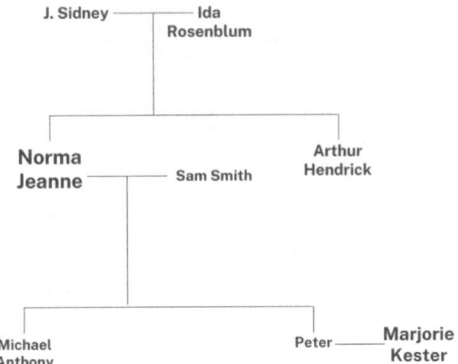

Chapter 1: Birdseye

A Don Juan doctor has a gun raised to his back by a woman behind him – Agnes Birdseye – one whose silence, whose feeling of being casually and consistently sloughed-off – will now be broken – not by words but the blast of a revolver.

The small thunderclap of short-range fire.

The shooter in this scandalous scenario being merely his assistant (and after-work plaything), she can seem a figure once meek and dependent forcefully and finally giving non-verbal voice to all she has felt. Attaining agency by way of ballistics.

Agnes Birdseye appears a quiet character who has finally exploded. A non-entity, for long periods, now seeking to be seen. As a volcano for eras appears impassive – a background feature – until its fiery, magmatic overflow. Its sudden, convulsing reassertion of presence.

Agnes' sister has a nursing degree – but Agnes merely works in a para-nursing capacity without such a credential. She has always been more shadow than fully fleshed-out personage. Never quite forceful enough to get what she wants even when occupying a role that should yield such perquisites on its own. A medical professional. The lover of an accomplished man. She should have things coming to her.

But she eventually stored a gun in a desk in a doctor's office, a domain whose first rule is *Do No Harm*.

She began slowly to contravene professional and social guidelines. She is at a breaking point when she finally yanks it from its drawer to shoot. Someone taken for granted will insist she never be so overlooked again.

Not even by someone with the charisma, power and connections of Dr. Milton Thomashefsky (which are far more considerable than the title of "doctor" simply suggests; he is New York royalty, in a way).

So Agnes Birdseye can seem – at the very moment she aims her weapon at the doctor's vertebrae.

But was she really a long-dormant character by rage awakened? By what sad, sluggish process, slow-moving molten flow, did she actually reach her eruptive point? From whence does the disregarded woman emerge?

Becoming Agnes Birdseye, gunner:

NEW YORK CITY LOVE TRIANGLE, 1931

An album compiled by Agnes' father himself – Lewis E. Birdseye I.

A very quick and very dry history of patrilineal descent (though this is an antiquated and utterly unfair way to tell history, admittedly) – from the Birdseyes who first settled America to Lewis E. Birdseye.

CHAPTER 1: BIRDSEYE

Deacon John Birdseye was a Puritan born in Reading, England, in 1616, who sailed to the New World – specifically, to New Haven, Connecticut – two decades later in 1636. He and his second wife helped found Milford, Connecticut, in 1689, and he died a year later, on April 4, 1690.

Deacon John had a son named John who had a son named Abel, who in 1727 became a lieutenant in the Stratford Militia of the Colony of Connecticut. Abel died in 1747, upon which time an inventory of his estate documented his ownership of a black slave, a Native American slave and a "mullato" slave.

Abel's second-to-last son was also named Abel and born on January 4th of either 1724 or 1725. Two decades later, this younger Abel married a woman named Phebe Thompson and fathered six children, including one Captain Jonas Abel Birdseye, who fought in the Revolutionary War at the age of 24.

Captain Jonas Abel had his own son named Abel, who moved the clan from the state of Connecticut to New York, siring Julius Hiram Birdseye in 1826. Julius Hiram stayed in the western New York region, working as a farmer and fathering a son named Arthur with Elizabeth Kliner in Waterloo, Seneca County, on Aug. 21, 1858.

This was Lewis E. Birdseye's older brother – they together represent the ninth American generation of Birdseyes – and Arthur would gain prominence as an insurance salesman and as a member of the Connecticut State Legislature, after moving to Hartford and then Farmington.

His work in the legislature was considered outsized, at least by one account. "In the face of powerful and wealthy opposition he forced to passage the bill known throughout the country as 'Birdseye's Money Shark Bill' prohibiting the loaning of money at exorbitant rates to wage earners."[2]

This bill was said to be a vital tool in the jailing of the famed loan shark D.H. Tolman for usury in Sing Sing. Tolman had long evaded jailing through a series of clever and dastardly tactics (most of which involved shell companies and myriad young women working as front-people).

From the start, Lewis E. Birdseye led a very different life than his brother, in part due to the massive gap between their births. Lewis was born in 1873, a full 15 years after Arthur. Their mother died when Lewis was 4, in 1877, and their father Julius Hiram died when Lewis was 12, in 1885, at which point a parent-less Lewis was enrolled in the DeVaux School in Niagara Falls – originally created for "Orphans and Destitute Children."

Its enrollment was about 50 such young men when Lewis Edward Birdseye entered, and the school made the boy sign a form promising he'd abstain from tobacco use; he was also a member of one of its fraternities (he is figure #2, in the back row, below).

After Lewis graduated at 19, in 1892, his brother Arthur found him a job first as a clerk at an outpost of American Express at 65 Broadway and then at the East Side Bank, at 135 Grand Street – or in the thick of the Lower

CHAPTER 1: BIRDSEYE

East Side population that so avidly patronized the Yiddish plays of Boris Thomashefsky.

But in 1895, rumors of East Side Bank's potential insolvency led to a run on the institution from which it never recovered. Lewis then spent a year as a bookkeeper before finding his first true professional calling: as an extender of credits for a public meatpacking firm – Schwarzschild & Sulzberger.

He was obviously something of a talent in the role, for in July of 1908, the American Meat Packers' Association asked him to address their annual convention in Chicago.

So he did – at the convention's second session, Monday, 2 p.m., Oct. 12, 1908: He first referred to butchers by a nickname by which they were apparently known in New Orleans – "mushrooms" – then said the more apt comparison was to "the Arab, who folds his tent and silently steals away."

"The faults arising from the packers' contractual relations with this class of tradesmen are not without remedy," he continued, "neither is the butcher the only one to be blamed for the evils that have crept into our business...Now, here is where the credit man becomes a good asset to your business. He should be alive to catch the first signs of lack of capital, especially with a new customer."

Though Birdseye was perhaps keenest in the nation at spotting a butcher unable to pay back his debts, he nevertheless was about to leave the Chicago and Kansas City-dominated meat trade – to move rather shockingly for someone of his professional training into big city politics.

Of course, he couldn't very well do that as a single man – not in his era and perhaps not yet in our own; but as it happens, the stern clerk, 5 feet and 7.25 inches tall, with brown hair and blue eyes, had been married on Valentine's Day 1900.

* * *

Florence Gedney had been born in 1874 in the village of *Milton* (what's now referred to as Rye, New York, a suburb just north of the city in Westchester), an area whose every feature practically bore that name, coincidentally or portentously or both: *Milton* Harbor, the gateway to the area from the Long Island Sound, had been built up in 1679, nearly a century before the country itself was founded, and the area featured both a *Milton* Avenue and *Milton* Point.

That name would mean so much more to Florence after her daughter Agnes' downfall.

Florence came from a line of seamen, and her father Abram, captain of a market sloop who'd chosen to become a mariner at the age of 11, carried produce (and possibly other goods) up and down the Northern Atlantic coast until he passed away at 40, reportedly a "nervous wreck" from the commercial situation then troubling shippers and the physical distress he endured manning his boat – often alone and for days and nights on end without sleep.

Florence was just two-and-a-half years old at the time, and her mother, Agnes, took up "fancy sewing" as a profession in the wake of the death, to gain some small income.

But really, Florence was alone in the world, left behind. Her mother wound up dying when Florence was 15 – and it was after this woman that Florence's first child, Agnes, was later named.

First, she met a meatpacking man of an early American background who'd nevertheless similarly grown up without the advantage of parents – Lewis Birdseye. They tied the knot on the auspicious date of Feb. 14, 1900.

CHAPTER 1: BIRDSEYE

A young Lewis Birdseye in profile.

In that particular year, Valentine's Day in New York was also marked by the auction of all the artsy worldly possessions left behind by the recently deceased Henry Hilton, a Tammany Hall judge (and the former head of Central Park) who out of an ignorance of science and detestation of its research had ordered in 1871 the destruction of a $12,000 model hadrosaur then being created based on the first dino fossil ever unearthed in New Jersey and later earned himself further infamy for his role in an American sort of Dreyfus Affair, when he refused to admit a Jewish financier into his hotel in Saratoga Springs in 1877.

Hilton having died in 1899, the turn of the century now saw, on the same day as the Birdseye wedding, the dissipation of all the valuable objects the Boss Tweed-endorsed, Tammany Hall Democratic Know-Nothing had accumulated in life but could never take with him.

Meanwhile, the Birdseyes began a proper family. Agnes was conceived so quickly after their nuptials, she was born to Lewis and Florence in December of that same year – Dec. 18, 1900 – in the Bronx. They further bore Lewis Jr. in 1903, Elizabeth (known in the family as "Betty") in 1906 and Eleanor ("Chico") in 1910; the family meanwhile moved homes, living in New Jersey, Yonkers and Flatbush.

The birth of Chico, this final child, coinciding with her father's entrance into politics, is to me no coincidence at all. Lewis and Florence's turn into the heart of the Republican machine can be seen firstly, perhaps, as the natural next step of wedded orphans who've made for themselves already a name in business. It's a logical progression in that generic Horatio Alger tale of American bootstrapping that politicians have always cynically cited to boost their credibility but that the Birdseyes seemed truly to embody. They descended both from historically notable people and those who'd had to resort to fishing for days alone; they were children of the American revolution who found themselves orphaned and then working at a meatpacking firm.

But perhaps more profoundly, the Birdseyes' political turn can be seen as a response to the ignominious behavior of the Democrat whose goods were dispersed on the day of their wedding – to the excesses of a corrupt New York political machine that a fastidious meatpacking credit clerk must have found utterly anathema to all he'd been taught on his journey from Niagara Falls to the convention in Chicago at which he spoke.

And now the Birdseyes had a family – three daughters and a son. To submit their kin to life in a crooked city without attempting to modify it for the better, to make it more livable and wholesome both, would be a betrayal of those they'd brought into the world.

As Ben Hecht in "Perfidy" wrote: "All was serene in my domain. Love, hope, gratitude abounded in my home…And yet the world continued to arm itself, to scream at itself…In this contrast between my home and the fi-fo-fumming of statesmen lay the measure of the sickness which has smitten the mind of man."[3]

Lewis E. Birdseye, no doubt excited over the prospect of proximity to power, was nevertheless more persuaded to change careers, I believe, by the opportunity that change afforded him to bridge the Hechtian gap – between the serenity of his new home and the chaos of the city just beyond its doors.

On Oct. 20, 1910, New York City's 94th mayor, the recently-elected William Jay Gaynor, who'd go on to become the only city mayor ever to be felled by an assassin's bullet (albeit one whose effects killed him after a three-year period, the slug having been lodged in his throat when a Hoboken dockworker had shot him as he boarded a ship to Europe in 1910, the very year of his election), named his new police chief:

James Church Cropsey, a 36-year-old Columbia law school graduate and resident of Brooklyn who'd served as a legal counsel to the cops in his borough from the age of 24 (at a salary, in 1897, of $2,500 a year).[4,5]

Gaynor further named Clement J. Driscoll, a city editor at William Randolph Heart's Evening Journal newspaper who'd been highly critical of the mayor in that capacity, first deputy police commissioner.[6] The mayor had earlier in the year appointed as fire commissioner Rhinelander Waldo.

Soon, Lewis B. Birdseye would be interacting with all these figures, and perhaps not as suddenly or as unexpectedly as such associations might seem.

James C. Cropsey's American origins were not dissimilar to Lewis E. Birdseye's, after all – Cropsey had a long lineage in the country but his predecessors were nevertheless humble folk, and his mother had died rather tragically. Ancestor Joost Casparse had moved from Gronigen in the

Netherlands to Brooklyn in 1652 as a bonded man – an indentured worker. His fare to reach the new country having been covered by a man named Bergen, Casparse – which name would in later generations evolve into Cropsey – had to work Bergen's farm in the neighborhood of Bay Ridge until he'd repaid the fee.

Centuries later, James Cropsey's mother died a full decade before he'd ever be appointed top cop, ostensibly, per one Brooklyn paper, from an extended shock at having witnessed the prior year the Windsor Hotel fire on Fifth Avenue, which engulfed and burned down the structure so rapidly multiple women were seen jumping from its higher floors to their grisly deaths below.[78]

So Cropsey, now head of police in late 1910, tabbed fellow Brooklynite Lewis E. Birdseye as his private secretary, which move occasioned this notice in the meatpacking newsletter The National Provisioner: "The trade was taken by surprise this week by the news that one of its best known figures had deserted it for a more strenuous life in a high official place…

"Mr. Birdseye probably has as wide an acquaintance in the meat and allied trades as any man in them…

"The position of private secretary to New York's Police Commissioner is a difficult and arduous one, requiring talents of a peculiar kind, and especially tact unlimited, qualities with which Mr. Birdseye is especially well equipped."

Within months, Birdseye was pictured at the head of a police parade down Fifth Avenue terminating at Madison Square Park – just north of the Flatiron Building at 23rd Street and just south of the Berlitz School of Language building a block up.

There he mingled quite literally with all of the aforementioned pooh-bahs – Cropsey, Assistant Commissioner Driscoll, Fire Commissioner Waldo and Mayor Gaynor himself.

CHAPTER 1: BIRDSEYE

NEW YORK CITY LOVE TRIANGLE, 1931

From left to right, that's Driscoll, Gaynor, Cropsey, Birdseye – right in the center, closest to the lens – and Waldo in the back, hovering, eyeing the photographer with displeasure.

That Waldo does hover in the back, a figure of some small menace if you pay his facial expression heed, is apt – for just six months following their collective appointments, Mayor Gaynor asked for the resignations of all the new cops, Cropsey, Driscoll and Birdseye included – and Gaynor installed Rhinelander Waldo of all people, former fire chief and background figure here, as the new police commissioner, writing in an open letter:

"I want you to banish from the Police Department, as you have from the Fire Department, even the appearance of appointments or promotions going by favoritism or by purchase."

The mayor added that there were 48 "illegal" appointments made by prior commissioners – illegal, in his mind, because they were taken from a list prepared by the Civil Service Commission not in the order of that list but in the order deemed most appropriate by the police commissioner.

CHAPTER 1: BIRDSEYE

Whether that numbered list was somehow the last word in meritocracy – or a fairer system would have demanded the free judgment of the commissioner himself in choosing from the list – was a matter that was debated for many months beyond the firing.

The entire Cropsey police team took it not to heart that Gaynor had kicked them out of office within a half year –they were proud of the reforms they'd begun to initiate – and within another half year, Cropsey was running for District Attorney of Kings County (Brooklyn); one partisan newspaper said the Republican ticket "will knock Tammanyites COLD: Cropsey, O'Laughlin, Law and Devoy."[9] As it turns out, all four won on Nov. 7, 1911 – for the positions of district attorney, register, sheriff, and county clerk.

Two months later, three days before Christmas, James Cropsey, district attorney-elect, gave a dinner at his home for all the lawyers in his office plus his just-announced new chief clerk – Lewis E. Birdseye, "a personal friend of his for years," who'd take in $3,500 per year for the work.[10] Cropsey bumped up Birdseye's salary to $4,000 not long after and to $5,000 two years later.

Cropsey, from the George Grantham Bain collection

The cases Birdseye worked on were as varied (and lurid) as the borough he helped oversee: in 1913 he helped petition authorities to move an accused killer from a jail cell to a sanatorium on account of the accused's case of tuberculosis (despite his having bashed in another boy's head with a rock, allegedly); the next year he requested bail be set at $10,000 for a serial forger of property deeds who, on the basis of those fraudulent documents, would sell properties he did not own, using 20 names in the process and evading capture by detectives for 18 months.

Birdseye meanwhile mingled in the office with a stunning array of legal talent, including Herbert H. Kellogg, a Yale-trained lawyer who'd later become a federal DA and whose son of the same name would become such a prominent figure in the field of metallurgical engineering that he'd be put in charge of America's national strategy for the production of titanium.[11]

Birdseye, along with several assistant attorneys in the office and a handful of detectives, was especially lauded for his work in the 1914 case against

Joseph Anzellotti, 31, whose house was staked out for a week from a horse stable across the street, in the service of developing evidence sufficient to raid the home on suspicion, later proven, that Anzellotti was both a drug distributor and white slaver – the latter, disquietingly racial, term known then to mean a kidnapper and sex-trafficker of (white) women.[12]

The judge pronounced Anzellotti a practitioner "of the worst vices of the devil," in handing down 40 years hard labor at Sing Sing, adding, "The full penalty of the law is none too severe for you."

One newspaper on the occasion said the instance should serve as a reminder to all citizenry that the crime they imagined so distant from their own lives in the city was in fact far closer and more related to their existential capsules than they'd ever considered.

"Secure in the safety of a higher moral plane, far removed from temptations such as are the stock in trade of the agents of vice, [they rather] turn the head and shudder, than to face the actual facts..."[13]

Crime was very close indeed.

By the 1920s, it would quite literally find its way into the District Attorney's office in the form of a fugitive murderer turning herself in after knocking off her abusive lover – but that would happen later.

As Lewis E. Birdseye rose to prominence in what many might consider an uncultivated, raffish business – meatpacking – and then attained political power in part by dealing with society's most loutish members – its criminal deviants – he simultaneously built up the tight family unit he'd long lacked – assembled a circle whose intimacy might strengthen what parts of him were by the rough world worn down daily.

The obvious method was by raising properly those children he'd already sired with Florence, including eldest child, Agnes, and her brother, Lewis Birdseye Jr (both of whom are pictured above with their father in the hamlet of Cold Spring, just north of West Point along the Hudson River in New York, Junior being the occupant of the stroller while Agnes ambles beside it).

CHAPTER 1: BIRDSEYE

Lewis strove to render this domestic milieu wholesome in a manner reminiscent of Frank Capra's eventually-Washington-bound Jefferson Smith.

From the age of 41, he served as the scoutmaster of his son's troop – No. 62 – after its former leader, a Flatbush-based reverend, was transferred;[14] perhaps an exaggeration, Birdseye was reported to have been recruited by the scouts themselves, among them his son, Lewis Jr., after he'd impressed the kids with his hiking through the Ramapo Mountain area.[15]

(Who was a doctor at the Ramapo camp – Camp Matinecock – for Queens boy scouts? None other than Dr. Joseph Kasnetz, who'd later share an office suite in the Turner Towers with Dr. Milton Thomashefsky.[16])

After becoming their scoutmaster, Lewis Birdseye encouraged his charges to learn more about flora at the Brooklyn Botanic Garden (whose entrance stood a mere 130 feet from the site where Dr. Thomashefsky's office would a decade later be constructed in the Turner Towers) [17]

In December of 1915, Birdseye's Troop 62 set about raising funds to provide two impoverished families in their area a proper holiday, which monies were delivered on Christmas Eve.[18]

Birdseye insisted his scouts learn archery – and they indeed became the only troop in Greater New York so engaged; to raise money for the necessary equipment, Lewis had them stage a minstrel show, in which his own son, as part of a chorus, sang "Kentucky Babe."[19]

Lewis Birdseye, bringing his son to work in an age long before that was encouraged, also let Jr. roam around the district attorney's office, where he was "a great favorite" of its powerful prosecutors.

"He used to amuse himself by running the elevator while the regular operator was out to lunch," one paper reported.[20]

But Lewis Sr. attempted to fortify himself not only with his immediate family – long before the age of social media and genealogy web sites, he set about locating his cousins near and far and corresponding with them regularly.

Each Christmas he sent cards to relatives featuring the legend of how their shared surname was first acquired, the tale that spurred his tutelage of archery among his scouts:

In the year 520, King Arthur assembled a coterie of expert archers at Camelot and set a prize for the best shot. But the contest evolved into a desperate and harried call to arms when a long-tailed hawk began to scrap in the sky with King Arthur's prized pet falcon, a peregrine that evenly exchanged blows at first but soon began to falter from the numerous "brunts" it had received. An adroit youth named Hubert reacted with rapidity and precision, shooting the aggressor bird through both eyes. King Arthur, after asking for the lad's name, announced he'd henceforth be called "Hubert of the Birdseye."

Of course, these Christmas communiques were just openers for Lewis – his real interest was not in Arthurian myth but in setting correspondence in motion. No matter how mundane those letters exchanged with relatives might prove, the exchanges themselves expanded and fortified his familial sphere.

And a great many correspondent Birdseyes were actually quite distinguished figures.

Lewis communicated with his cousin GFH Birdseye, Inspector in charge of the Post Office Department of Cincinnati, and GFH's son, Claude Hale Birdseye, Chief Engineer of the Topographic Division of the US Geological Survey.

CHAPTER 1: BIRDSEYE

Claude Hale Birdseye in the Grand Canyon

Claude Hale was essentially a modern-day explorer: In 1923, he led a major expedition to map out the Grand Canyon, which had only been entirely traversed to that point by 27 people and never precisely mapped out at all (to commemorate this pivotal, 76-day excursion, a four-story protuberance from the Canyon, a mountain 6,500 feet above sea level, was named Birdseye Point).

Lewis E. wrote to Henry Ebenezer Birdseye of investment house Blodget & Co. – and to Henry's brother, Clarence Frank Birdseye, a 5'6" Congregationalist Christian and lawyer, who went to prison in 1919, along with son Kellogg, for grand larceny after the pair and a third conspirator took control of Pittsburgh Life and Trust and then stripped it of all its assets.

Lewis E. wrote to Clarence Frank's son — Clarence Frank Birdseye II, of Gloucester, Massachusetts, whose U.S. Patent #1,773,079 for the double-belt freezer essentially inaugurated the manufacture and sale of prepackaged frozen foods. Yes, *that* Birdseye.

One surviving reply from Clarence, dated Oct. 30, 1930, addresses his cousin Lewis by the nickname "Lucien" and then references an actual meeting of the families in the recent past:

"A few days ago I ran across a negative of the 'family tree' which we discussed when you dropped in to see me at Gloucester last summer…We were very glad to get the picture of your daughter Eleanor, who evidently is a mighty fine girl. The family was also glad to receive the snapshot of the two youngest kids and myself."

Another missive back from the inventor of frozen victuals to Lewis, dated March 13, 1931:

Dear Cousin:

I am "sorry" that the wheel did not bear more directly on the Birdseye branch of the family. It is the only part of Father's genealogical Records which I have run across…

The Eastern Point House is progressing on schedule, but we are not planning to move into it until about the middle of June.

Sincerely yours,

Clarence

CHAPTER 1: BIRDSEYE

GENERAL FOODS COMPANY
GLOUCESTER, MASSACHUSETTS

DEVELOPMENT DEPARTMENT

March 13, 19 31

Mr. Lewis E. Birdseye
The Jewish Hospital of Brooklyn
Classon and St. Marks Avenues
Brooklyn, New York

Dear Cousin:

I am sorry that the "wheel" did not bear more directly on the Birdseye branch of the family. It is the only part of Father's geneological records which I have ran across. If anything else turns up you may rest assured that I shall be glad to send it along to you.

The Eastern Point house is progressing on schedule, but we are not planning to move into it until about the middle of June.

Sincerely yours

Clarence

Clarence Birdseye
EWH

Clarence's sister Miriam also received Lewis' Christmas card. She worked in the Department of Agriculture in Washington, D.C. – one of the few women in a position of federal power – developing extension courses for farmers to maximize their production. She wound up traveling to every state to spread her work.

Her reply to Lewis began: "Dear Cousin-Whom-I-Should-Like-Someday-to-Meet."

It ended: "When you next come to Washington, won't you let me know?"

There's no extant record of Lewis E. Birdseye Sr. making such a trip to D.C. to meet Miriam, but then again, he'd never required physical proximity to feel the kinship of these cousins – to increase that feeling of domesticity he lacked as a boy once sent to a school for orphans.

He found ample connection in the writing, and it sufficed.

His wife Florence embraced a kind of larger networking, too – only her reaching out was of a political nature. She was a member of the New York State Woman Suffrage Party in the 1910s.

While national suffrage for women was achieved by way of a constitutional amendment in 1920, certain states put the issue of women voting to the public earlier – New York State among them, in 1917.

The state's official party authorized Florence to be one of its poll watchers for that vote.

Florence oversaw the tabulation of yays and nays in Kings County's Assembly District 2, Election District 4 – the surviving document from which records 179 votes in favor and 131 opposed (plus 10 left blank and 4 that were for some reason or other voided).

And so women in New York, herself and many Birdseyes besides, achieved the right to vote.

Her daughters were nearing the age when they'd be able to exercise that right: Not yet 15, Agnes Elizabeth Birdseye graduated PS 99 in Midwood in 1915[21] and a year later, attended a Saturday evening surprise Halloween party (on Oct. 28) for her friend Violet Smith, on which occasion the clique surreptitiously decked out Violet's house in seasonally spooky colors and waxed the floor, so that everyone might dance after playing parlor games.[22]

Agnes then studied in the Packer Institute,[23] a junior college originally founded to be a highly Christian institution for girls in the early-19th century but that was now more attuned to topics less prayerful and more political – almost confusingly so – after its first site had burnt down:

"Packer likes to call [its political philosophy] progressive conservatism or sometimes conservative progressiveness. Some say that it is neither conservatism nor progressiveness, but liberalism. It is necessary to examine these terms which mean such different things on different lips."[24]

CHAPTER 1: BIRDSEYE

A public-domain photo of the Packer Institute (Brooklyn Museum).

Soon, Lewis Jr., once the plaything of every counselor in the DA's office, would be a high schooler at Erasmus Hall and then a student of the New York State Nautical School, from which he was the only graduate in 1922.

Licensed as a third officer in the Merchant Marines, he'd then set sail aboard the steamer East Cape for India in July of 1922. A year later, Agnes would finish her studies and begin work as a nurse-assistant in the office of a handsome ear-nose-and-throat doctor.

Chapter 1A: 1931

Becoming Agnes Birdseye, gunner: It's a story complicated after the shooting by its teller — a hospitalized Dr. Milton Thomashefsky — her victim. What incentives does he actually have to be totally forthright about what has happened between him and his female subordinate (whose suicide means she cannot speak for herself)?

In his hospital bed, the doctor claims Agnes had no reason to be jealous of anyone. But then he concedes they've been out to the theater together, for joint leisure motoring trips — that she has even been inside the apartment he shares with his mother (who was absent during the chloroform incident as she was vacationing in the mountains, at the time).

Becoming Agnes Birdseye, gunner: It's a story obfuscated by what her own mourning, ashamed relatives will and won't admit, by their silences and omissions — and by the narrative distortions of her rival's family, too.

Six months earlier, Agnes showed her sister an engagement ring — a diamond solitaire. But no one will now say who bought it. The ring has been found in Agnes' purse at the scene of the crime, as well as another ring — a marriage band. No one will say who bought that piece of symbolic jewelry either.

Artist Norma Jeanne Bernstein's father insists his daughter never had any liaisons with this Dr. Milton Thomashefsky - no matter that the police and press have in their possession a love letter written by Norma Jeanne to the doctor that concludes: "Oh, did I remember to tell you, dear, darling Mickey, that I miss you so much?"

The press does see through the prevarications and outright lies. The first graf of the Brooklyn Times Union: "Woman's unrequited love and the shadowy portrait *of another girl in the scene stood today as the basis for the probably fatal shooting of Dr. Milton Thomashefsky."*

The Brooklyn Times Union even learns there was a religious element to Agnes' agonized longing:

"Miss Birdseye resented this friendship of Miss Bernstein and the physician...and often had quarreled with the doctor about it...Difference in religious faith, Miss Birdseye's being Christian, also caused the pretty office nurse much worry."

And the Times Union picks up on one more tidbit from the cops: *"In questioning Miss Birdseye's family it was learned that shortly before the shooting the nurse telephoned to her sister and cried during the conversation."* By way of explanation of these plaintive sobs, Agnes offered only the promise that she would clear up everything later that night. Except she never made it home.

She was dead before 7 o'clock.

And perhaps this is the most confounding detail in the development of Agnes Birdseye, gunner — in the reconstruction of her evolving character and final motive: the way Agnes seemed so betwixt and between just before the episode — the strange paradox of her behavior.

If she wanted to keep this man, ensure he didn't fall completely into the hands of her rival, why had she ostensibly attempted to cut off his penis (of course, we don't know that she even did make such an effort — only that the doctor insisted it happened and everyone in the world, media and police included, took his word as gospel)?

And, on the other hand, if this woman had felt betrayed by a lothario otolaryngologist, if there was premeditation to her actions, if she knew in her heart she was going to vanquish the man who'd metaphysically shattered her and then depart this Earth rather than face the legal consequences, why had she promised her own family she'd be home that night, that she'd explain the sordid mess then?

What does it mean to carry around both an engagement ring and a gun?

Chapter 2: Thomashefsky

In the summer of 2024, I reach out to Dr. Milton Thomashefsky's famed musical nephew – world-renowned San Francisco Symphony conductor emeritus Michael Tilson Thomas. He is the son of Milton's brother Ted Thomas (original name: Theodore Herzl Thomashefsky), a deceased Hollywood producer.

But an assistant replies that Michael Tilson Thomas is sick – he's suffering from glioblastoma multiforme, essentially an aggressive, stage IV brain cancer that rapidly diminishes and debases a person, quickly strips him of those qualities that render him unique – his personality, cognition, capacity to speak. Somehow, Tilson Thomas has survived for three years with the disease. But Tilson Thomas will likely never be able to sit with me, the email says.

More than a decade ago, Tilson Thomas did produce an entire stage-show (which was adapted for the screen and aired on PBS) about his family, which I watch. It very clearly elides over _both_ shootings – for there was another Thomashefsky love triangle whose outcome was death and paralysis decades before Dr. Milton ever found himself shot by his nurse.

Yet the show artfully tells the remarkable true story all the same of how the Thomashefsky family – how Milton's parents – gained tremendous fame and fortune as the first acting family of the Yiddish Theater in America.

And when you learn of Dr. Milton's family, perhaps his father most especially, you realize very quickly how essential they all were to his becoming an object of obsession – or, put another way, a wanton seducer.

CHAPTER 2: THOMASHEFSKY

* * *

When Bessie Thomashefsky, famed Yiddish actress and estranged wife of the even more famous Boris Thomashefsky, first met her cowriter on a memoir project in 1914, they conversed all day and all night in Café Royal, a hub of Yiddish theatrical schmoozing for that world's stars and intellectuals.

Bessie, crying intermittently, asked him whether anyone might be interested in the story of her ruined life.

"What they call a 'ruined life' is an interesting life for me," Tenenholz replied.

* * *

Brukhe Baumfeld-Kaufman was born in Tarashche, Kiev, Ukraine, on May 30, 1873, in a period of great Russian oppression of Jews (what else is new?) but also infighting among various branches of Chasidic dynasties. Her father, Shlomi (Solomon) Baumfeld, a merchant with many side-hustles (he was listed as a *"handler"* later on his US immigration papers) was a devote of the Talner Rebbe, known as Duvidl, "who was renowned for his sharp wit, healing abilities, and powerful sermons."[25]

Shlomi's wife, Molly, was an even greater follower of the Talner Rebbe, whom she believed in as much as God, per her daughter's later memoir (whose narrative has the quality of a folktale at times, though whether that indicates a bending of the truth I can't say).[26]

Soon Molly would need the Talner Rebbe's services urgently: After eight years of happy marriage, all three of her children had died in a week. Molly was convinced the cause was Shlomi lighting up cigarettes and smoking them in the field on Shabbos (a grave violation of the prohibition against starting fires on the day of rest).

And so she petitioned the Rebbe to help her obtain from her husband a Jewish divorce, or *get*, for his evil had brought death to all of her offspring. Had ruined her life. But the Rebbe convinced Molly that another baby was on its way and he himself would name it when the time came. Sure enough, Molly gave birth yet again – and the Rebbe named her redemptive girl "Chaya," a play on the Hebrew word for "life" (this newborn much later went by the anglicized "Clara").

And then Molly had yet another girl and once again felt obliged to seek a name from the Talner Rebbe who'd so wisely advised her to stay in her marriage earlier – only this time it was the dead of winter, absolutely frigid, and so Molly had to wrap the newborn in a pillow and swaddle that whole mass in a large fur coat to make the journey she considered compulsory, despite her own deep chill.

The Rebbe called this second girl "Brukhe"– or the Hebrew word for "blessing." And it had a double meaning of sorts, was both fact and entreaty – that the baby was a present blessing to formerly bereft parents but should also herself by virtue of the name receive grace and beneficence for the remainder of her life.

The girl was not immediately endowed with good fortune, however. After falling from a bed and sustaining a head injury, she lost the ability to speak, a faculty no doctors or witches or amulet pendants proved able to restore. Slowly, she did begin to stutter but just couldn't smoothly enunciate a sentence – much to her chagrin in front of her peers, when she'd sometimes even hiccup in the middle of a pronunciation.

Finally, her mother heard of a healer in the town of Baslav who strove to help everyone, even the *"kalikim"* – the paralyzed. As the girl herself would later refer to the healer in her memoir – he was real *"toter"* – a quack.

For the stuttering girl's remedy, for Brukhe, the man scribbled all over scraps of yellow paper, dropped them into a pot of boiling water, which he served to her in a thimble, for drinking, once the yellow had faded away and the water had become clear.

Owing nothing to this treatment, Brukhe did manage to lose her stutter over the next two years – and became quite talkative besides – leading her mother to curse the healer for restoring her daughter's capacity to speak.[27]

But she enjoyed her childhood in Kiev, despite the superstitions. She played on the ice with the *goyim* in winter and even when she fell through its cracks and blacked out, they hoisted her up and saved her from drowning.

And then the "Fiddler"-esque tales took a darker turn. As it turned out, her cool-Chasid father who dared to smoke on Shabbos, Shlomi, was a member of a secret nihilist group working to undermine governmental activities called The Red Banner. In 1881, four members of the nihilist movement, using two bombs, assassinated Czar Alexander II as he returned to the Winter Palace in Saint Petersburg.

The police arrested Shlomi but his family managed to spring him out on 10,000 rubles-bail (apparently, even the authorities couldn't believe Shlomi was involved in such a subversive cause). But in 1882, the dead czar's ignoble successor, Alexander III, implemented the May Laws, which forbade Jews from acquiring new properties outside the swath of Western land known as the Pale, as well as criminalized the issuance of mortgages or leases to Jews.

The family decided to make an escape, in separate units; Shlomi and Brukhe, all of 9 years old in 1882, first together took a horse and buggy to Radziwill, Poland, where they set off on foot across the snow-draped fields. They were joined by other refugees, who'd arranged for sleds to be waiting for them in the heavily Hebrew-populated city of Brody.

But one 10-year-old boy could not stay silent in the group of refugees with which Shlomi and Brukhe fled, even as the group heard a gunshot in the distance and dropped hard onto the frigid white snow to hide. This boy cried. The group berated both boy and mother, the latter of whom, began to cover the boy's mouth.

Finally, Shlomi and Brukhe reached the sled they'd been churning toward for hours. There was a another sled, as the group could not all fit on one. And as Shlomi and Brukhe glided toward their new future, they suddenly heard a squeal.

The mother of the boy had cupped his mouth and nasal passages so tightly and for so protracted a period he'd suffocated. The others shook the boy, doused him in water, but it was no use. He was dead.

The Talner Rebbe had named her "Brukhe" – so that she might be blessed even when she was merely called. But during this escape mission, her own father decided to dump his surname for "Kaufman" so as to avoid the possibility of being arrested for skipping bail.

The full family sailed on the S.S. Australia from Hamburg, Germany, to New York in the summer of 1882, arriving at the Castle Garden Emigrant Landing Depot, at the southernmost point of Manhattan, two days after Independence Day – July 6.

Shlomi was 38, Molly 37, Brukhe merely 8.

The processing center, the predecessor of Ellis Island, was so chaotic it gave birth to a Yiddish slang term for a place of great disorder – *kesselgarden*.

"In Kessel Garden, we wandered for three months among a lot of people with a lot of bags, so like sheep," Brukhe would recall 34 years later, "until we were sent to Baltimore. My father, I remember, called it Balta Morea."

By any name, this new city made the now-10-year-old long for home desperately. "This land is not flat land, but a piece of rock, and the more you plow, the more stones are found, but no earth," she'd write. She missed Russia though it had nothing but scorn for her kind. Home was still home.

"How my young heart was then torn by longing for Uzin (a Ukrainian city in the Kyiv Oblast), for the beloved town of Tarashche, there where I was so well off, where I had a healthy rich father and knew no care and poverty!"

There was only one small upside to the uprooting – one she could only appreciate later.

The departure from all that she knew "caused me deep wounds in my heart and made me feel strongly, more deeply than my friends, even my sisters. Maybe this was a help for me to become an actress, I should be able to feel the sufferings and joys of the heroes that I play."

She'd go by "Bessie" here.

CHAPTER 2: THOMASHEFSKY

געווידמעט מיין ליעבענדער פרוי
מיין טרייער לעבענס בעגלייטערין
מאדאם בעסי טאמאשעפסקי

"Madame Bessie Thomashefsky" reads this new-world, theatrical glamour shot.

Boris Thomashefsky was born in July 1866 just towns away from Bessie's shtetl in the Kiev region. Originally named "Baruch Aaron," he came from a long line of *chazzanim* – cantors – and this led to him being sent, at age 11 or 12, despite any personal hopes the boy may have harbored, to the singing school of Reb Nisan Belzer of Berdichev, Russia (Boris' own father, though a violinist, was also, of course, a chazzan).

A soprano, Boris was recognized immediately for the quality of his singing — but also for his vanity and transgressive tendencies. He fell for a girl in the community named Bashka, making sustained and obviously flirtatious eye contact with her even as he performed in the synagogue. "I no longer sang my solos for the Berdichev public but for Bashka alone," he'd later write. [28]

For such insolent in-shul behavior, Reb Belzer first slapped Boris in front of the entire congregation and later whipped him privately.[29]

Boris' family fled to America in 1881, arriving just 10 days after he turned 15 (and just two years before the aforementioned Russian May Laws forbade Yiddish theatrical productions in his now-former homeland).

Boris worked in a Lower East Side cigarette paper factory – at Chatham Square, the bustling intersection of eight different streets and quite a few cultures, where earlier in the year, in February 1881, three Chinese men had been badly beaten.[30]

This was the area whose gang wars had made its former name synonymous with vice and violence: Five Points. But it was now the home of countless Asian and Eastern European immigrants.

Chatham Square was also home to a synagogue[31] and a hotel run by a revolutionary for Irish Independence formerly imprisoned by the British – who then planned bombings on English soil from his new base in New York (Jeremiah O'Donovan Rossa – to whom alone a whole book could be devoted).[32]

Boris, while working his cigarette gig in what had once been the roughest neighborhood in town, took up cantorial duties at the Henry Street Synagogue, the president (or vice-president, perhaps) of which so liked his voice he invited the teenage cantor to his house to regale his Shabbos lunch guests with tunes.

At one such meal, Boris convinced his host there was great value in the business of the Yiddish theater – in fact, he knew of one Romanian troupe presently performing "Koldunya" ("The Sorceress") in London who might command large crowds in New York.[33]

It was thus that, in July of 1882, the same month he turned 16, after importing star actors with his patron's money, Boris mounted what some consider the first Yiddish theater production in America at the Winter Garden on the Bowery.

But not without substantial protest: those more settled and powerful Jews – the race's earlier-arriving upper class who greatly worried a vulgar show in the tongue of the old land might jeopardize the entire community's chances of acceptance — ordered Boris to call off the show, lest they be forced to "drive [these theatrical newcomers] out of America," to send them back "by ship to Russia and then onto Siberia."[34]

These were taken by powerless and impecunious actors as serious threats – many of those Thomashefsky strove to use locally were getting their meals by way of free charity lunches provided by a saloon on Canal Street owned by a Mr. Schreiber.[35]

Perhaps most ominously, given where this story ultimately ends, one grave warning, insisting the show must not go on, was lodged by a *City coroner* named Livay on Opening Night. In fact, the show's cowed star refused to sing in the production as a result.

Who stepped into her prima donna role of Mirele?

None other than Boris Thomashefsky himself – whose pubescence had not yet deepened his soprano and whose seductive good looks apparently lent themselves to rather convincing cross-dressing.

Of course, as with all Jewish matters, a counter-narrative exists: that the first Yiddish theater production ever, titled "Schmendrick," was held one year prior to Boris', at the same Bowery Garden Theater where his own show eventually opened; that tickets for Boris' initial production were not, as he later claimed, sold out in advance; and that Boris stepped into the leading actress' role merely because she was hoarse (that Boris' one son not involved in show business wound up performing surgery as a throat doctor is perhaps, then, not an unrelated or desultory development, but more on Milton later).

Boris' first success, if it may be called that (he certainly would have), led to him playing further women's parts, as part of a theater troupe composed of Golubok. Spector, Barsky, Rosenblum, Boyarsky, Bernstein and Zshupnik. Boris' father Pinchas was even involved.

Staging plays on Friday night and Saturday afternoon – a seminally secular move, as both slots coincided with Shabbos – they put on shows by the already-famous author Avrom Goldfaden, a rabbinical school dropout who'd written "Koldunya" and "Capricious Daughter," and also works by the mononymous Shomer.

Much of this work was altered just before showtime or semi-improvised, with the help of a line-feeding "prompter," a human positioned just beneath the stage, and nearly all of it was leavened by moments of musical outburst not always anticipated by the dramatist.

Boris sang as a girl quite a lot and to apparent acclaim.

It was a theater that had to straddle old world and new; that had to pander to tired, working class masses but also, on occasion, elevate them (otherwise, how was it any different from a cheap revue that could be seen elsewhere?); that had to define what made an immigrant American — how much of the old world should be retained and how much of the new absorbed — when the answer was still unclear to those behind the curtain.

If that sounds too much a burden for an art form to sustain, that's because it was, at least initially. Those putting on Yiddish theater were not yet fully aware of their intended message; the target audience was likewise not quite ready to receive it.

The crowds Boris envisioned never materialized.

And then he underwent his own personal change. His pubescence robbed him of the lithe soprano that had enabled him to play women's parts, forcing him into a yearslong acting hiatus, at the end of which he was a baritone.

But he was still an ambitious business mogul-manque.

He reassembled his old gang (some of whom had gone into the shirt-

CHAPTER 2: THOMASHEFSKY

making business) and set out on a national tour. Its 1887 stop in Baltimore, however mundane it might have first appeared on the calendar, would alter the history of the nascent Yiddish theater — and the course of Boris' life. It would also set in motion the violent events at the heart of this book.

A certain Bessie Kaufman, 15 years old, was then working menial jobs in Baltimore (she ripped the veins from tobacco leaves, at one such gig) — a city to which she'd migrated just four years earlier.

Bessie's sister had, by total chance, married a man who handled the arrangements of visiting theater troupes— a man whose great hyping of a certain new production at the Concordia Theater (where Charles Dickens once gave readings in 1868),[36] made a teenage Bessie desperate to attend the show. And so she acquired tickets with a friend, Annie, but kept the plan a secret from her father, whose disapproval of the theater and its ostensibly wanton purveyors she already knew.

He found out anyway and forbade her attendance, but she snuck out of the house with the help of her more-understanding mother.

She ran to her friend Annie's house and then with Annie – through a pouring rain – to the theater on Eutaw Street, a gilded palace of red-velvet seats. They were utterly soaked. Their seats were in the balcony. The curtain came up rather late, at 9 pm, and Bessie was "trembling with fear."[37]

The show was "Aliles Dam" or "Blood Libel"– a production in which Boris played many roles – a woman who lights Shabbos candles, a Chasid who's exiled to Siberia, another singer besides.

The plot: A fetching, peyes-bedecked Chasid with entrancing green eyes refuses the come-on of a *shiksa* – in return for which, the spurned gentile women and some henchmen plant a child's corpse in the Jewish home.

This triggers the general populace into perpetuating the infamous blood libel – that Jews are killing off their children so that they might make matzohs with their blood, an alleged crime for which the Jews are jailed and also sent to Siberia. Miracle of miracles – they're ultimately freed in the fifth act and absolved of the slanderous charge.

Afterward, Bessie and Annie stood outside the stage door, waiting to meet this tall actor with an "hourglass face" who'd embodied the Chasid role, but her brother-in-law told her – no, this actor is frayed at the nerves right now, on account of having played not just the Chasid role but that of the woman who lights the Shabbos candles and of the actor who sings the couplets.

Bessie ignored him, ran straight to the tall actor, looked him in the face without saying a word, then hurried back to her brother-in-law.

"What's his name?" she asked.

"Boris Thomashefsky."

* * *

At home, Bessie began to act out those scenes she had just observed on stage. "I felt in me something that I had never felt before," Bessie recalled. "Something had spoken to my heart."[38]

As her brother-in-law was in charge of hosting the local troupe, Bessie found this actor she suddenly idolized invited to her own dinner table.

Boris arrived to his first meal at her home wearing a brown coat and patent leather shoes and his signature stovepipe hat, a walking stick in hand. At one point, Boris patted Bessie on the head and, in so doing, pricked himself on a pin in her hair. He then sucked the blood from the tiny wound in a suggestive manner.

After Boris' second show in Baltimore, he snuck up on her in a blonde wig and red velvet suit as she waited in the stage wings. He planted a kiss on her cheek and said, "Hey, baby."

(In later years, Thomashefsky tasked an aide with scouting the crowd for comely admirers whom he might make out with in a special box in between scenes.)[39]

It was a self-possessed adult's playful seduction of a teenager who'd never been so frankly pursued — and it's possible Boris conducted it entirely for fun, at least at first.

But then, Boris' acting troupe returned to New York, and he stayed on in Baltimore and ran a small dramatic school for Bessie's family and friends — as if he knew, in spite of his more superficial inclinations to flirt, he might have a chanced upon a connection more profound and promising .

That didn't stop him from toying with her emotions. He had the acting club put on a production in which he kissed her on-stage (she played the bride in this show). And then he left Baltimore — only to return to the city and ignore her at the train station in favor of his male buddies who had come to greet his arrival.

Then he gave her a bracelet from New York with both their names engraved on it and made his pitch: He had refined his notion of the role she was to play in his life — she should be his partner in romance and theater both. Should star alongside him in a Boston production of "Shulamis," Goldfaden's 1883 opera about a rustic girl on her way to Jerusalem who, after getting lost and falling down a well, is rescued by the man of her dreams.

Of course, Bessie's father reviled the notion: He saw Boris for the vain, fanciful, lusty thespian he was. He detested already in Boris that habit that would ultimately land the actor's son in a violent 1931 tabloid scandal (besides wrecking Boris' own marriage first):

The mixing of work and play, employment and enticement. Never mind that Bessie was still practically a kid.

"Take care of yourself and leave my child," Shlomi, her father, begged the curly-haired stage Casanova. "She is still too young to have her head turned even by the wind in the field."

But Boris did not relent. Perhaps he had great convictions about Bessie's latent stage abilities. Perhaps he'd finally found a woman who promised to be more than just another theatrical fling. He just knew he could not progress further in life without her by his side.

Finally, after Boris' father wrote an attestation of his son's above-board intent (Bessie would perform in "Shulamis" and then be returned to Baltimore), her father relented.

But of course, nothing went according to Pinchas' letter. Bessie did not return after the great success of "Shulamis" nor after several other productions.[40] Finally, her father threatened to get her arrested if she would not come back to Baltimore. Bessie's brother-in-law suggested she marry Boris, which would render empty her father's legal threats. They were married in 1889.

Bessie had gotten what she wanted (or what Boris had manipulated her into needing).

She gave birth to Esther in 1889, Harry in 1895, Milton in 1897 and Ted in 1904.

Esther died of diphtheria the same year Harry was born – and Harry would in a small number of years become a child star on the Yiddish stage. Ted, born the day after Theodore Herzl died, had actually been named after the pioneering Zionist (he was "Theodore Herzl Thomashefsky" originally), but he'd soon truncate his surname to simply "Thomas" – all the better for advancing in Hollywood, where he'd go to work for the new film studios.

Only Milton would keep his distance from show business – and yet he, of course, would find himself caught up in the most dramatic narrative of them all.

Dr. Milton Thomashefsky, scion of the two great Yiddish stage stars, would be the child to reenact his father's unseemly, almost predatory, workplace seduction.

Chapter 2A: 1931

There are those after the event who'd rather believe Dr. Milton Thomashefsky entirely a victim — if only to resolve the dissonance at the heart of the case — who'd prefer to ignore any exploitative (or even seductive) behavior on his part that has come to light.

How did the esteemed Dr. Milton Thomashefsky himself become a patient (one paralyzed and with a grim prognosis)? Certainly not via the sort of provocative behavior once exhibited by his own father. Oh, no.

Agnes was merely another female hysteric — perhaps one so confused by the world of regular social relations she mistook professional courtesy for romantic overture. She was a dizzy dame, she had gone quite mad, perhaps from those illusions that overtake solitary ladies who withdraw from the real world into literary fantasy.

The Herald Tribune two days after the trigger-pulls:

"Miss Birdseye was overcome with jealous fury...a blonde who, police say, had reached her thirty-fifth year without ever apparently having been interested in a man...For two years, she was said to have nourished a secret affection for the doctor, who is of striking appearance. The quiet little woman, who studied medicine at night in the hope of becoming a doctor herself, became so demented in her jealousy..."

Later: "Detectives learned that Miss Birdseye lived by herself and was very lonely. She had few companions and amused herself when not studying by reading romantic novels. Her friends said that despite her quiet life, she was sentimental."

Case closed, then — this front-page shooting is perhaps not so complex after all — just a woman whose reading and re-reading of romantic literature so warped *her view of reality she believed her boss her beloved also — believed that her own feelings, however private she kept them, surely must be requited in the doctor's bosom — that this handsome man from a famous acting family was surely not just her otolaryngologist overseer but also her hero — the strapping beau destined to rescue her from a mundane, pitiful life of isolation (and books).*

Only the Herald-Tribune account turns out to have a few issues: Agnes was not in her 35th year when she pulled the trigger — born Dec. 18, 1900, she was a few months shy of turning 31. So she was still 30. Maybe an old maid by the era's standards but a person hardly out of her 20s, strictly by the numbers.

More importantly, she was not a cloistered, obsessive, involuntarily abstinent bookworm. She lived with her sister and drove around town in her own car — a Ford Coupe — and owned flashy jewelry — items a mere assistant would have struggled to afford in those first years of the Depression — without a male benefactor of some kind.

Cruising Brooklyn boulevards in bling — does that sound the hobby of a neurotic reader, an overly-chaste woman carried by fiction into murderous madness? (Also, has literature ever turned anyone actually into a paranoiac killer?)

Of course, if Agnes had not been provoked by the imagined, she must have been greatly troubled by the presence of something — or someone — very, very real.

She must have had an actual rival.

Chapter 3: Bernstein

There is the question of what parents build for their children and the degree of expectation they should have that this thing into which they're investing so much will ultimately benefit that next generation.

A question of potential loss and frittering away. Of chance romance and potential deviation.

Ponder the New Hampshire house I find myself exploring in summer 2024: Norma Jeanne Bernstein would move up here with her eventual husband, after the shootings, in 1940, on the industrial advice of Armand Hammer, the chairman of Occidental Petroleum who sold lead pencils in Lenin's Russia, collected art, funded cancer research – and is perhaps more commonly known now as the great-grandfather of the disgraced actor with a cannibal-kink Armie Hammer.[41]

The elder Armand had spotted an empty factory up here, in Newmarket, New Hampshire, Norma's husband might be able to convert for his own use. This is what led her to leave New York City.

Now, in 2024, Marjorie Diane Kester Smith, daughter-in-law of Norma Jeanne Bernstein, leads me from the garage into the house. Had we entered through the front door, we would have first encountered a painting now to our left – a portrait Norma executed of New York stage siren "Tamara" – aka Tamara Drasin, a refugee of Ukrainian pogroms who made her (stage) name in the 1933 musical "Roberta" opposite Bob Hope and Fred MacMurray.

Norma's portrait of "Tamara" was slated to hang in the lobby of the New Amsterdam Theater on Broadway, and the New York Times photographed her working on it, in a series on artists capturing their subjects (a decade later, Tamara would die in a plane crash over Lisbon on a USO tour).[42]

The piece is somber and tenebrous; the actress appears to commune with the onlooker from the shadows – her almost ambery-pink eyes, highlighting inky-black pupils, indicating hers is a past more haunting than her singing suggests.

"Everybody who knows anything about art, and I am not in that group, speaks about how skilled she is at capturing the essence of a person," her daughter-in-law Marjorie says.

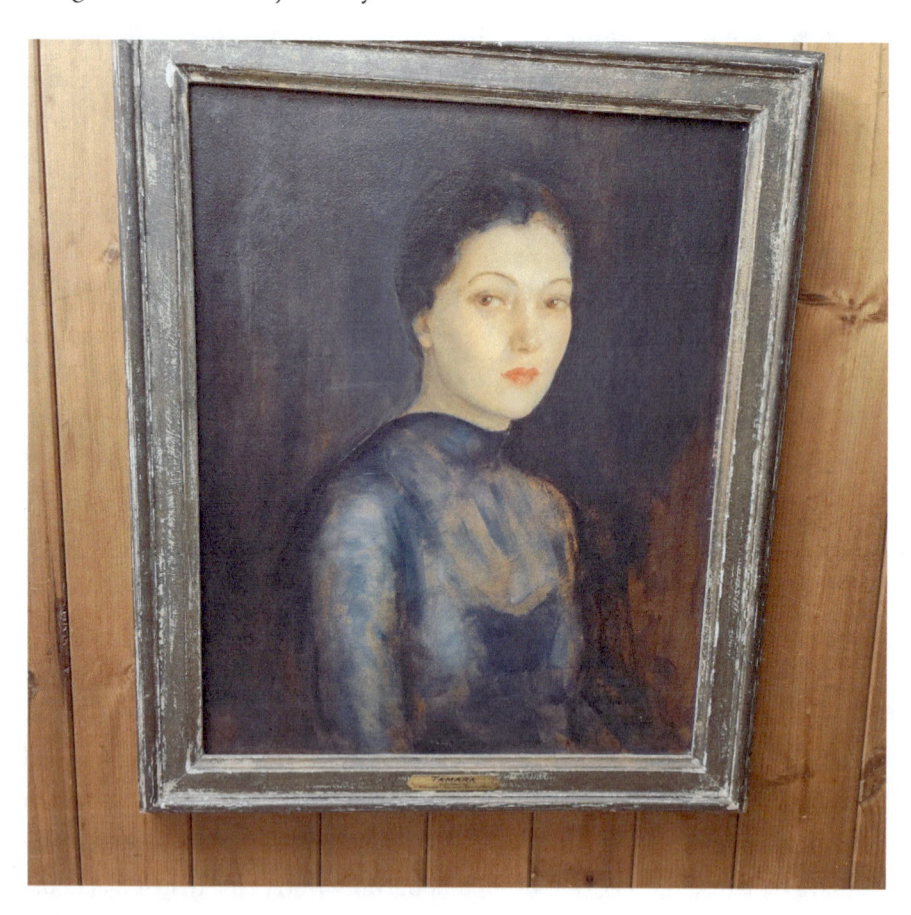

CHAPTER 3: BERNSTEIN

Norma painting Tamara. Credit: Times Wide World/The New York Times/Redux

Marjorie, 83, favoring one side, limps through the wood-paneled dining room – all the walls of which are covered in Norma's art, including a nude that Norma gifted her husband upon their marriage (not of herself; it's titled "Mimi") – and soon we've mounted a staircase, her hitched gait resulting in a slow, almost-diagonal ascent. We climb just a few carpeted steps, toward a landing with a cushioned love-seat and a window overlooking lush, green trees.

There in one of two bookcases that surround the stairway lie several guides to Mount Katahdin – the northernmost point of the Appalachian trail, in Maine, and a mountain that her late husband, Norma's son, Peter, climbed yearly for 60 years.

We keep moving – from the landing to the second floor. Were we to bear left, we'd enter Marjorie's bedroom, which also contains her office, including the computer and printer by which she produces all her campaign materials (she's up for reelection again this fall; she believes commercial printers are wasteful).

But instead, we bear right, into a vast, cabin-like, sun-bedecked atelier – the rustic studio in which Norma once painted – now ornamented with many of the portraits she produced and featuring a palette of dried-up paints and a large tin can filled with brushes.

There's also a couch, a beaten-up brown leather club chair, a metal bucket of political buttons of yesteryear, a fireplace, a cloth-draped piano and in the center, a table on which Marjorie has piled materials for my research:

A catalogue raisonné of Norma's work, full-size photocopies of newspaper pages from 1931, two of Norma's hand-written diaries (from when she was 17 and 20) and…what appear to be the love letters she actually received from Dr. Milton Thomashefsky.

And what's more, I discover there are letters here he drafted before the shooting – which I'd no idea still existed, let alone were awaiting me – but also some he apparently wrote her in the days and months *after* he'd been shot – which I'd never known existed at all.

Nobody had.

And a photo of Dr. Milton he gifted her, presumably that summer they met in the Adirondacks.

It's all too much.

Wasn't Norma's husband upset that she retained all these mementos from her tabloid courtship with Dr. Thomashefsky? I ask.

Marjorie shrugs.

Nobody is sure Norma's husband even knew, Marjorie says. *They found these envelopes, this photo of Doctor Thomashefsky, in a drawer of Norma's desk after she died in 1984.*

Norma may have kept them close to her, surreptitiously, from the time of the incident until she passed – or for more than 50 years, across residences in New York City, Nassau County, New Hampshire.

She'd never for a moment let go.

CHAPTER 3: BERNSTEIN

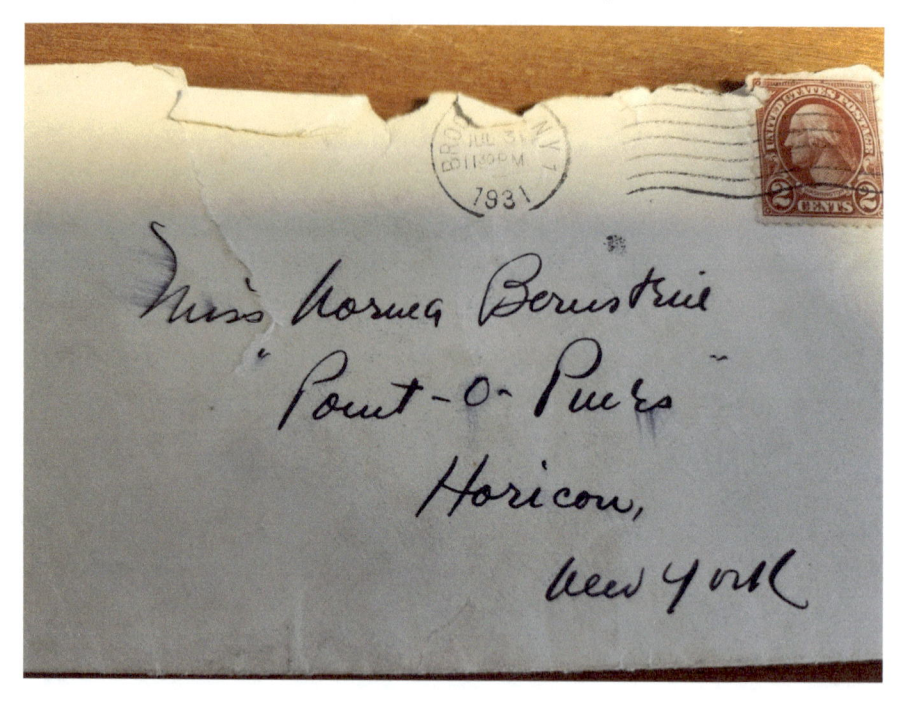

NEW YORK CITY LOVE TRIANGLE, 1931

CHAPTER 3: BERNSTEIN

[Letterhead: MILTON THOMASHEFSKY, M.D. / 135 EASTERN PARKWAY / BROOKLYN, NEW YORK / STERLING 5252]

Sweet Norma - It's so good to have you to think about - It's become chronic - acid in the past week several acute exacerbations - one when Miss Birdseye (really!) told me a Miss Bernstein had called and would call again - probably a patient but - and again when Bill Pines made casual mention of Norma - andagain when Alvin Roxcroson dropped in to say that Arthur Freund was in town - he never called to tell me how you cried when I left - and to-day, two letters about Norma - one written by herself and mis-directed so that it travelled to a few post-offices - and the other from a snake. I havn't the slightest idea who he is, but he writes quite peculiarly to "Dear Doc Mickey Thomas", tell me he has referred a customer - and then - I quote from the letter from Iago: "Didn't I see you out a few times with little Miss Bernstein? I passed her one night early this week by the side of the road necking to beat hell with one of Dr. Shields patients." Know, Miss Bernstein, little Miss Bernstein, that I love you! Know, little Miss Bernstein, that I adore you! Know that I long for you! Know that all the things in the story books have ~~ever~~ happened to me on account of you. Know that I never want to see you

A close-up of the photo Dr. Milton Thomashefsky gifted Norma Jeanne Bernstein

From whence did the artistic rival lover, Norma Jeanne, emerge?

Norma's father, Jacob Sidney Bernstein, moved rapidly in society and with tremendous ambition. With the drive and zeal not of an immigrant out to better his lot (though he technically was) but with an upper-class desire to manipulate matters to his liking; a man possessed of a determined, perhaps even ruthless, political strain.

J. Sidney, as he preferred to be called, was born in Russia on May 9, 1877, but raised in Canada. He arrived in America at the age of 20 in May of 1897, and by June of 1900, he was both a naturalized citizen and the holder of a law degree from NYU.

On New Year's Day of 1905, J. Sidney, 27, married Idalia (Ida) Rosenblum, the 19-year-old daughter of a Chicago grocer who was second-oldest of 10 children. The ceremony took place in the Cadillac Hotel, at Broadway and 43rd in Times Square, in the older wing of which Eugene O'Neill, eminent playwright, had been birthed in a suite a couple decades prior (on his deathbed, O'Neill reportedly said, "I knew it. I knew it. Born in a hotel room — and Goddamn it — died in a hotel room").[43]

Very quickly, the couple was monied. The year after their marriage, in Ida's name, they sold a four-story tenement building on East 9th Street. How they acquired it and the price at which they let it go are unclear.[44] J. Sidney also frequently fronted real estate transactions for his legal clients – perhaps this was another case of that, although if so, it's a bit odd that it was done in Ida's name. No matter – either way, J. Sidney profited.

They couple itself lived in a predominantly Jewish section of Harlem, at 3 West 112th Street, along with a live-in Polish maid named Jennie Friedrick.

Meanwhile, even as he was marrying, swapping real estate and working as a lawyer (mostly on realty transactions but also in cases involving bankruptcy – later he'd handle more salacious cases), J. Sidney was endearing himself to the Democrats who held a firm grip on the politics of swaths of Manhattan – that is, the leaders of the Tammany Hall Club.

This was not as simple as it seems, for Tammany Hall was a divided and hierarchical institution whose base was composed of hyper-local clubs filled with quarrelsome men given to polemics.

To rise in Tammany required either a great polemical conquering of these clubs or the abetting of another's conquest.

In J. Sidney Bernstein's 31st District, the Tammany Hall leader from 1899 to 1904 had been a man named Isaac Hopper, who owned the firm that constructed Carnegie Hall in 1891 and who also built the Third Avenue Bridge and Marie Antoinette Hotel and had won the contract to create the power house for the subway system.[45]

Hopper, who'd long presided over the Sagamore Club, Harlem Democratic Club, Occidental Club, Lexington Club, and Massasoit Club, was the man whom J. Sidney sought to aid in 1904.[46]

And though Hopper had been named the city's Superintendent of Buildings early that year, he'd lost enough popularity by the summer – perhaps there was those who'd found his power alarming – that the race to lead Tammany's 31st District was suddenly seen as an even one.

Hopper's opponent was Lewis A. Abrams, formerly an assistant district attorney in Manhattan and a state assemblyman for two years. He further had taken part in the Change of Grade Commission, which was a bizarrely powerful group created by the city in 1893 to settle claims arising from the alteration of city streets to accommodate depressed tracks on the New York and Harlem Railroad. In its lifetime, this group would wind up disbursing $100 million.[47]

By day, Abrams was canvassing house by house for his candidacy to run Tammany Hall in the 31st District. At night, he debated his foes vigorously in the aforementioned clubs.

On a Saturday night in August, Abrams spoke for three hours across two conclaves – only for seven different allies of Hopper to try to shout him down – *J. Sidney Bernstein included.*[48] If Hopper won, this disputation would surely be recalled and rewarded.

On Tuesday, Aug. 30, 1904, Hopper – and J. Sidney by proxy – won the race against Abrams by a score of 2,593 votes to 1,174.

The favor was immediately repaid: With the backing of his Tammany Hall Leader, J. Sidney ran for state assemblyman in the 31st District later in 1904. He actually lost to the Republican by a count of 11,104 votes to 9,115, but state legislature terms were but a year, and so in 1905, J. Sidney had a chance to vie for the position once more, and this time he won.

J. Sidney lost again in 1906 – but it didn't matter. He was now an insider – positioned to benefit when Tammany Hall did and even to wield some of the influence of the party when he backed certain projects (much later he would at least publicly appear to back a swimming pool with a sand beach in the black section of Harlem).[49]

In fact, when the Tammany Hall head of the 17th District, Samuel Marx,

CHAPTER 3: BERNSTEIN

died in 1922, J. Sidney not only filed his will (the deceased had assets worth approximately $100,000) but placed the ad in The New York Times that "respectfully requested" – *demanded* – all 17th District members attend the funeral services.[50]

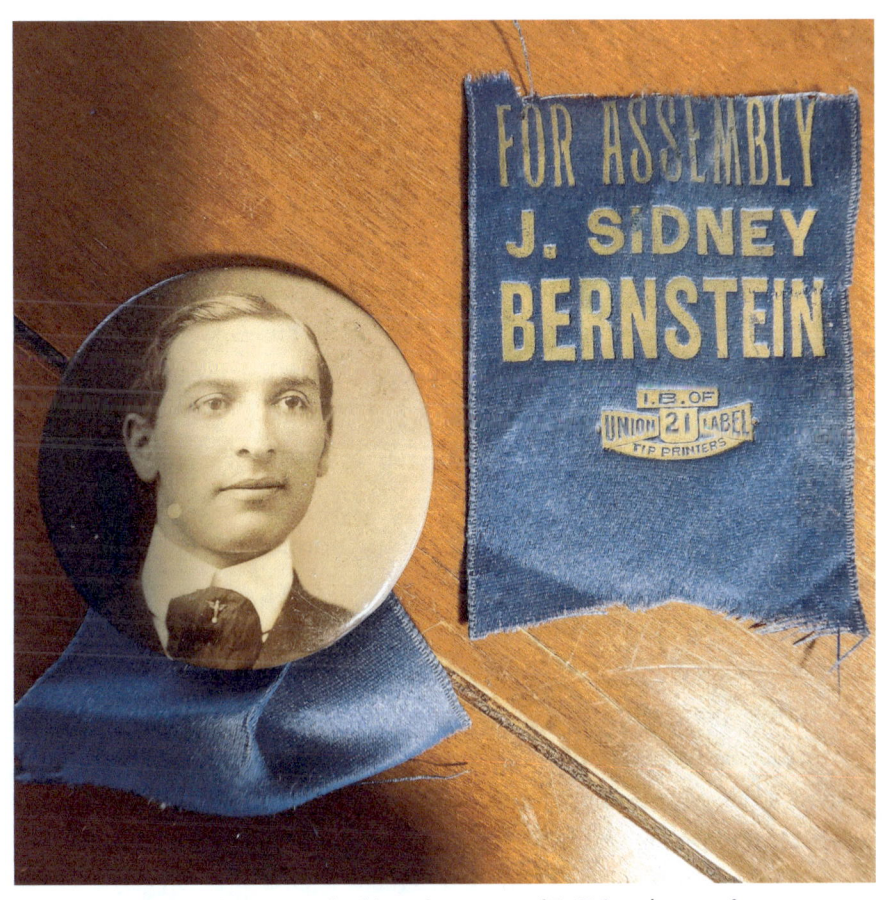

A campaign button and ribbon from one of J. Sidney's runs for state assemblyman.

By 1907, he was in charge of law firm Stroock & Stroock's real estate team, and by 1908, he had a practice of his own. He was involved in all manner of cases, some more sensational than others (those being the cases I find worthy of citation):

He represented an Ohio-born man who'd made it big in New York, as the owner of a textile facility in downtown Manhattan, whose showgirl wife Gilda was suing him for "alienation of affections" (J. Sidney negotiated a settlement in which the Ohio man had to pay $12,500).[51]

A Greek naval admiral who'd just taken part in a successful 1925 coup days later sued a Greek-born New Yorker for insurance fees allegedly collected on a steamship sunk by a submarine during World War I – J. Sidney represented the defendant being taken to court by the coup-enactor.[52]

He also represented a Harlem landlord whose tenants refused to pay a rent increase the landlord had attempted to rationalize on the basis of the particularly salubrious nature of his row homes (owing in part to the positioning of their windows). The New York Times story on this case, featured on the front page of a Sunday section, was headlined: "Death Rate So Low He Boosts Rent."[53]

Late in 1929, Anna Morlock, living in the Hotel Pennsylvania, walked into a jewelry store owned by Max E. Werner, a recent widower, who proceeded on subsequent occasions to woo her – and not just in New York but in Havana and Miami, saying, "Fate brought us together" and penning a whole host of love letters.

Werner hosted a big dinner party to announce the couple's engagement, presenting Anna with a five-carat, square-cut diamond engagement ring.

And then Anna got the phone call at her residence from Max: They should discuss some recent happenings over dinner, a proposal to which Anna agreed. An hour later Anna mentioned the dinner to a friend, who replied: "Why, haven't you heard? He got married last Thanksgiving Day."

Werner wound up offering Anna $2,000 to forget their engagement. She sued him instead for $50,000 for breach of promise, promising to present in court, as the Daily News termed it, "a packet of love letters, bound with a pale pink, tear-stained ribbon."[54] She was represented in the suit by J. Sidney Bernstein. The case should have made at least one thing painfully clear to all involved – counsel included: This was a city in which love letters could change everything.

CHAPTER 3: BERNSTEIN

***

Ida, though the daughter of a grocer, spoke several languages and could translate documents.

Her refinement, J. Sidney's cases, the couple's attainments and priorities – all of it inured to their children's benefit – or at least, it enabled them to do things – what a fateful error we make conflating the two.

J. Sidney and Ida had Norma Jeanne in February of 1906 and Arthur Hendrick in December of 1907. (If the names convey an unseemly degree of desired upward enterprise for a Jewish couple, one can at least respect the hustle, if not the pretension).

J. Sidney in an auto with Norma (right) and Arthur (middle) in the early to mid-1910s.

On her 17th birthday, Norma Jeanne – wearing formal evening dress for only the second time – saw David Warfield play Shylock in David Belasco's production of "The Merchant of Venice" at the Lyceum Theatre.[55]

Her party – was it composed of family *and* friends or just friends plus Arthur? – then tried to celebrate further at the Biltmore but was denied entry because her younger brother wasn't wearing a tuxedo. So they decamped instead to the Plaza, "where we ate and danced and made merry till the wee small hours of the morning," Norma wrote in her diary.

She wasn't merely spending dough – she wrote that in March she attempted to sell to Fifth Avenue store buyers up to two dozen pearls (seemingly from Deauville, France) she owned or was gifted so as to supplement her $5 allowance (which she was going to ask "papa" to double soon).

She enjoyed the piano lessons in popular music J. Sidney funded. But among the assortment of life choices and opportunities presented her, Norma Jeanne gave herself over to two above and beyond all others – two that didn't quite cohere one with another but would mark her equally – one by leading her to the cataclysm that would make tabloid headlines and the other by cultivating within her the gift that would earn her, however briefly, a separate and more wholesome fame (one that should be today restored):

She fell hard for high-class summer camp and the study of art.

In 1923, when she was 17, Norma Jeanne spent the summer at Camp Rondack for girls in upstate New York – 230 miles due north of her apartment building, not far from Lake Placid – which, "equipped with every modern device for the comfort and pleasure of its guests," covered 165 acres on the shore of Schroon Lake and hosted 185 campers (and featured a golf course and riding stables, at least in later years).[56]

Each year the camp culminated in an acted-out pageant. Norma attended in 1923 as possibly the oldest camper, the ages allowed then seemingly being 10-17.

She made the most of her final year. "Wonderful time in summer camp," she wrote in her diary. "Was better than ever. Got into the honor society, too. I made up my mind that I wanted to get in, and I certainly succeeded in doing it – in fact I was the first one put in this year."

A member of Bunk A, she referred to her roommates as "very nice" and posed with them in goofy photos she preserved for the remainder of her life (below).

The camp doctor this particular summer was no lothario but something of a female trailblazer: Dr. Anna Harvey Voorhis, who'd end up on ship called the American Merchant in July of 1932, setting off from New York for what she thought would be a two-month vacation in Europe, along with 93 other passengers, only for the ship's doctor to die – and for her to declare him dead and assume his role, making her the first woman ever to have medical charge of an ocean-liner.[57]

Back in camp, Norma referred to the experience as the "pleasantest summer ever" – while also mentioning a "Dr. Carl" and his theory of suggestion. "I wonder if there is something in [it] after all," she said. And one can't help but think about Dr. Carl Jung, already famed then, and his argument we believe ourselves in control of forces that instead actually have us in their grip .

When camp ended, Norma made her way to Albany, meeting up with her parents and embarking on a road-trip – to the Canadian side of Niagara Falls and then Chicago, where they stayed four days. They then returned eastward "via the southern route," staying overnight "at a couple of one-hotel towns" and then in Washington, D.C. and Atlantic City – hitting 10 states overall. "I really can appreciate 'lil Old New York,'" she wrote upon her return.

Captions: "Our Gang for a Change" and "Wide Awake at Taps – Per Usual"

NEW YORK CITY LOVE TRIANGLE, 1931

Dressed up for a change

CHAPTER 3: BERNSTEIN

When Norma returned from that road trip in the fall of 1923, she had her first encounter with a man whose name would pop up again and again and whose affections would not always be requited – Lloyd.

"I haven't had time to write about such unimportant things as going out with ditzy he-males," she wrote, "but this really was funny."

"Had a date with Lloyd Yom Kippur Eve – of all nites," and he "took advantage of the momentous occasion to invite me out to dinner, theatre, etc."

One can imagine this 17-year-old in a temple not even attempting prayer, giggling, while some ridiculous smooth-talker in a suit slightly too big for him speaks sweet nothings in her ear. All the same, she found not just the situation comedic but Lloyd himself quite funny. That would change.

But the reason she didn't have time for "ditzy he-males" was that other passion her upbringing afforded – her education in fine art.

From 1921-1923, that is, from the ages of 15 to 17, she'd attended an art-minded quasi-college, which was both humble and yet distinguished – the New York School of Applied Design for Women, a forerunner of Pratt, at Lexington and 30th.

While founded by a single woman looking to elevate working class females who might otherwise never be exposed to a suitable trade, offering classes in textile design, advertising and even architecture, it was nevertheless elevated by some of its personnel and patrons into much more than a vehicle for social mobility.[58] Somehow, at one point, it saw donations from Queen Victoria's daughter Princess Christian.[59] The great Art Nouveau illustrator Alphonse Mucha, renowned for his posters of Sarah Bernhardt, had taught there while on an extended tour of America and lectured there as late as the spring of 1921.[60]

In fact, the oldest artwork of Norma's preserved in her former home dates to her period attending the institute — a self-portrait sketched in pencil from November of 1921 inscribed to her mother:

"To You of Me by Me From Me With Love Norma"

But now, in the fall of 1923, Norma had applied and been accepted to the Art Students League of New York, an altogether more serious and demanding school than the institute – and she'd no time for he-males because how she fared there meant everything to her.

And yet, from the outset, she evinced a strict interest in portraiture that defied the broader curriculum the school imposed.

Her diary: "Took an exam to get into Mr. Bridgeman's (sic) Life class – and miracle of miracles, I passed. I don't see how I did as he only chooses forty of some big bunch – most of them really very good."

This is a reference to George H. Bridgman's class on drawing the male figure, which had been taken by Norman Rockwell just 12 years earlier, around 1911.[61] During Norman's time in his class and Norma Jeanne's, Bridgman would rank his students' work in numerical order at the end of each week (one of Norma's very first rankings in his class was 39 of 40).

(In just a couple decades, Norman Rockwell would illustrate an advertisement for Norma Jeanne's husband's shoe company – but we're jumping ahead.)

"I've learned a lot by taking life," Norma Jeanne wrote in her diary, "but I can't see as I'm crazy about it. It gets sort of boring doing the same figure all week. *I'm crazy about portrait class.* We started in by drawing heads, but thought I'd rather paint. Two weeks ago I started to paint my first portrait in oils.

"It certainly is fascinating work and I love it. Maybe some day I'll get good enough so that I will be able to make money doing portraits."

Her portrait instructor was Frank DuMond, who'd studied in Paris, illustrated Harper's Monthly and taught Georgia O'Keeffe 15 years earlier in this same class.[62]

NEW YORK CITY LOVE TRIANGLE, 1931

The first portrait Norma completed in Bridgman's class.

On Dec. 5, Norma wrote of pulling a 22 in Bridgman's Life class, "which is decidedly better than a 39. At any rate, I am improving. Am also improving in portrait painting – so Du Mond (sic) says. Rather encouraging to say the least."

On Dec. 27, she managed an 18 in Life, and then Jan. 19, 1924: "The portrait I did last week is the best I've done so far. Du Mond thought so too. Going to fix it up a bit and bring it in to him for another crit. next week. I sure do love to paint portraits."

March 19, 1924: "Did a pretty good pastel of Bee Powers on black paper last week. I like them on black. Very effective. Doing that other old man this week. He's the cat's eyebrows."

By the end of 1924, Norma Jeanne had attained ninth in Bridgman's class and formed a friendship of sorts with DuMond's son, Joe – an illustrator whose intense primate fascination would lead him to establish a hybrid zoo-conservatory called Monkey Jungle in Florida a decade later. In the end, though – that is, when her first three year spell, from 1923-1926, at the Art Students' League had ended – it was neither Bridgman nor Du Mond whom she credited as her most influential teacher, but a portraitist whose class she took the following year who'd spent his fair share of time around the Ashcan Realist painters: Dimitri Romanovsky.[63]

All the same, by the end of her first year at the league, Norma had received her first paid commission – a portrait of one Sylvia, painted for $25.

Also, early in 1924, she had been encouraged by the sales manager of a major Tin Pan Alley composer to submit a title page illustration for sheet music – and so she'd listened to a new single composed by Fred Fisher — "Monavanna."

Norma Jeanne was convinced this would be another number-one hit for Fisher. She had one opponent in this contest for the frontispiece and there was a race against time to convince Fred Fisher to go with her selection before he sent the tune to EB Marks' sheet music publishing house. Fisher chose her rival's work, which she scorned as inferior.

But Norma at another point won the right to design the coat catalog for the furrier B. Blosveren, whose showroom was adjacent to the Plaza on West 57th. And Norma's catalog, a beautiful contrast of long angular limbs and plush, luxuriant curvature, concealed chicly the firm's humbler business (the Blosveren family had another enterprise, apparently, located in the garment district, that once offered discounts to vaudeville stars on novelty coats made of squirrel and seal[64]).

CHAPTER 3: BERNSTEIN

B. Blosveren
43 West 57 Street NEW YORK.

Number 3822
Silver Muskrat
Border, Collar and cuffs
of Natural Muskrat Backs
46 inches long $ 195.00

NEW YORK CITY LOVE TRIANGLE, 1931

B. Blosveren
43 West 57 Street.   NEW YORK.

NUMBER 2609
Susliki Cocoa Color
Cocoa Kitt Fox Collar,
Cuffs and Border

46 inches long $ 395.00

CHAPTER 3: BERNSTEIN

Yet even as she buried herself in work, she found time to inquire about some new camp started in 1922 by a Bronx hustler named Andrew I. Albert. He was said by the papers to run colleges and had spent somewhere around $10,000 buying 55 acres of land in the Berkshire mountains – on the shores of Lake Pontoosuc – and fixing up two sections of it to be camps for boys and girls (the dormitory for the latter was a converted chicken coop that had once housed 5,000 birds).[65][66]

In the fall of Norma's first term at the Art Students League, she "went to see Mr. Albert about getting a position as a councillor (sic)" on the girls' side – Camp Wahconah.

At that New York meeting, her art and camp worlds for the first time converged: "He was interested in what I could do for the camp magazine."

There's something astounding but perhaps all-too-authentic, precious, in the 17-year-old precocious pupil of Rockwell and O'Keeffe's tutors nevertheless still being intrigued by work for a camp magazine.

The periodical was dispatched to former and future campers year-round, such that even before Norma Jeanne's first summer there, once she'd signed a contract with Andrew I. Albert, she began work on it.

"It's pretty good," she wrote, after that first issue arrived by mail. "I'm angry because they didn't use one of my poems and they made a mistake and put me down as assistant art editor instead of art editor."

It's all right there – the promise of her future and this extended adolescent sphere that will one day put that future in awful jeopardy.

Eventually, she would indeed attend this camp on the western shore of Lake Pontoosuc, being stuck at a table of anemics such that she was responsible for getting them properly fed, writing the following May: "It thrills me when I sit on the dock or on the beach or in the woods all alone." Before July 4th, she'd paddle across the lake to reach her friend Hilda's house and spend July 4th observing the fireworks with "Bill" Lennie Bronner. All aglow, he'd ask her out, only for her to say "I intended to have a nice time in *my own way*." They'd wind up attending a camp show and walking around the perimeter of the lake for their date.

And there's the third element – yes, camp, but also men.

Rewind to late 1923: Norma Jeanne had so many male admirers she could afford to turn some away – and did. She had such youthful charm, natural appeal, her very presence might imbue mundane situations with a tension non-platonic. She was suggestive to men in ways she didn't even intend to be.

She was already enamored of a doctor, too.

A blossoming 17-year-old, just months from her next birthday, right on the cusp. In the midst of Prohibition and the Roaring Twenties.

"Lloyd was supposed to come over Friday night but he had to go to Lakewood instead. I suppose I'll see him soon, tho. *No sleep lost over that.*"

"Herb was singing opera to me all evening. He has a fairly good voice. He's a nice boy."

"Got a very nice letter from Doctor H. He evidently hasn't heard what I said about him – and which unfortunately for me, his sister happened to overhear. I guess I won't talk about my body for a long time – especially in front of a third party."

"Last night, Bill Taft was over to discuss our plans for New Year's Eve." She'd recently played bridge with him. "He's certainly a dandy chap. He's going to take me to a farewell party at the Arcola Country Club and if the party breaks up too late I'm going to stay at his house that night. Has a big house in Weehawken."

The doctor was coming over to spend "the evening. First time I've seen him since the event in Cincinnati – last June. Lloyd's coming over tomorrow night. I guess we'll go to the movies."

Christmas: Leo Phillip's friend is dressed as Santa at a house party while Leo mixes cocktails. Leo hands Norma half of a small glass of his concoction. "Gee – it sure got me groggy…Leo is awfully nice. I hope he calls me up. He doesn't like music, tho, so there must be something wrong. I don't understand a person who doesn't like music."

Dec. 29: "Gerald surprised me yesterday morning by coming into N.Y.… He took Hilda and me to the movies. Lloyd was supposed to come over but the dumbbell never showed up. I guess there must be something wrong somewhere. I'll never look at that fellow again. He's got a heck of a nerve,

CHAPTER 3: BERNSTEIN

I'll say."

"The doctor was over Thursday night. I nearly fell asleep. For a fellow of 25, he's got one foot in the grave already."

"Bill Taft called up to say that the New Year's Eve Party was changed. The Arcola Country Club shut down or something, so it's going to be in the Orange Room of the Hotel Astor. That means I'll come home that night. I'm rather disappointed as it would have been fun making a night and day of it the other way."

New Year's Eve: Norma Jeanne drank and had "loads of fun" with Bill Taft and didn't get home until 5 am. One Thursday night she and Bill took a little walk and then talked till 1 am. "He's interesting to talk to. So far so good."

Later, she and Bill walked to Columbia, where he would become a pitcher for their baseball team, which had just featured on its roster Lou Gehrig, who left for the Yankees in 1923. Bill would send an Norma an inscribed photo of himself in his uniform on campus:

NEW YORK CITY LOVE TRIANGLE, 1931

CHAPTER 3: BERNSTEIN

Lines began to get crossed.

Her fellow Art League students seemed to be the ones always confiding *in her* their own love issues, to the point that Norma referred to herself in her diary as Beatrice Fairfax, an advice columnist for the lovelorn in The New York Evening Journal.

At the end of 1923, Norma was reading the Fannie Hurst novel that had just come out in October, priced at $2 – "Lummox" – about a rotund and inarticulate maid named Bertha whose silent serving of all manner of New York families enables her – she who was born beside the garbage barges of New York Harbor – now being in the right place at the right time – to help innumerable suffering humans.

Helga to Bertha: "You're like one of those tanks you are…You're all on the inside of yourself."

Norma in her diary: "Last night, I thought 'n thought 'n thought – in fact, I got quite a hit of satisfaction out of thinking for myself. I felt happy in a cry-y sort of way. I get that way occasionally after I finish a cry-y part of a book."

There was a price to the overwhelming, gleeful, outwardness of constant youthful liaison (later, in Camp Wahconah, she'd go out "every single blessed night"), and she yearned for that inwardness needed to bring herself into balance. And she seemed to understand also the proximity of sadness to happiness. There is something indeed melancholic in a fullness that feels almost brimming over.

Norma clearly had a whole host of thoughts unresolved. She could feel to a greater degree than she could articulate. An artist-in-training who still adored all things camp.

There were older men who knew well how to turn such inconsistencies against a girl – who by way of forcefulness could appear to compensate for every uncertainty and contradiction of which she was conscious.

And yet Norma would first be steeled against such simple and predatory enticement – she was heading to Paris to further her art education.

Chapter 3A: 1931

The timeline is given entirely by Dr. Milton Thomashefsky, for he is the only person who survives the love triangle's cataclysmic moment in time while still very much occupying it: Norma Jeanne Bernstein, his other ostensible lover, was up in a summer camp in the Adirondacks (despite being a highly accomplished painter) during the shooting. Agnes, the nurse who turned on her doctor and took him down with one shot to the spine, then blew her brains out — silencing her voice, precluding her own future testimony.

So it's the word of Dr. Milton against no one else's. Now, Dr. Milton, paralyzed and barely able to breathe, lies in a hospital bed in the very same institution where he himself worked for many years.

He is likely asked about the bizarre connections between the three families involved in this tragedy. Norma's father is a major Democratic former state-assemblyman and future judge deeply connected to Tammany Hall bigwigs. Agnes's father is the very superintendent of the hospital in which Dr. Milton lies — and a major Republican figure who's the former chief assistant to the head of the New York City Police Department.

And Dr. Milton's father, Boris Thomashefsky, is such a famous actor he can sell out theaters all across the US, Europe, even South America. Even non-Jewish folks know his name — he's the Yiddish Barrymore and also its Ziegfeld. His productions/follies are reviewed in the New York Times, his actions are reported on in Variety.

How could these families come into contact, let alone crash into each other with such sudden, grotesque violence?

But if Dr. Milton is posed this more grandiose question, his answer is *nevertheless very limited and specific and peculiar.*

Also, confounding.

He says his nurse Agnes, before she offed herself, admitted to him that she'd secretly acquired a passkey to his apartment before this present week (it's now sometime on Thursday).

Monday night, she used that passkey after midnight to sneak into Dr. Milton's apartment after he'd already gone to sleep, chloroformed him with a rag Hollywood-style, and attempted to mutilate his genitals— slice off his penis, seemingly — but stopped early on in the procedure, when she became overwhelmed by the notion, and by the blood, and bandaged him up. Meanwhile, he snoozed in his etherized state oblivious to the procedure first and her abandonment of the scene second.

And here's where the doctor's testimony on his hospital bed, before a crowd of his former hospital colleagues and a few cops and assistant district attorneys who seem willing to believe whatever he says, gets incredibly odd, per the Herald Tribune:

He knew Agnes was the perpetrator from the moment he awoke bandaged on Tuesday morning: "I thought that it had been Miss Birdseye who had attacked me."

As for Agnes, he says, "She came to work on Tuesday and Wednesday as if nothing had happened. It was not until that [Wednesday] night (of the shooting) that I accused her of the stabbing."

No one questions Dr. Milton's version of events, but it makes no sense on two levels — one, his nurse was no cat burglar and his apartment house had a 24-hour doorman. How had Agnes obtained a passkey and slipped inside so stealthily? That is, why was she really already in Dr. Milton's flat when he was soundly asleep on his bed? Why was his comely young assistant in his bedroom after midnight for real?

And then that odd delay: If Dr. Milton knew by Tuesday morning that his assistant had knocked him cold the day earlier with an anesthetic and then gone to work on his genitals with a knife during that period of insensibility, why had the doctor let Agnes work all day Tuesday and then all day Wednesday before bringing up the topic?

What existed between these two — doctor and assistant — that made the former

CHAPTER 3A: 1931

so unwilling and hesitant to confront the latter about such a horrific attack?

Was there some history of prior betrayal — did the doctor have his own misdeeds to hide — did he fear his own malfeasance would come to light if he called out Agnes on her own?

Otherwise, why not simply fire her?

And when Dr. Milton did bring up the scandalous assault on his nether regions, in his account to his fellow hospital physicians while lying in bed, he specifically noted he didn't merely discharge Agnes — not at all. He began talking about relationships.

"She said she was madly in love with me, even though she knew I was going to marry another woman."

Sorry, your involvement with a third-party romantically has some bearing on her employment status after she has knocked you out and lacerated you?

Oh, and while Dr. Milton lies in the hospital, near-death, one of his brothers — perhaps to cover up heterosexual promiscuity, to throw newspapermen off the scent, but curiously all the same — proclaims that the Thomashefsky family always believed Dr. Milton to be a "women-hater" — i.e. gay.

Who was Dr. Milton Thomashefsky?

Chapter 4: Thomashefsky

What if what happened to Dr. Milton Thomashefsky – and Agnes Birdseye and Norma Jeanne Bernstein – in August 1931 had already happened a generation earlier – what if it had precedent in the doctor's family history?

What if this was the *second* time a Thomashefsky had been paralyzed by gunfire as a result of having two lovers, one of whom had then offed him or herself?

Enter Boris Thomashefsky's sister, Emma — Dr. Milton's aunt. Of course, she, too, worked in the Yiddish theater.

She was just a 16-year-old chorus girl when she had run off in 1893 with an actor and theatrical manager and divorcé named Morris Finkel, who was either 34 or 44 or somewhere in between, depending on which document you believe. Their elopement and union proceeded without incident for a number of years, resulting in the birth of children, including daughters who'd go on to act themselves.

Then, at the turn of the century, Emma became a leading lady of the Yiddish theater, and Morris was forced to sell his stake in a major theater of the time to Jacob Adler (a producer, but also famed acting coach Stella Adler's father). Jacob Adler, having obtained Morris' theatrical ownings, then hired Emma, Morris' wife, to act in his productions.

And so Morris' jealous nature came to the fore in ways it previously hadn't. And Emma, initiating divorce proceedings from her domineering and miserable older husband, began an affair with another actor – one David Levinson – an affair her husband possibly learned about from a private detective he'd hired to tail his wife. Finkel also allegedly thrashed his now-distant wife once in Central Park.

In the summer of 1904, Emma – needing to escape the city – she was being surveilled and possibly abused – took her children to a farm in Orange, New Jersey – without her husband but with her lover.

But Morris, enraged, showed up anyway, found his wife walking with the man she'd been seeing extramaritally, withdrew a gun and fired – first in the direction of Emma and then a second time, at himself.[67]

By one account this all took place in front of the couple's six-year-old daughter, Bella, who'd go on to marry the 1930s Hollywood icon Paul Muni (star of the original "Scarface").

The bullet Morris fired toward Emma pierced her spine – paralyzing her. The one he fired at himself was fatal.

As she lay dying in the hospital – to the doctors' minds, anyway – Emma was married to her lover, Levinson, by a Rabbi.[68]

Meanwhile, in the Yiddish press, a different side of the tale was reported: that on her deathbed, Emma asked whether Morris had been arrested, having no idea he'd committed suicide.[69]

She survived, but was an inpatient of 11 hospitals in the next seven years.[70] In 1922, Emma embarked on a trip to "medical springs" in Czechoslovakia.

But despite all that, the show did go on: Emma did return to the stage. In most of these shows she found literal and figurative backing in her lover Levinson and her children, singers Lucy and Bella. She apparently leaned against items. She performed in "Cleopatra" in 1911, in a show eerily titled "The Second Wife" in 1912.

In December of 1911 she made nationwide news when she was pronounced "cured" – that she would dance again in two months because of a sensational surgery.[71]

It wasn't to be. Emma died in Atlantic City in 1929, her Daily News obit opening: "Emma Finkel, famous twenty-five years ago..."[72]

This was Boris Thomashefsky's sister – shot in the back for having two lovers at once, one of whom then killed himself. A precedent.

But what if it wasn't the only one – just the first?

What if Agnes Birdseye acted so violently because she – *and her father, too* – had born witness to the vengeance of another spurned lover a generation after the Emma Thomashefsky incident – this woman abused and aggrieved very nearby? What if that case had touched every person Agnes' father Lewis had looked up to in his Republican political career? What if the final act of violence had occurred within eyeshot of the Thomashefsky family home?

Chapter 5: Birdseye

How wholesome, civic-minded and spirited was Lewis E. Birdseye – now, in the late 1910s, chief clerk to Brooklyn District Attorney Harry Emerson Lewis?

In 1919, he convinced his colleagues in that office — as well as a Democratic judge and the former DA and police chief, James Church Cropsey, now also a judge — to take the train from Brooklyn up to New Canaan, Connecticut, and then hike 12 miles to Birdseye's family farm/summer house in Branchville, where his wife served everyone a chicken dinner when they finally arrived.[73]

Hell, Birdseye even agitated for the group — as if it were the Boy Scout troop he led — to walk back to New Canaan after dinner; the group declined and took a direct train from Branchville, showing up to work the next day "stiff, lame and tired" in the words of one paper.[74]

All the same, Birdseye's enthusiasms for justice and nature had induced that initial hike out of politicians with sufficient power to move about the city without making even minor exertions.

Birdseye.

And then on Dec. 13, 1921, a woman named Lillian Schaffer Raizen walked into the Brooklyn District Attorney's office where Birdseye and Harry E.

CHAPTER 5: BIRDSEYE

Lewis and most everyone on his wholesome hike worked. She confessed to those present she had shot Dr. Abraham Glickstein in his house the previous Saturday.

"He destroyed my life," she said, "and I decided to kill him."

It was perfectly true but also an abridgment of years of tawdry and torturous behavior by Glickstein.

Seven years earlier, Dr. Glickstein, an NYU medical school grad then known as "the cocaine and opium king," had been sentenced to a penitentiary in Atlanta, convicted of the mailing and marketing of coke and the manufacture of smokable opium. The judge in that case stated how outraged he was by Glickstein's sheer number of Zombie victims, whom he called "human wrecks."[75]

His medical license was revoked upon his conviction but after his imprisonment, in June of 1915, he was pardoned by President Woodrow Wilson,[76] and so he reapplied for his medical license.

He was not reformed, however.

In November of 1915, the good doctor stayed out partying on Coney Island till 2 am one early Friday morning and drove home anyway – his system perhaps flush with intoxicants – no test was ever done – bashing his roadster into a tree at Ocean Parkway and Avenue Y, which crash expelled himself and two passengers. One passenger suffered a compound fracture of the leg, another a lacerated face and broken nose and the doctor sustained a concussion.[77] In 1916, the doctor was charged *in another incident* with driving recklessly, this time definitely while intoxicated (his passengers were also charged for their inebriation, incidentally, including a dentist).[78] In 1917, he drunkenly crashed his car again – this time into a Brooklyn street trolley, injuring a woman inside it.[79]

Meanwhile, the good Doc set up shop as physician first on South 5th Street in Brooklyn and then in a home with his family at 535 Bedford Avenue – just one block down from the home of Boris and Bessie Thomashefsky and their sons, including Milton, at 549 Bedford Avenue. Dr. Glickstein and the Thomashefskys were, incredibly, separated by mere houses.

About this time, the Doctor – a husband and father of two teenage daughters – began to see Lillian Schaffer as a patient. He was 36 in 1915 and she was 22; he had known her family since she was child on the Lower East Side.

Per her retelling of events to the members of the office in which Lewis Birdseye worked, which events were never really disputed by prosecutors or judges:

During Lillian's first appointment, Dr. Glickstein forced himself on her – raped her, though that term was not used – and thereafter, they continued having relations, which were far more consensual in many senses but, of course, still originated in that initial assault and were always tainted by the power imbalance of his being *her family physician.*

He also performed two operations on her that left her sterile. Whether those were medically necessary or some sort of perverse malpractice was unclear.

And he always boosted her ego during their trysts: He complimented her singing and intellect, told her she could study medicine and become his partner.

Naturally, all of this – her affair with a married man that had its roots in rape, the operations, the doctor's blandishments – left Lillian dazed, so much so that in 1918 she dumped her sweetheart since childhood, a toy-maker named Charles Raizen with whom she'd always discussed marriage and begged the doctor to find a way to ditch his family for her or at least become a bigamist.

Ostensibly, Lillian tailed the doctor when he made house calls. Brought him silk shirts from the factory in which she worked as a bookkeeper. Gave *him* a diamond ring. Threatened him with death were he not to marry her and make of her a decent woman.

"Why don't you kill me, then?" the doctor replied at one point. "Have you got your gun with you, kid?"

Lillian Schaffer was going insane, if not by the clinical definition of the day than by every layman's metric.

But she did something rather mundane that could have been her entire salvation in 1920: she sent that childhood lover she'd broken up with – Charles Raizen – a birthday card. He was surprised but quite pleased, and that one gesture led to him visiting her and their deciding to resume their longtime courtship. They planned a big wedding together, though somehow the Doctor found out about it and ridiculed the engagement: "Use your brains," he said. "Be an intellectual, and do not marry."

But this time, Lillian Schaffer persisted.

In the spring of 1921, as she was about to pick up her trousseau from a shop, Dr. Glickstein telephoned her and invited her to his office to speak. She believed he wanted to apologize before she was married. Instead, he tried to force himself upon her again – only this time she was able to fend him off and escape from his office.

Utterly unnerved, she sought out counseling in several figures, including a Christian Scientist healer whom she'd wind up inviting to her wedding.

She indeed married in May, and on the second night of her honeymoon in Atlantic City, Lillian Schaffer Raizen burst into tears and told her husband everything that the doctor had done to her – but in the light of the era, all the story seemed to amount to was that she'd been a prominent physician's mistress.

"My husband was never the same since," she said after the shooting, awaiting trial in a local jail. "He loves me, he is kind to me, but I see in his eyes whenever he looks at me that he remembers, try as he will to forget."

She was suddenly startled by every bit of noise – a telephone, a car passing her house. She cried, she "brooded perpetually about the babies she could never expect to have."[80] Her husband recommended she see a psychoanalyst, who himself advised Lillian travel to Florida and convalesce in the sun.

But Lillian "wandered through Florida hotels, a sort of present-day Ophelia, singing bits of nothing."[81] She wrote her psychiatrist a note from the Sunshine State: "I have thought of putting an end to myself, but why should I do that? That skunk must go first."

Her husband replied in his own missive, directed to her when she was staying in Palm Beach: "Don't carry vengeance in your heart, for vengeance is only making us – you and I – carry the brunt."

Of course, she did – to the degree anyone driven mad by myriad conflicting feelings bears but a single notion in mind or heart. She was quite literally so confounded by all that had transpired to her that even after the murder, while sitting in jail, she called the doctor "almost a god" and the "greatest mind I have ever known."[82]

And yet she knew that genius was the cause of internal disquiet, not to mention her husband's unsubtly-hidden disapproval. So she acquired a gun in Jacksonville, returned to New York City, hid the gun in a fur muffler on a December day and, conveying it so hidden into his office on the second floor of Dr. Glickstein's house, she shot the doctor straight through the heart. He was seen collapsing from the instantaneously-fatal salvo by women in his waiting room.

Lillian ran away – but her single act wound up bringing about more death than she'd anticipated (not that she could be reasonably blamed for these secondary departures, though she was by all the papers):

At the doctor's funeral, his grief-stricken mother literally collapsed over his casket and died. Five months later, the doctor's widow jumped out a window to her death.

Three days after the shooting, conveyed there by a team of lawyers, Lillian entered the office in which Lewis E. Birdseye and his fellow hikers worked, led by DA Harry E. Lewis, and Lillian confessed. When she later went to trial, the presiding judge was none other than Lewis E. Birdseye's friend and mentor, James Church Cropsey, who'd first roped Birdseye into city affairs a decade earlier when Cropsey was police chief and who'd also been part of the 1919 hike to Lewis's farm.

Both these major figures in Birdseye's life could have sent a message in this case – that while the killing was to be condemned, the woman herself was to be pitied for the way in which she had been so horrifically maltreated by her victim (just a block away from the Thomashefsky home on Bedford Avenue). That Lillian had, in fact, been victimized first.

This may seem an attempt to judge early-20th Century legal minds by the standards of the 21st , but even a few contemporaries noted the ways in which both players, the DA and the judge, could have better served Lillian and thereby sent a message to the entire city that despairing women in unjust relationships had their attention and sympathies; in so doing, perhaps the prosecutor and judge might have even averted the commitment of further violence – homicides and suicides both – by those feeling aimless and without resource while enduring brutal relationships.

Where did they go wrong?

When DA Lewis heard that Lillian's defense team had hired four alienists (or psychologists deemed capable of evaluating a person's sanity) to assess her and that all four had found her insane, he sought to confer with alienists hired by his own office, determined, *by his own admission*, on countering whatever the other side would present at trial rather than on actually assessing the validity of those initial reports — on learning the truth of Lillian's condition.[83]

(His immediate successor in that office, as the case sprawled out over years, wound up attempting to suppress a report by two DA-hired alienists that also found Lillian insane, in favor of a more expensive and later-commissioned report that finally, somehow, found her sane – at a cost to the taxpayers of more than $10,000. This seeming prejudicial effort to secure a report in the DA's favor was noticed in the press of the day. The Daily News even said, "The highest priced specialists won.")[84]

Meanwhile, Judge Cropsey, who'd recruited Lewis Birdseye to be his secretary when he was police chief, essentially belittled Lillian's manner, made her out to be a strident, querulous figure, accused her of faking the mental illness even the DA's first alienist report had found all too real.

At one point, just as Lillian was to relay her state of mind upon entering Glickstein's office with her gun, for apparently she had contemplated merely killing herself in front of him, Cropsey interrupted her, saying: "If you want the jury to hear your story, you had better talk to them, instead of *whining* about it."

Later, Cropsey asked Lillian why she did not answer her lawyer's questions, and when she replied, "I didn't hear," Cropsey retorted, "Oh, yes, you did."

Later, a Dr. Kirby, who was sympathetic to the defense, had the stand. Judge Cropsey asked him: "What do you mean by her weeping?"

"Crying, shedding tears," Kirby said.

Cropsey replied: "It doesn't mean whining as she is doing here in this trial." And moments later, "You have heard her whine, haven't you?"

Wrote one appellate judge:

> *I think error was committed by the learned trial justice in two respects. The first involves what seems to me an expression of opinion by him indicating that the defendant was neither truthful nor candid, a view that was extremely detrimental to her... I am constrained to say that the attitude of the court was tantamount to a denunciation of the defendant as a malingerer, and that what occurred was calculated to convey to the jury the court's opinion that the defendant was endeavoring to deceive them,* and was pretending emotion. *It seems to me difficult to entertain any implication from what occurred other than that the trial court expressed his opinion that the defendant was falsifying emotion.*

He could have added that Cropsey, in his transparent attempt to portray Lillian as a shrill harpy, was quintessentially misogynistic.

One truly unfortunate implication of the entire ordeal was that a woman done wrong by a man and therefore impelled – however immorally – to commit a crime was better off simply offing herself thereafter than throwing herself on the mercy of the courts.

Why stay alive to be called a whiny bitch from the bench of a courtroom?

Of course, Agnes was in Brooklyn while this all went on amongst her father's colleagues and mentors. And a block over from the Glickstein house, the Thomashefsky family was capable of eyeing every bit of the aftermath.

Another precedent, a generation later, in 1921.

Chapter 6: Thomashefsky

The Thomashefsky house at 549 Bedford Avenue, a block away from the home and office of an ex-con drug-dealer and doctor named Abraham Glickstein, was actually only half-filled, was missing two major family members, for *at least a decade*. The reason for this prolonged and portentous absence goes to the heart of the Yiddish theater created by Boris and Bessie – alongside Boris' ill-fated sister Emma and brother Max and father Pinchas.

It was a theater of disputation, rivalry and constant reinvention (both in terms of the churned out plays and personae and in the euphemistic heisting of competitors' work).

Even after Boris convinced Bessie to join him in his troupe in Boston in "Shulamis," he may have left that group altogether "due to a difference in opinion."[85] He fought with the very people he'd recruited, including his future wife.

Boris re-established the troupe in Philadelphia in 1889, when he first met and cast a curious Jew named Sam Kasten, the first cousin of Bessie, who'd come to America penniless and fatherless, began selling matches on the streets of Philly, then became instantly enriched when his sister won the lottery and his family bought for him a farm in the New Jersey hinterlands.

That purchase was induced in part by the family's knowledge that Kasten wanted badly to pursue a life in the theater as an actor – they were against such a move. Kasten lived briefly on the farm but wound up returning to Philly regardless. He could not stay away from working, even as an extra, with the great actors of the era. He particularly revered Sigmond Mogulesko but was fond also of Thomashefsky's work. He'd become integral to the latter's shows once Boris and Bessie had their major falling out.

For now, in Philly, Boris' new troupe established its home at Dramatic Hall at 5th and Gaskill, right in the middle of the city's Jewish Quarter, but also played midweek shows, for richer, earlier-arriving German Jews, uptown on Callowhill Street, at the Thalia Theater (not to be confused with the Thalia on the Bowery in Manhattan, where Thomashefsky would later bring his troupe).

At this time, Boris staged work assembled by his father, Pinchas: "Yankel Yugatsch" and "The Spanish Inquisition," the latter of which involved a *"shegetz"* – a gentile – Spanish prince falling in love with a Jewish girl and then slaying an uprising of antisemitic Spaniards thirsty for a vengeful pogrom.

Boris, needing a new play, returned to New York, attended a performance, scribbled down the entire plot on a sheet of paper, presented it to his father in Philly – with whom, in three days, he wrote entirely new dialogue for the plot he'd heisted on a napkin and cobbled together some old songs for the show's compulsory musical component. And thus, in a most unsavory way, Boris and his father created yet another show – "Hannah and her Seven Sons," based loosely on an apocryphal tale from the Biblical book Maccabees II.

The Thomashefskys' work in Philly was highly praised. "An Oppressed Nation's Art," read the headline of an English language newspaper that had dared to send a reporter to a Friday night show at Dramatic Hall.[86]

He described a furious rush by patrons who'd scored the cheapest tickets – 15 cents for a Gallery seat – to secure a chair at the front of that section, the nosebleed seats in the highest balcony. Other tickets cost 25, 35 and 50 cents (the last for a front row view in what was not called the orchestra section but the "parquet"). Concessions included peanuts, soda pop, apples and pretzels.

(Once, in a rush for a gallery seat, the Hungarian theater fan known as Moishe Gulash fell over the railing and down a level, leaving him with a limp and a medal for a kind of theatrical dedication otherwise unknown, which medal he promptly pawned for 95 cents.[87])

"The scenery, the singing, the acting and the audience were all foreign to anything ever seen in Philadelphia. There were about 500 men, women and children in the theatre, Russians, Poles, Austrians, Germans, Hungarians…

"The gallery was packed. Children played in the aisles, and men and women got up and walked about when they got tired of sitting…The opera was apparently very funny, for the audience applauded vociferously. *There was very little handclapping. Men and women stamped their feet.*"

The reporter, calling the show "a family affair," added of the doomed Emma Thomashefsky, Boris' sister: She is "a very clever little comedienne, quite pretty and full of dramatic promise."

But that family dynamic was about to be altered: Boris had a falling out with his own father, and, the latter beginning his own company, the two began to compete for an audience in rival troupes – while casting aspersions on one another in the Yiddish press.

"Even the great Moliere could not have come up with a more ridiculous plot,"[88] Bessie wrote later. "The father announced that he and only he is the true Thomashefsky… The son responded that he is certainly the only Thomashefsky. The father then wrote that his son is a 'rebellious son.' The son answered that 'Father is a lame transgressor, a complete nothing and not an actor.'"

Another rivalry: Boris' troupe had to square off also against that of impresario Jacob Gartenstein, who'd rented out the uptown Thalia Theater on Callowhill. But the fight for patrons was a far dirtier affair than merely scooping up a theater your rival used.

Gartenstein put up a poster that read, per Bessie's recollection: "Extra, Extra! Jews, do not attend the other toilet which they call theatre, for only clowns perform there, not actors; don't let them fool you into paying good money! Jews, workers, ladies and gentlemen—come to our theatre, we are true artists."[89]

With these underhanded acts, Gartenstein proved himself ready for his next act – he became a Chicago politician.

Naturally, Boris had to retaliate (there was no taking the high road in such a brawl), and so he did, printing this poster: "Irresponsible language: Jews, Sisters and brothers! That Bastard is a bluffer and an embarrassment for all Jews, for the whole Jewish nation. What he says is comparable to a dog's howling, and I am turning over a shoe and let us say Amen."[90]

The poster featured an image of a shoe. *Take that.*

But the rivalries didn't always result in name-calling and direct competition. If a particular star decided to come to Philly, Boris and his troupe might simply go on a tour of another metro area, say Pittsburgh or Baltimore or Boston.

Strangely, one such tour led Boris and Bessie to a theater in Chelsea, Massachusetts, the town where in just a few years, Norma Jeanne Bernstein's future husband would be born – the man who may never have known Norma had kept Dr. Morris Thomashefsky's love letters from the 1931 incident.

And sometimes the regional moves sparked partnerships between the Yiddish public's revered personalities – Thomashefsky having decamped for Chicago, he wound up collaborating there with the great actor-impresarios Mogulesko and Jacob P. Adler (Stella's father), although those temporary all-star teams generally dissolved amidst a clash over roles or money.

(In Chicago once, Thomashefsky tried desperately to fix up a new theater, only for the recently-added varnish on its seats to adhere to the backsides of the opening night crowd, forcing Boris to pay everyone for their ruined finery;[91] a great Sigmond Mogulesko story – he once inserted into the show a song-and-dance during rehearsals of a play called "Siberia" written by Jacob Gorin, the fecund playwright who was something of a moralizing stiff; Gorin protested, so Mogulesko proclaimed Gorin an anti-Semite and just left.[92])

Teams might dissolve over affairs: both of Jacob Adler's two women, his wife Sara Heine-Haimovitch and his lover, Sophie Goldstein-Karl, were actresses who'd left actor husbands for him. But those who'd been cucked continued to act alongside those who'd left them alarmingly often.[93]

This was a world of powerful personalities who often had it both ways – all the ways they wanted to, in fact; Adler, the German translation of which is Eagle, called himself *Nesher HaGadol*, Hebrew for "the great eagle," and would print a two-headed eagle on his theater posters.[94]

Sam Kasten, who left Philly and was seeking to establish a Yiddish theater in the muddy shtetl of Brownsville, Brooklyn, merely by staging Boris Thomashefsky's work where it had not yet been heard (with his permission), later recalled the powerful spell cast by the Yiddish acting personalities:

"And it was no wonder that I was so frightened of them, of the famous actors of that time. There was something about them that really plunged you into fear and yet really stirred the imagination; They had innumerable fans, who were ready to 'jump into fire and water' for them."[95]

These fans, known as *patrioten,* also treated their theater much like a sport – even when it wasn't unfolding before them, they argued over drinks and deli about who had the best deliveries, technical skills, pathos.

The Litvaks hung out at the Essex Café, noshing on the seven-course, 12-cent meal – made and served by a Romanian proprietor named Manilevscu, who believed these customers utterly ignorant of what constituted great theater. Romanian theater fans tended to gather at the Campus Café on Delancey, whose posted slogan was *"Est un lacht* – Eat and laugh.

But everyone – Morris Finkel (soon to paralyze Emma Thomashefsky), Mogulesko, the great David Kessler – and their lager-swigging loyalists – mingled in Schreiber's Saloon, at 33 Canal, a long and narrow pub – featuring a mahogany-and-brass-rail bar and an area in back with wooden tables and unpainted chairs.

Schreiber's commonly gave out free food (knishes, a Romanian cornmeal porridge called *mamaliga,* herring, pretzels) to those theater folk who'd yet to make it. Bellies slightly fuller, they'd look for work at Schreiber's, see if they could latch onto, in any role, some present production. Get their break.

Boris and Bessie, after relentless touring, finally did begin to get their own bigger breaks – after a career that had truly begun at Schreiber's, for the Romanian actors Boris had imported from London for his first show in America had sustained themselves on Schreiber's free meals years before.

The couple was already tremendously successful by the turn of the 19th

Century, but its biggest hits in New York came precisely in that last decade of the 1800s and the first of the 1900s. And so, too, the seed of their secret family schism and all the turmoil it occasioned in the heart of a young doctor-son.

In 1892, Boris and Bessie starred in "Aleksander, der kroyn prints fun yerusholaim," – or, "Alexander, Crown Prince of Jerusalem," at the Thalia Theatre at 46-48 Bowery, a neoclassical building that had opened in 1845 and burned down four times only to be rebuilt anew after each calamity (it hosted all manner of Vaudeville and minstrelsy before purveying Yiddish fare).

"The role of 'Alexander' gained him many fans," Bessie wrote. "He played a prince even better than any prince, simply with his good looks alone! Even many men could not stop being dazzled by his good looks in that role…

"One evening a woman in the audience had an attack of nerves and it became necessary to take her to a hospital. 'My King,' she screamed out. 'He is my King, the handsome Alexander.'"

The Alexander role involved Thomashefsky sitting astride an armor-covered horse – which had worked an ice wagon all day – Boris' upper body exposed, his legs bulging against shimmering gold tights. Once, per a later recollection in Commentary:

> *Tomashefsky (sic) was engaged in a long and fiery apostrophe about life in general and nothing in particular when the horse committed a nuisance on the stage. Despite cries of 'Order! Order!' by the more serious minded, the house burst into hysterical laughter. Tomashefsky, unaware of the cause of the laughter, continued his monologue like the good trouper he was, but the prompter ordered the curtain lowered on a greatly astonished Prince of Jerusalem. Tomashefsky's only comment was: "A ferd bleibt a ferd" – "a horse is just a horse."*[96]

After a 1901 trip to Europe that saw Boris and Bessie act in Berlin, the pair, now in charge of the People's Theater, on the Bowery, which boasted the second largest stage in the city, behind only that of the Hippodrome at 43rd and Sixth, produced its memorable "Green Season" – a season in which Bessie played a series of immigrants, all of whom, like the patrons, were so-called *greenhorns* seeking to assimilate and climb the social ladder. That some were men hardly made a difference – Bessie could play a yeshiva boy as well as Boris could ever play a sensual lady.

These works were: "Di grine moyd (The Green Girl)" (based on the English melodrama "Rachel Goldstein"), "Di grine kinder (The Green Children)," "Di grine vaybl, oder, Der yidishe yenki dudl (The Jewish Yankee Doodle)," and "Di grine bokher (The Green Boy)."[97]

[Sheet music cover: "Popular Songs sung by Mrs. B. Thomashefsky in the play דער גרינער בחור / THE GREEN BOY. 1. YIDELACH-BRÜDERLACH, 2. ICH BLEIB A BUCHER, 3. DER GRÜNER BUCHER PARADE. By LOUIS FRIEDSEL. Piano, Violin. Published by THEODORE LOHR, 286 Grand St. (near Eldridge St.) N.Y."]

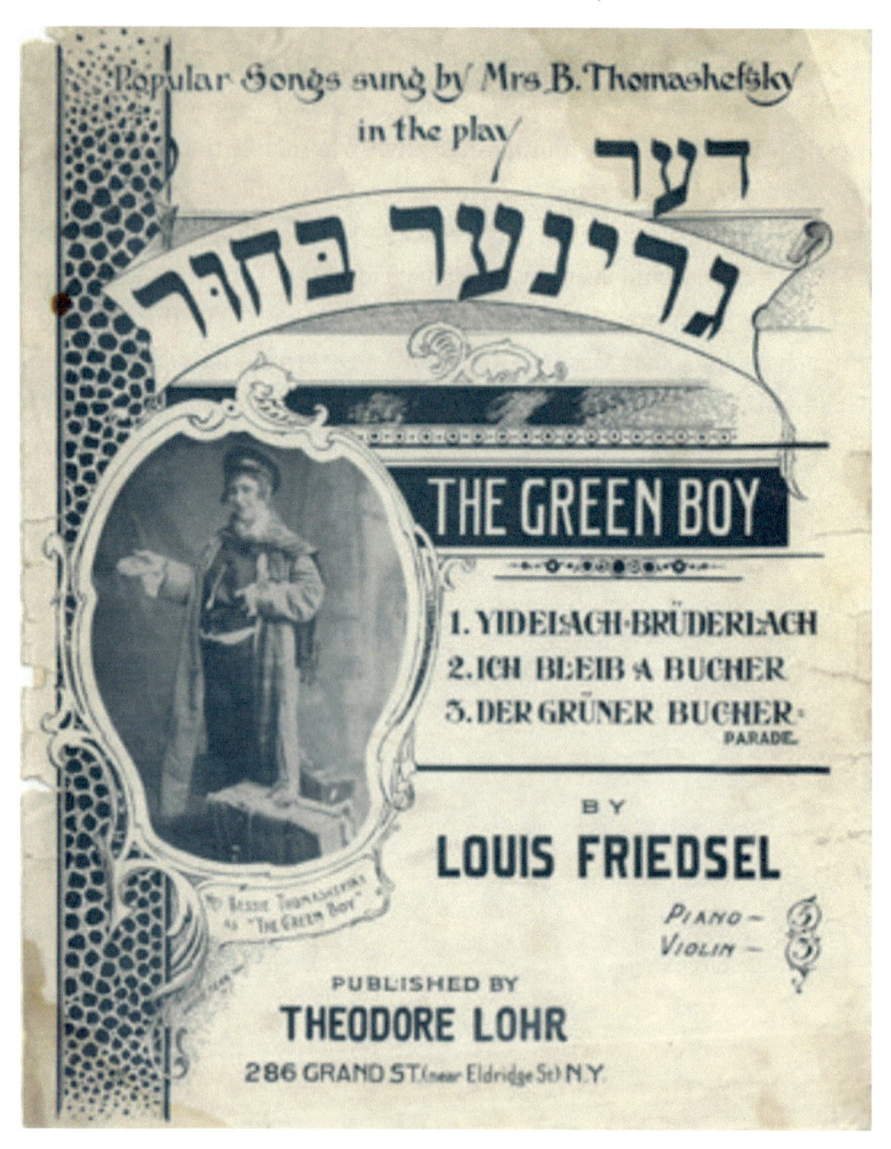

The final mega hit of this era, though it was by some critics derided as *shund*, or sentimental claptrap, was "Das Pinetele Yid," or 'The Jewish Spark," of 1909 – an operetta in which young George and Ira Gershwin paraded down the aisles of the theater as part of the "Bar Mitzvah March" number.[98]

Boris and Bessie's son Harry, now a child star, had a major role, too.

All this success led Boris to open a new theater, Paradise Garden, in

Hunter, New York, in the Catskills Mountains, beside his vacation house. Oscar Hammerstein's son William had previously used the title "Paradise Garden" for the name of a rooftop summer venue atop the Victoria and Belasco Theaters. Boris just took it without a second thought.[99]

Opening up a theater adjacent to his villa was hardly Boris' only luxury. Earning $45,000 per year, he spent a big chunk of it on keeping two motorcars running at a time when that was incredibly costly and something akin to keeping private jets; maintained a Japanese butler at the Bedford Avenue home; and installed a mistress – an operatic star of Austria, a diva whom he'd met in London in 1908 – in a home across from his own, at 544 Bedford Avenue.[100]

This last move had begun as a savvy business act: After Boris first spotted Regina Zuckerberg at the Pavilion in London and convinced her to come to America, a bidding war commenced between Boris' People's Theater and his rivals, the Grand Theater and the Kalich Theater, to sign her.[101] His eye for talent was no less legitimate than the lust often attached to it.

As soon as Boris had signed Regina, however, he began flaunting her in a way that clearly diminished his wife's standing. He took 21 members of his troupe – plus a chorus – on a tour whose promotion billed *Regina* as "the *Greatest* Yiddish Prima Donna."[102] They hit Cincinnati and St. Louis and Chicago playing Dimov's "Schmai Yisroel" and Goldfaden's "Ben Ami" and occasionally "The Merry Widow."

That these are included in the repertoire, wrote Tribune drama critic Burns Mantle, "means something to you if you are Yiddish."[103]

Well, not quite. Even those who staged "Ben Ami" would later argue vociferously over what it was intended to be artistically.

"Ben Ami" was an effort of the great Yiddish writer Abraham Goldfaden — author of "Shulamis," in which Bessie had made her debut in the 1880s — in his weaker final days (he died in January of 1908).

In Bessie's recollection, Goldfaden, knowing he was fading, urged Boris to treat what would be his final work with sobriety – to omit the often-plot-agnostic operatic songs so discordant with this drama. Boris, as director, refused to heed the dying author, unashamedly.

In Boris' recollection, Goldfaden managed to watch two rehearsals from a loge seat just before he passed. "Thomashefsky," Goldfaden said, "you promised me that I would be crowned for my 'Ben Ami,' and I say that you must receive the crown for your direction of my 'Ben Ami.' I can see from these rehearsals that you brought my characters alive, you planted a soul into my thoughts."

Which instruction Goldfaden actually issued hardly matters – that Boris and Bessie publicly relayed such contradictory accounts speaks to the great antipathy between them almost from the moment Regina Zuckerberg, known as the "Yiddish Tetrazzini," entered the scene as prima donna.

On the other hand, given the way Boris had wooed a young Bessie Kaufman to leave her Baltimore home behind her father's back 30 years earlier, perhaps matters were destined to reach this point of lascivious triangulation eventually.

And Bessie suspected Boris had badly mismanaged the great funds she, too, had accumulated from her craft.

And so she decided to leave the Thomashefsky manse at 549 Bedford Ave. She would still work with him on stage, of course, and even Regina, too – but from this moment around 1913 on, Bessie would live independently, not in a house with such a disloyal, narcissistic, irremediable cad. And she'd soon be examining the various accounting books the theaters had kept.

Bessie established herself as a brilliant artist independent of Boris, particularly in the show "Chantshe in America," but their slow and agonizing separation never went way – remained a shadow over their work to those in the know.

And yet there *was* joint work – even, amazingly, a 1920 show called "Parlor Floor and Basement" whose lyrics brothers Harry and Milton wrote together (including one tune about being an American boy who listens to rag time, dances in jazz time, and roots for the Yankees because here, sports are everything – sis, boom, bah!)

Amazingly, this show ran in February of 1919 with Regina and Bessie both starring and with Sam Kasten – Bessie's first cousin who'd become a notable character actor after his early days imitating Boris in Brownsville, after he rejected lottery winnings and farm life to pursue theater – also slotted in the cast.

The New York Public Library seemingly has the notebook in which the play was written or transcribed for the first time – seems like the writing work took place in Boris' villa in the Catskills, in Hunter.

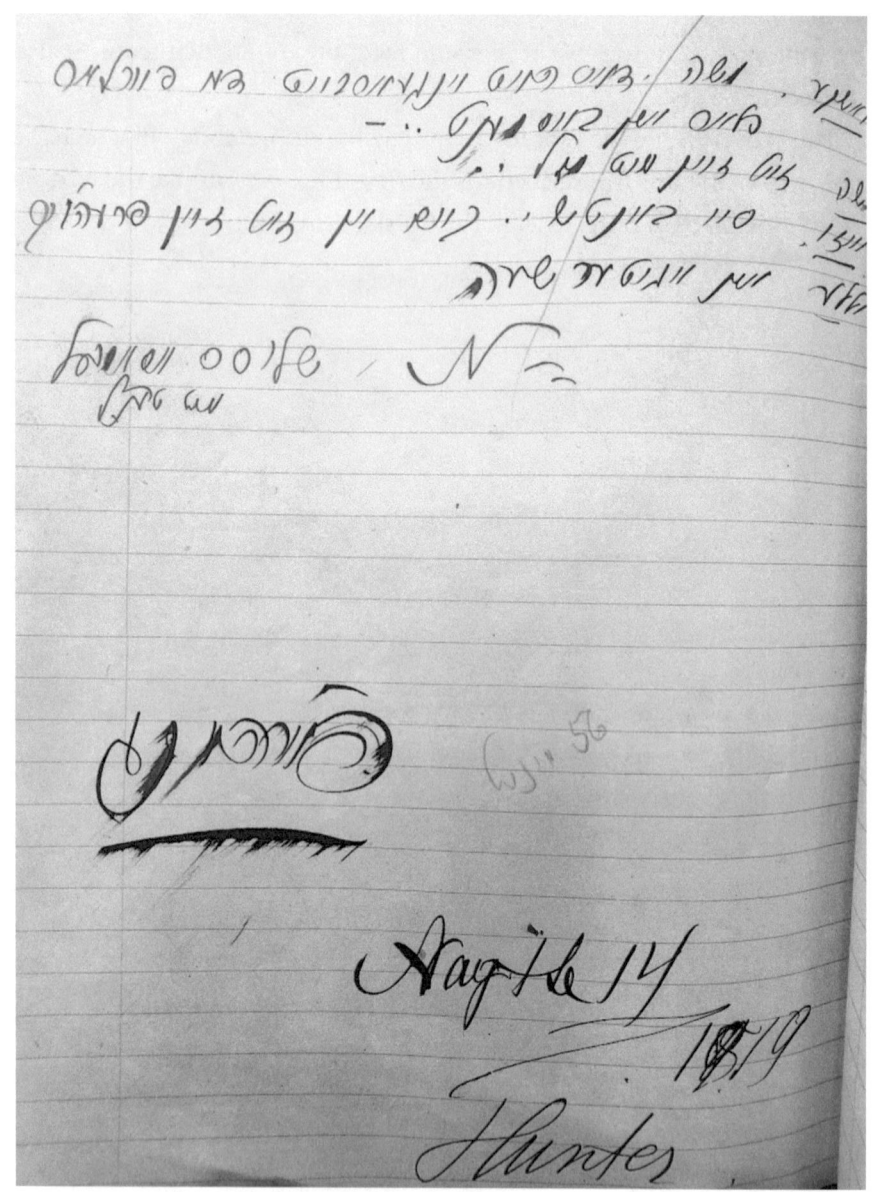

"Forehang," the word bottom left, indicates the curtain comes down – it was how each act in a Yiddish script concluded. The later pencil notation at the bottom reads, "56 minutes," perhaps the time of just the third act with music included.

CHAPTER 6: THOMASHEFSKY

But it was a family reunion of the most superficial kind.

In 1921, Regina Zuckerberg's husband – for she had been married the whole time she'd palled around town with Boris, until obtaining a divorce in Chicago in 1920 – sued Boris for $100,000 in damages for the alienation of Regina's affections; that move made, Bessie then sued, too – to recoup a $20,000 loan Boris owed her and for support payments, for what had become a decade of separation, totaling $80,000.

Now it was the year 1923 and suddenly Boris could feel the heat. He was eyeing expensive court cases that could see his already considerable debts swell, and he was suffering from an illness never disclosed but seemingly of some relation to his overall predicament. He was rushed to Brooklyn Jewish Hospital, where by this point, Milton Thomashefsky – the son who'd spurned the theater for a life in medicine – was finally an intern.

Milton himself was allowed to perform the surgery his father required (Boris must have pulled some strings or the one account that mentions this – Variety in April of 1923 – must be wrong).

Bessie felt compelled to visit Boris in the hospital. In Bessie's later words, she and Boris suddenly "agreed to forgive and forget, to make a home for our three sons where we had lived when they were children. And I was to return to the stage with him, just as it was 10 years ago, before this Mrs. Zuckerberg came into his life."

Bessie filed a discontinuation on all three of her lawsuits – only to return home to 549 Bedford Avenue to startling news: Boris had reneged on the deal or it had been a ruse from the start to get her to drop her suits.

Boris had settled out of court with Regina's husband in that alienation of affections suit, meaning he'd had money with which to pay Bessie; but far worse, he'd cast Regina in the role that was supposed to symbolize their great reunion, the lead female in "The Three Little Businessmen" he'd promised her.[104] Which would have been in a Broadway theater – the Nora Bayes Theater.

"I believed him when he said he would return to me," Bessie said, "and that's why I discontinued my three suits. He has deceived me and deeply wounded my heart."

Now, sons Harry, 28, and Milton, 26, had to make a decision, having witnessed their father's behavior, this awful exploitation of his illness, this manipulation of their well-meaning mother. Bessie had come home to 549 Bedford and wound up staying just a single night – she thought she was coming home for good.

Either son could follow Bessie out and stand up for a betrayed mother – make a statement in her defense with his feet – for both were single.

Milton, though still young, was, in one telling, thought by his family to be a "women-hater" – gay, in other words, although this was said by Harry in the wake of a sordid and unthinkable heterosexual incident perhaps to obfuscate the truth, as a kind of damage control (Harry would later go into PR after a long period of unemployment in the entertainment world).[105]

Harry, meanwhile, had indeed been married – in March of 1916 – only to find himself divorced by the following February, accused in court by his complainant spouse Ida Schwartz of being a wife-beater.[106] The judge in that case, who'd awarded Harry's now ex-wife $50 a month in alimony, was none other than James Church Cropsey – or the former NYPD chief who'd recruited Lewis E. Birdseye to be his secretary and then made Birdseye his chief clerk when he was a district attorney.[107]

And when Harry Thomashefsky asked for a retrial, on the grounds that he'd never properly had an opportunity to respond to the abuse charge, his petition was heard in 1919 by Judge Lazansky – another Brooklyn judicial mind who was friends with Lewis Birdseye and had attended the Birdseye hike that year up to his Connecticut farm for dinner.

In fact, earlier in 1923, before his father had cruelly tricked his mother in the hospital, Harry had already been arrested for nonpayment of alimony, in partial reparation for which he handed over to a deputy sheriff $425 in cash on the spot.[108]

Now, the two single brothers faced a choice of which parent to back. Milton, who in just a few months would hire a nurse named Agnes Birdseye, supported the woman deceived into believing she'd found love again with her soulmate. Was there for her. He walked out with his mother and lived with her in her new apartment.

CHAPTER 6: THOMASHEFSKY

Harry decided to continue devoting himself to his father's work, including a big Broadway debut, and by extension, his father. He remained at Bedford Avenue, where "to let and for sale signs hang on the Glickstein house, empty since the murder of the physician, the suicide of his wife and the death of his aged mother across his coffin."[109]

A frenetic scramble of New York storylines was afoot. The pieces were nearly all in place.

Chapter 7: Bernstein

"Much emphasis was placed in the power of a brush stroke quickly placed, to catch with spontaneity, the unique character of a personality."

– From the catalog to a posthumous show of Norma Jeanne Bernstein's work

Just 20 years old, Norma Jeanne Bernstein set off for Paris on the SS Leviathan in December 1926, bound to study painting further in the city most known for art at that time in the world. It was the era of Picasso and Hemingway and Woolf.

And the ship on which Norma traveled was itself a lens onto the era.

Woodrow Wilson's wife, the First Lady, celebrated her own birthday aboard the Leviathan that year.[110] Princess Ileana of Romania, carrying aboard love letters from young American men, pondered possible Stateside suitors while on the ship.[111] Irving Berlin and his new wife cruised on the Leviathan to their European honeymoon, telling the press in a joint interview, "If we were doing it again, we would get married *aboard* the Leviathan."[112]

CHAPTER 7: BERNSTEIN

On board, Norma was swarmed with eager men, as had become the norm. A boat engineer named Pat Rooney called her stateroom and asked for her by name. She played deck tennis with one – then "he snapped my picture gosh darn him," she wrote. Additionally, "a nice old French man dragged me up to the gym before dinner and I tried out all the machines" (in the suave

Gallic gentleman's defense, Norma had been feeling sick from the choppy waters and did later believe her workout had relieved those symptoms).

Norma's mother and brother accompanied her overseas, and before she began her studies in earnest, the trio visited Lucerne, Switzerland, for the winter holidays. They admired its "hand-painted houses" and the Statute of the Dying Lion. On New Year's, all three fell asleep before midnight, only to be woken by the town's chimes signaling the arrival of 1927. They drank a glass of port to their absent Papa. After a train trip, they then visited Nancy, France, including certain areas that still bore signs of bombardment from the Great War.

In Paris, Norma Jeanne settled into a small *pension* run by Madame Bertillon at 4 Square Lagarde in the 5th Arrondisement. She seemingly already had contacts in the city, including a family named the Coucrats, who fed her rabbit for the first time and who found great comedy in her American manner and linguistic difficulties (she was also worried her culinary intake would leave her "elephantine").[113]

On the evening of January 3, she reviewed a letter from her best friend Hilda and her father and a boy named Eddie, before drifting off – her first day of school in the morning.

Only, quite in keeping with the spirit of her era, Norma really had no set plans on how to obtain the training she sought in the City of Light. Or rather, she wasn't just some rich American indulging a whim or hobby. She had real artistic sense by now, a direction. She knew she was a portraitist in her heart. Finding a teacher who would suit that instinct and build on her prior advancement – that was the difficulty.

A pastel Norma did of her mother Ida, two years prior to arriving in Paris.

Norma Jeanne signed up for a month at the Académie de la Grande Chaumiere, founded in 1902 on a small block of Montparnasse in the 6th Arrondisement, near the Jardins du Luxembourg, that was to become a haven for aspiring artists.

Her first day was exactly as awkward as scholastic debuts have always proven: For some reason, the school was more crowded on Tuesdays, the day of the week her term began. As a result, she got a bad seat, including a "shaky easel, slippery canvas." Then she returned to her pension, her home for the year, to make herself "cozy" – only her room lacked heating, and "she was cold as the deuce."

Day One.

Paris was glitzy, Paris was grimy.

Alberto Giacometti, just five years younger than Norma, had just concluded a half-decade of sculpture study at the Grande Chaumiere under Professor Bourdelle.[114] The Cubist-Symbolist-Proto Pop Artist Fernand Léger, whose tubular, mechanistic representations of the modern world cast that whole 1920s milieu through the lens of an ocean liner's engine room, would teach at the Chaumiere in just five years.[115]

But the Chaumiere was also a meat market – a gathering place for migrants and bohemians looking to pose nude on frigid days (formerly models were professionals – not hippies – and they had assembled to be selected for such work at the Carrefour Brea in Montmartre).

"Around the stove of the ante-chamber of the Grande Chaumier every Monday during the winter season crowds the haphazard, happy-go-lucky mass of models looking for work," the Associated Press reported.[116]

Norma Jeanne's second account of class: "The work — getting Renoir-ish *avec* the knife. The antique professor came in and criticized me today – all in French – someone helped interpret so it wasn't as meaningless as it should have been."

Later, on her work: "Mine is the *only* colorful one" (the emphasis is my own). Besides mentioning her heavy use of a palette knife for application, Norma Jeanne also called her process "painting my slapstick way."

She kept at French, practicing reading aloud to her pension proprietress

Madame Bertillon. Visited the Bon Marche on a rainy day, Au Printemps for tea on a separate occasion. She took in the offerings of the Musee du Luxembourg, finding those paintings "sort of modern" quite agreeable but those "very modern" "rotten."

It began to occur to her, however ambitious or naïve it may seem, that her professor at the Chaumiere was "terrible" – "an awful idiot." She did at one point enjoy chatting with four of her classmates, all of whom spoke a different language, including French, Russian and Hebrew ("much interpreting"). She bought art books, taking particular note of the style of Swedish painter Anders Zorn. Visited the Independents Exhibition at the Grand Palace. "Terrible stuff," she pronounced, "and loads of it."

She wandered the neighborhood around her art academy on a day with a hint of spring in the air, marveled at little kiddies taking donkey rides in the vicinity of the Jardins. She visited an American art alliance in search of a better instructor – and got the address of Armenian-American painter Hovsep Pushman, whose most intriguing works to Norma would have been his keen and compassionate portraits of women (see his "Marguerite #47").

A broken tub at issue, Norma hadn't bathed for quite a while, to the point where she feared she'd soon be able to peal the grime off her skin with a knife. She coveted a gold and turquoise bracelet she spotted in a shop, which her mother, who'd stayed on in Paris to oversee Norma, though from a distance, eventually bought her.

Norma Jeanne visited the studio of Madame Mela Muter, who only took on four students at a time, for 400 francs per month. That was four times what Norma Jeanne would pay elsewhere but an enticing opportunity all the same.

Muter had been born to a Jewish merchant in Warsaw in 1876 as Maria *Melania* Klingsland. In 1899, she'd married an art critic named Michal Mutermilch; they'd moved to Paris in 1901 (her brother Zygmunt was an art critic and legal adviser in the Polish Embassy there).

Wrote the Women's Art Journal of Muter, "She was especially praised for her studies of… (her artist) friends."[117] She also painted quite well the desultory cast of urban, impoverished souls she came across. As she matured, she increasingly appreciated the expressionistic stylings of Cezanne and Van Gogh.[118]

Whose application was sometimes quite impasto-heavy.

In other words, Muter could have seemed to be the perfect teacher for Norma – their interests utterly aligned. Muter had also studied at the Grande Chaumiere and had presented her work at the Salon des Beaux Arts. But that's the vexing nature of such artistic tutelage: a correspondence in ideals by no means ensures one of approach.

And so Norma and Muter came to despise each other, to the degree teachers and students can and do.

It's perhaps fitting that their arrangement was consummated almost by default. At the end of January, Norma Jeanne brought her work to the Ecole des Beaux Arts in the pouring rain. "Terrible place," she later reflected, "a pack of animals for students – yelling and hooting at the first sight of an American."

One imagines it was more specifically to do with her being a *female* American, but anyway:

A professor there, Lucien Simon (a portrait of whom hangs in the Orsay and whose accomplished work of bathers, to give one example, can be found in a fine arts museum in Buenos Aires), was greatly interested in Norma Jeanne's "old lady avec color and done with a knife." But his class was entirely booked for the term – she'd not be able to enter till Easter.

CHAPTER 7: BERNSTEIN

The painting Lucien Simon found impressive, later titled "Paysanne." Norma first described, in her diary, creating this "avec a vim and a vigor – oodles of paint, color."

And so Norma was left with Madame Muter, who, unbeknownst to her new American pupil, had suffered quite a great deal in the years preceding Norma Jeanne's 1927 arrival in her studio.

Muter had had an affair with a wounded French war veteran left so disillusioned by the *guerre* he'd become a radical communist. When Muter's affair came to light, she divorced her husband in 1919 – only for lover Lefebvre to attend a communist conference in Moscow the following year and disappear forever on his return back in a boat, perhaps the victim of international foul play (Le Figaro was certain he was assassinated by the Soviets).[119] Then Mela Muter's son died in 1924 and poet Rainer Maria Rilke – who'd dedicated poems to Mela, as if they were lovers – died at the end of December 1926 (in Switzerland – at precisely the moment Norma Jeanne Bernstein and her mother and brother were vacationing in that country).

Muter, in other words, was eyeing Norma's work each day having just been totally altered as a person (in fact, she wound up converting from Judaism to Catholicism as one consequence of the experiences). But Norma very likely knew little, if any, of this.

And so the two pursued life and art honestly in a shared search for the essence of things. Which meant Mela disapproving of all Norma's choices.

There are but allusions to these blow-ups in Norma's diary but they're evocative all the same.

February 4, 1927: "Commenced at Mme. Muter's — she made me draw first - then a horrible clash of personalities. Went home dead tired - physically, mentally and possibly spiritually."

February 15: "Mme. Muter and I were at 'loggerheads' again this morning – Darn her, anyway.

March 2: "Simply cannot stand Mme. M. Had another battle this morning. She will not teach me any way but exactly her own - Stubborn – and such a funny way of looking at things – little pieces at a time instead of the thing as a whole with large masses. It's killing me."

Norma Jeanne's social life, or its absence, proceeded:

Often at nights, Norma read from French books with Madame Coucrat and Madame Bertillon. She despaired over receiving no letters from home – she who had been so popular in New York. "Lonesome as hell tonite," she wrote in her diary once – before meeting up with Sam Hollander, on his return from Leipzig, while wearing a black and gold dress and hat and her new bracelet; Sam is the boy who took the photo of her on the ship from New York, featured above.

Norma Jeanne wandered the Boulevard Clichy, with its "millions of little Greenwich Village places and studios and cafes with all the funny types sitting out in front drinking and regarding the passersby."

At odds with Madame Muter, Norma Jeanne nevertheless painted in her studio a portrait that lies on the floor of the studio in which I research her life nearly 100 years later and entrances me (it's not always shoddily propped up against drawers; Norma's daughter-in-law just likes to rotate the locations of paintings) – "Man with Gold Scarf":

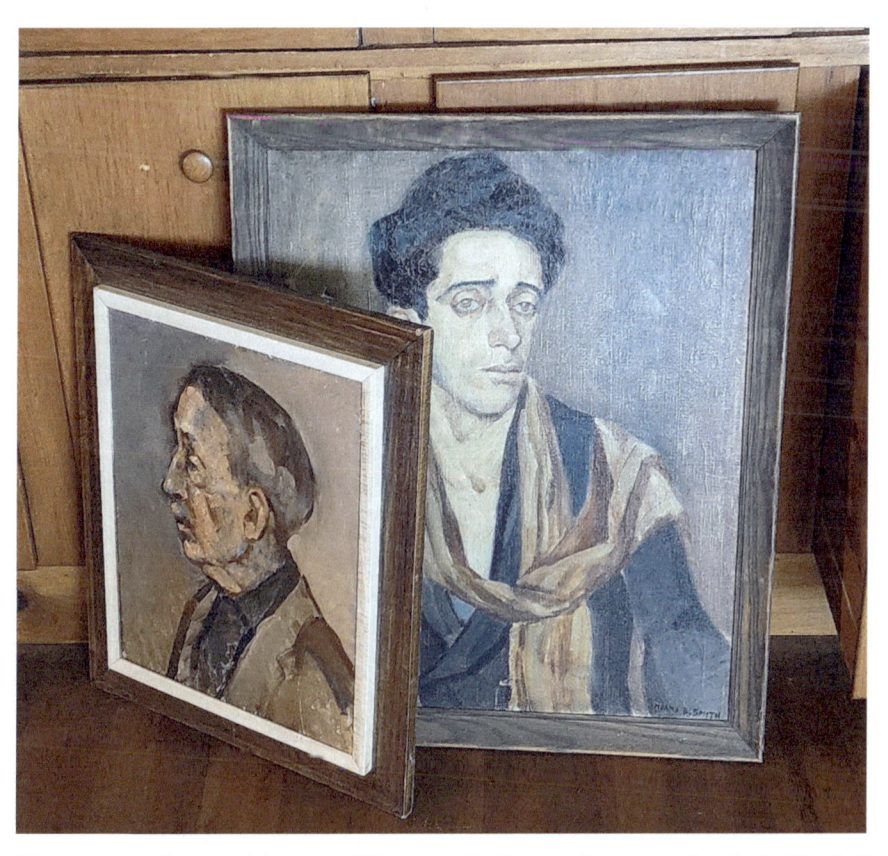

Norma was also working on a likeness of a figure she termed only "a Hindu,"

the completed version of which appears here:

Finally, she found her favorite artistic guides – she took the class of Professor Laurens at the Académie Julien in the mornings, and the class of Henri Morisset at the Académie Colarossi in the afternoon.

CHAPTER 7: BERNSTEIN

The latter institution had been founded by an Italian sculptor, Filippo Colarossi, in 1870; its star pupils had included Gauguin, Modigliani and Helene de Beauvoir, sister of Simone.[120][121]

Henri Morisset, Norma's professor, was himself distinguished: he'd studied under Delaunay and Gustave Moreau, and one of his works had been acquired by France itself for its national collection in 1896, when he was just 26 (several other acquisitions followed). He was named a Knight of the Legion of Honor in 1912.

On March 7, 1927, Norma described a "dandy model" at Colarossi's – "a sort of Oriental Cleopatra." The next day she met Morisset, describing him as "very nice and quite interesting."

By March 11, three days after making his acquaintance, Norma wrote, "I'm crazy about him – Charming personality. Gave me a good criticism, too – Very interesting and comprehensive – Like the school.

April 5: "Prof. Morisset gave me the most interesting criticism today. Really quite frank — all about how *little* professors can really help one – and that I should just go ahead and work things out myself because that was the only real way to learn – and not to pay attention to everything that everyone and every prof. will say about my work – That I'm the only one who really knows what I'm after, etc; not at all like the nice polite things most profs say to the students – at last I believe I'm with some one who sees things my way or at least the way I feel is right. Just as long as I have some idea I'll be able to plug things out by myself."

April 8: "Prof. Morisset didn't like my pictures as much as he did last Tuesday - said I spoiled it with the finishing touches - so when I get back he wants me to make two a week instead of one - until I get over my funny finishes - etc. which got me furious because I knew it so well myself. He's a darling man."

Thusly, Morisset convinced Norma Jeanne, who was both tremendously independent-minded but also still impressionable and young, that she was so natively capable she didn't need to keep fidgeting with her portraiture forever, that she could feel secure in the work she'd put in the work. That she knew in her soul when she had captured someone else's.

On May 16, she wrote, "Got a splendid at Colorossi's of a fisherman. This time I vow I won't spoil it" – as if somehow her prior portraiture would have been perfect if only she'd known when to stop fidgeting with it.

A "Carmen"-type, in Norma's words. "Done with a knife and ought to be on the type of old lady that everyone seemed to like so much," she added.

CHAPTER 7: BERNSTEIN

On the day Norma Jeanne turned 21, February 14, 1927, she records in her diary that she went shopping for some underwear "and ate some chocolates with the following contents" – here she glued into the notebook labels for Cointreau Triplesec and Grand Marnier:

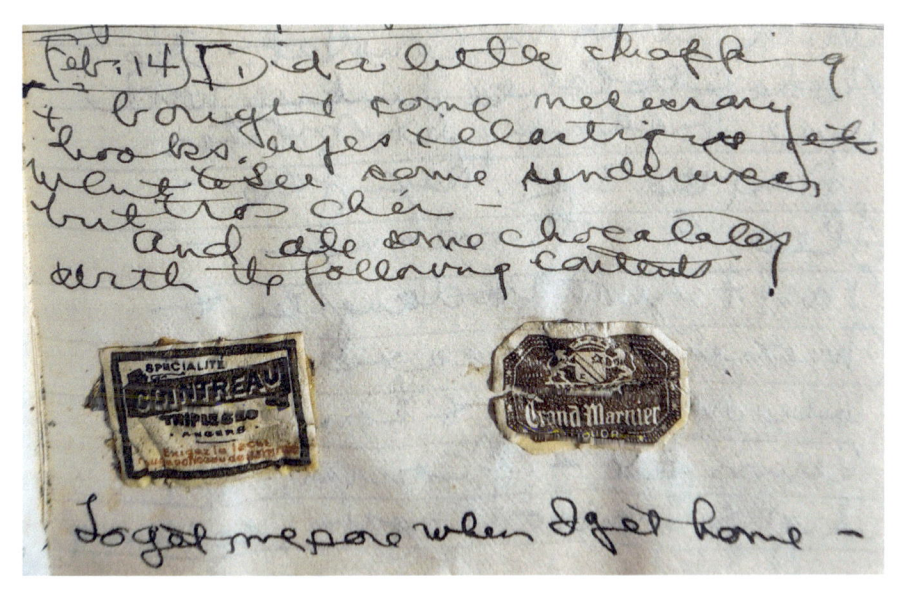

There's something amazing about those labels for having stayed in place and faded only slightly in the last 100 years. And while occasionally mundane, it's touches like these that make Norma's diary in some places incredibly cute and endearing.

And yet there is a single entry, mired in an ugliness no matter how unintended or naïve, that seems all at once to adumbrate, if not eclipse, the rest of the book's charm. I somehow believe that both things can be true: a document never written for a public audience, and bearing the not fully-formed thoughts of a young mind, the diary can be both winsome and repugnant. And it almost feels unfair to reprint the following because it just reads as so damning to any contemporary sensibility.

But in March of Norma Jeanne's year of study in Paris, at the Académie Julian, she was painting a black model, a handsome man whom she termed in her diary "tres interessante." But afterward the man approached her, "made eyes" at her and said, "I love you" albeit in "broken English."

The problem is the racially-predicated fright this approach appears to have engendered in Norma, the way the passage so clearly treats the model not as another lover-manque making a pass at her but some threatening figure in an eerily Emmett Till-like tale.

And it does so while using the most vile racial epithet (not "negro," for the record).

March 28: "Alors – Today I started in painting an *n-word* at Julien's. Tres interessante - but the *damn n-word* came over and made eyes at me [and said] "I love you" in broken English."[122]

It's so twisted, so repulsive in stereotype, that it matters not that Norma was outwardly a fan of Josephine Baker, whom she saw perform in Paris or that she painted famous black actors of her day back in New York upon her return from Paris – Ethel Waters and Richard Harrison and Isabel Washington. That she married a lifetime member of the NAACP, raised a New England liberal of a son who went to DC to help craft the Civil Rights Act and Voting Rights Act of the mid-1960s, which work was hailed by Representative John Lewis. That her father advocated for a swimming pool in the center of black Harlem.

I asked Marjorie, Norma's very liberal daughter-in-law, what exactly she made of Norma's views on race. Her answer, to my recollection, was that Norma, while socializing cordially with Harlemites for her work, did not really engage with the great social struggles for equality that occurred in the latter part of her lifetime.

My own take, which I share not to absolve her but to clarify matters: The diary entry, unleashing epithet so reflexively, emanates from an upbringing that failed her greatly in its conversations on the real meaning of rights. I doubt she was a racist, though the anecdote as written by her 21-year-old self certainly reads as such. Instead, I see her as someone who perhaps never advanced past certain notions transmitted to her in the earliest days of the 1900s, even in a Northern city like New York of which we'd like to think, especially of its so-called liberals, so much more.

And just maybe her racial epithet is not unrelated to the strange dichotomy of her persona – that even as she was advancing as an artist under the aegis of the world's most pedigreed teachers, she nevertheless was living out an extended childhood – a girl born in 1906 was in 1927 still most at home in a place we associate with mere children – summer camp.

That may seem a strange reductionism.

But there is another entry of salience from the diary of that year, written mere pages apart from the one about the black model who attempted to flirt with her and seemingly made her cower and curse:

"Brought home marshmallows and toasted 'em on electric heater. Sang camp songs until *I and everything was quite homey.*"

A complicated woman, not always sympathetic, not always a woman at all, on her road to a tragedy that would sever her from her youth while also preventing her from ever truly advancing past it – for whom only camp could somehow make everything alright.

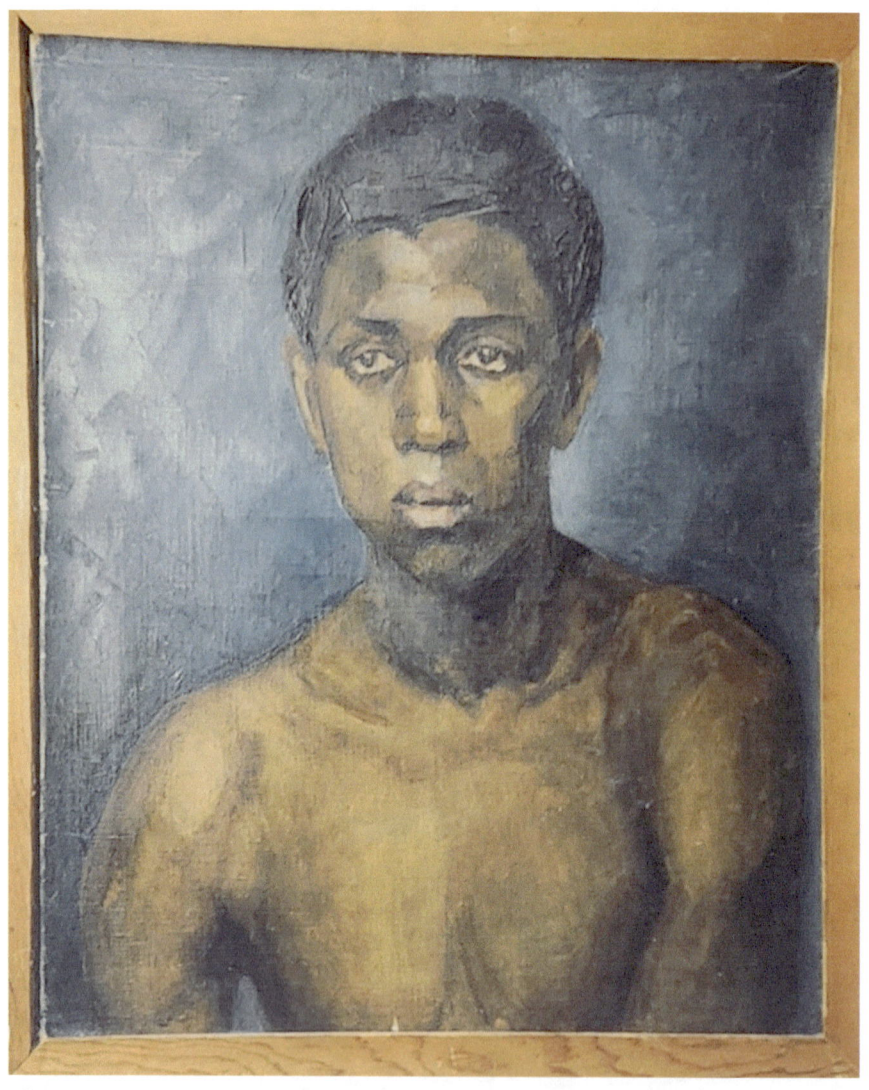

"Black Man Bare Chested," the portrait Norma made of the man whom she so derogated in her journal.

CHAPTER 7: BERNSTEIN

Norma Jeanne's portrait of black actress Ethel Waters.

NEW YORK CITY LOVE TRIANGLE, 1931

Marjorie Smith, Norma's daughter-in-law, sitting between two of Norma's works – that of a black girl from 193rd Street named Marjorie Albertha Holmes and of a "Chinese Girl," also the name of the painting, which was the winner of an "important exhibition," according to the New York Sun of May 7, 1930 (it's also a painting whose mood and color Marjorie appreciates especially).

On July 23, 2003, black civil rights icon Representative John Lewis of Georgia stood up in the house and said the following about Marjorie's husband and Norma Jeanne Bernstein's son – Peter Smith: "Mr. Speaker, I rise today to recognize a great contributor to civil rights and to the empowerment of people in this country."

Chapter 8:
Birdseye-Thomashefsky-Bernstein

In November of 1922, the Democrats took Brooklyn by storm, winning the election for the role of district attorney by a whopping 74,000 votes.

For the Republican lifer and chief clerk to the incumbent DA, this electoral sea-change meant Lewis E. Birdseye was suddenly without a job – and possibly without a direction.

But he had been a straight arrow his entire career. That wholesome hike up to his farm, the honest connections he'd forged with local power players that trip represented, would serve him again.

One of the hikers had actually been a Democrat — Justice Edward Lazansky (who'd handled the appeal of Yiddish theatrical scion Harry Thomashefsky's wife-beating divorce case a few years earlier).

Lazansky had served on the first board of an institution vital to the Brooklyn neighborhood Birdseye had long striven to advance – not just in the DA's office but as a Boy Scout leader (earlier in 1922, Birdseye had helped open a school to train adult scoutmasters[123]): The Brooklyn Jewish Hospital, which had opened in 1906 and quickly become a significant hub of the entire community.

These weren't just tenuous ties between Birdseye's colleagues and the hospital. Judge Lazansky had been additionally the first vice-president of its nursing school. Birdseye's former boss, former DA Harry. E. Lewis, who'd been made a judge himself in recent years and was therefore still employed despite being a Republican after a Democratic wave, would go on to become the vice-president of the Jewish Hospital.

And so the significance of the place to its surrounding populace, if not massively apparent to Birdseye already, was likely prevailed upon him by these political friends in the immediate aftermath of the 1922 election, when Birdseye was newly jobless and the hospital had the concurrent need of a fastidious overseer.

Though Birdseye had no experience in the medical field, he'd not had any in meatpacking, policing or prosecution when he took on jobs in all those fields, and his general competency had served him quite well, he'd assimilated whatever specific skills needed to succeed. He'd been sent to a school for orphan boys – he was going to work at whatever the task set before him. He had the resolve of someone never wanting to return.

So in July of 1923, his crew having vacated the DA's office, Lewis E. Birdseye became assistant superintendent of the Jewish Hospital, which had on staff a 26-year-old otolaryngologist, another son of the famous Yiddish acting clan Thomashefsky, only one who'd eschewed its theatrical way of life in favor of a more traditionally rewarding career: Dr. Milton Thomashefsky.

And the timing was intriguing, to say the least:

In the month immediately prior to Lewis E. Birdseye's arrival, Dr. Thomashefsky had overseen the care in the Jewish Hospital of his ill actor father Boris, on which occasion Boris had promised (falsely, it turned out) to reunite with his wife.

Now, within weeks, Lewis E. Birdseye was Dr. Milton Thomashefsky's supervisor (technically, in his assistant superintendent role, Lewis was more of an accountant overseeing hospital expenditures, and yet he was still part of the administration and nominally an overseer of the physicians).

Weirdly, the Jewish Hospital was intricately involved in the legal system Lewis E. Birdseye had just departed – as if somehow, Birdseye's assistant superintendent role, while not a sinecure, was nevertheless an extension of the district attorney's office. In 1924, a blonde, female attempted robber twice shot a cashier at a Nabisco factory in Brooklyn – and the DA was photographed discussing the case with Birdseye.[124]

The prior December in 1923, Birdseye petitioned the Brooklyn legal machinery for leniency – ostensibly in his role as a hospital administrator but clearly blurring his exact position in the entreaty. A well-regarded hospital employee of two years had drunkenly, stupidly, robbed a ring from a friend and received a five-year prison sentence for the relatively minor crime (the ring was returned). Birdseye asked the judge to reduce that punishment – and the latter did so, revising the confinement to 1-2.5 years.[125]

And so, though Birdseye didn't quite leave his former job behind, as he was not really expected to, he was well regarded in his assistant superintendent hospital role.

By 1925, Birdseye was therefore and unsurprisingly promoted to full superintendent (this isn't to say Birdseye, staunchly old school, got along with everyone; one of his doctors was accused of cruelty to animals in an animal research lab dedicated to the study of human pediatric disease;[126] when the Humane Society invited locals whose pets had gone missing to the lab to check whether their dogs were present, Birdseye, at first refusing the perceived agitators entry, scoffed, "This is my busy day.")[127][128]

After Birdseye was elevated to superintendent, he was Dr. Milton Thomashefsky's superior for only a few years – until at some point in the mid-1920s, the otolaryngologist opened his own office, while retaining admitting privileges to the hospital (a January 1928 article lists Thomashefsky as still being on staff).[129]

Meanwhile Lewis E. Birdseye labored for the hospital's expansion, its plan at the height of the stock market frenzy of the Roaring '20s to add three buildings at a cost of $4 million. Lewis can be seen below at the cornerstone laying for the project (he's the dour man in a white coat in the center, his shoulders even with a metal beam):

[Handwritten on photo: Brooklyn N.Y. / Corner stone laying / Jewish Hospital / Nov 4 1928]

Even then, as Dr. Milton branched out, Lewis E. Birdseye remained intimately connected to his work – for Milton hired as an assistant none other than Lewis's daughter, Agnes Birdseye.

Agnes' early working years had been marked by a commendable, if unusually achieved, independence. At 19, she worked as a stenographer in a bookbinding firm, while boarding in the home of her former high school's chemistry teacher – Ben M. Jaquish of Erasmus Hall (to be clear, Jaquish's four-member family, as well as two other lodgers, also resided in the house at 782 East 18th Street, Brooklyn).

Judged against this arrangement, Agnes' entrance into the office of Dr. Thomashefsky could be seen as a considerable improvement in circumstance – especially as the Doctor acquired fancy new digs.

In September of 1928, Dr. Milton and two other physicians rented a ground-floor suite in the Turner Towers – a $5 million, 15-story luxury apartment building opposite Grand Army Plaza – a building then tabbed the country's third largest residential structure.

Perhaps, then, Dr. Thomashefsky had hired Agnes as something of a favor to his sometime boss, her father, as a way of lifting her out of lowlier employment, although no documents survive to indicate as much.

If he did perform such a favor, it would have been in keeping with the reputation Dr. Milton had cultivated so far in his young life. A man who'd been exposed to the worst financial and personal excesses of show business, he'd turned away from that life to provide moral support to his spurned mother and medical care to his borough's sick.

He seemed, from the outside, a modest fellow in a family known for anything but that trait. He'd attended PS 16 on Wilson Street for elementary school; now, for recreation, he played in handball tournaments in a Reform temple on Eastern Parkway (he was neither a Class A nor Class C player – just Class B, bang average).[130][131]

If Dr Thomashefsky – ear, nose and throat specialist – was running anything but a standard medical office, an operation respectable and above-board, it would have been to most observers, Lewis Birdseye included, a wild surprise.

A massive shock.

* * *

On Norma's way home from Paris, she vacationed in Capri, where she captured a wonderful likeness, before hitting New York once more and beginning a proper ascent in the arts scene.

The stop:

She'd encountered an old man named Spadarro whom she privately called "Santy Claus." Her photograph of the bearded gentleman is a playful composition itself, possessing a sort of exaggerated verticality to match Spadarro's long, attenuated features – his facial hair and pipe and walking stick. Even his beret drooping down the side of his head like a Dali clock.

There is, too, the great balance between background and fore – a kind of three-dimensionality in the presentation, all of Spadarro's weight supported by his back right leg, while the left extends towards the viewer unbent, unbowed, in a free kick. Such unpracticed, continental cool.

Norma used the small snapshot as the basis for an etching, in which she decided to focus her attention on almost none of the aforementioned details but on the intricate lines of the local's tanned face and bushy eyebrows and woven sweater (plus that pendulous beret).

CHAPTER 8: BIRDSEYE-THOMASHEFSKY-BERNSTEIN

NEW YORK CITY LOVE TRIANGLE, 1931

And then she alighted back in the city and, after resuming class at the Art

CHAPTER 8: BIRDSEYE-THOMASHEFSKY-BERNSTEIN

Students' League, she began to put out into the world the pictures she'd been composing for the last half-decade. The result of intensive study interrupted at points by the great leisure her lifestyle afforded her. And camp.

In 1930, her "Portrait of Susie" was displayed on the fourth floor of the Grand Central Palace – a building in the style of Grand Central Terminal that no longer exists – as part of the Exhibition of the Society of Independent Artists (a group led by the eminent John Sloan and then mourning its first leader, founder of the school of Ashcan Realism, Robert Henri).

"Susie" as it hangs in Marjorie Smith's house today and in further detail (below).

NEW YORK CITY LOVE TRIANGLE, 1931

Forbes Watson, who'd written for the New York Evening Post and The World and The Times, who in the 1930s would advise FDR's Treasury Department on the procurement of painting and sculpture for federal building decoration,[132] working for The Arts magazine, assessed the show by making a "list of paintings that are not in the least slumberously conventional" and shared certain "invigorating characteristics" – particularly "freshness of observation" and unaffected honesty of expression."[133]

He listed Norma Jeanne's canvas *fourth* – ahead of work by many older and more accomplished artists, and from a show featuring 1,136 exhibits in total.

The New York Sun was more concise, calling Norma Jeanne's portrait "a warm and living thing."[134]

Norma parlayed these notices into her first one-woman show, from Nov. 17-Dec. 1, at the Morton Galleries on West 57th Street, whose owner, the eponymous Mrs. Morton, had always explicitly sought for her walls young American talent yet to be shown individually. She offered ardent young things an opportunity to show an equivalent aptitude.

Norma was given the chance to hang just 10 paintings. The game was on.

> YOU ARE CORDIALLY INVITED TO AN
> EXHIBITION
> of
> PORTRAITS
> by
> **Norma Jeanne Bernstein**
> at the
> **Morton Galleries**
> **49 West 57th Street**
>
> November 17th To December 1st   New York

The actual invitation to the exhibit.

Art News, Nov. 22, 1930: "With a deft palette knife and a genuine interest in character, Miss Bernstein demonstrates that she need not join the vast throng of society portraitists. Other promising canvases include…Grandma

Rieser, amiably resigned to her double chins."

The New York Evening Post, from the same day: "Miss Bernstein is a young artist, hardly beyond the student era, but her work reveals ability to seize characteristic physical gestures…Able and promising."

On Nov 23, The World wrote: "Ability to combine the personality of a sitter with physical likeness is an outstanding merit of a room of portraits by Norma Jeanne Bernstein."

That same day, a Sunday, the New York Times, which on all other days of the week abjured the use of photo to the degree the tabloids embraced it, ran per usual its lone exception to those ceaseless textual columns – its Sunday Rotogravure section, a graphic guide to events of the past week.

And just after a page featuring Babe Ruth, hand extended, picking up the chin of a hospitalized baby; and Albert Einstein, standing somewhat forlornly before a microphone, recording a phonograph side in Berlin; and a dark Soviet dirigible, looming not far above ground, like a giant floating melon, or an aerial orca, which had departed Moscow on a 1,000-mile test flight…

…there, just on the next Times page, gazed out at the reader New York City Judge Louis Wendel, as painted by Norma Jeanne Bernstein, the artist herself mentioned by name – a most incredible graphic inclusion in the paper of record.

Norma Jeanne took this opportunity to expound on the ideas behind her work in yet another newspaper article, to get at her quintessential aims in a world increasingly dominated by imagistic reproduction (and soon to be flooded with yet more images via the TV):

> *By means of a camera I could produce distortions as terrible as some I have seen at exhibitions. This could be done by placing a piece of curved glass before the camera's lens. That is the trouble with some painters who term themselves artists. When they work, there is, of course not literally, a piece of curved glass before their eyes. They believe they are creating, but the result is a mere distortion of nature. I see nothing deep or worthy in work of this caliber. Modern art would be placed*

CHAPTER 8: BIRDSEYE-THOMASHEFSKY-BERNSTEIN

on a higher pedestal if an interest in art would be re-born in its most valuable forms. Every artist should be able to see something different and yet vivid in the same subject.

She was just 24. And launched.

* * *

Norma Jeanne was also now a resident of the building in which I presently live today, on the Upper West Side – though she was bound in the aftermath of her greatly auspicious solo debut show, for the Caribbean: Her whole family boarded the French Line's Lafayette on Dec. 20 destined to spend the turn of the new year, 1930 into 1931, on a cruise docking in Nassau, Port Au Prince, Kingston, Cristobal and Havana.

Her obvious plan for the new year was to build on the artistic success she'd just had: Study, Paint, Show. Unclear is whether, by the time the boat had disembarked from the New York pier, she'd already decided in spite of that plan to spend the summer as supervisor of a camp in the Adirondacks – in Horicon, New York – called Point O' Pines.

To retreat into that slightly schlocky atmosphere she'd never ceased to find delightful.

Perhaps it was a notion she toyed with on-board the boat. Maybe each island she visited left her craving that stillness and peace and oneness-with-nature wooded, rural sites had singularly provided her. The decision could have been made by the time of her January 5th return to New York.

* * *

At the start of 1931, the Jewish Hospital didn't have the sort of surfeit funds one associates with leisurely holiday (no matter that institutions don't actually go anywhere). The hospital was strapped for cash quite seriously, in fact.

Lewis E. Birdseye spoke at a February confab in which the Jewish Hospital announced the issuance of bonds — $300,000 worth – that would allow it to make payments on *two* separate mortgages later in the year, in April and May.[135]

The Hospital assured the public that it had in 1930 secured sufficient donor pledges to have "entirely eliminated" its debt – only the Great Depression had prevented those promisors from following through on their charitable declarations.

The hospital used the same session in which it essentially begged the public for money – albeit while promising a six percent return in five years – to disclose care statistics for 1930 – numbers Lewis E. Birdseye never could have foreseen being impacted in the coming year by a bloody incident instigated by his own kin.[136]

In 1930, the hospital had seen exactly 15,217 patients.

No more, no fewer.

***

Dr. Milton Thomashefsky ran his medical office with the roguish charm and outrageous seduction of any well-practiced Don Juan.

Meek handball player and mama's boy? Hardly.

He was every bit the lothario his father was — only he'd done a far better job of keeping that behavior unknown.

This is one way to interpret, based on later testament (and evidence that nevertheless remains mysterious today), the envy and violence soon to ensue:

That from the moment Agnes Birdseye entered his employ, Dr. Milton Thomashefsky told her everything she wanted to hear, took her out for drives in his car, on dates to the theater, on trips to the apartment in which he lived (alongside that cast away mother).

Sometimes Dr. Milton and Agnes just parked their car in a slightly shielded area beside the road and made out (during one such session, a gang took advantage of their compromised position and robbed Agnes of all her jewelry – which baubles Dr. Thomashefsky then spent money to replace).

That "the physician and his pretty nurse had mixed *fervent love* with their professional relations, and had held *numerous trysts* after hours."[137]

In this version, Milton called Miss Birdseye "Boo Boo" outside the office and she called him "Mickey" in return. For years – to the point that some friends of the pair considered them engaged.[138]

He was just three years her senior – not a tremendous difference. She was going to study medicine at night, too – become more of his avocational and intellectual and social equal.[139]

Of course, they were from totally different worlds – he was highly Jewish, albeit tied to that ethnicity and culture in unusual ways. His father was the most famous Yiddish actor in the world, who'd be referenced by Groucho himself in the 1931 Marx Brothers film "Monkey Business."

She was a direct descendant of the Puritan deacon who'd settled Milford, Connecticut, in the 1600s. A daughter of the American Revolution (if not by registration than by patrimony). Her father's Boy Scout troop had met for years at Wells Presbyterian Church.

Their one obvious social overlap – her father overseeing the Jewish Hospital in which Dr. Milton had worked – was the subject the couple absolutely could not broach, at least for now. Lewis E. Birdseye, superintendent, couldn't learn of Dr. Milton's highly physical canoodling with a daughter entrusted to the doctor's employ. He would have felt shamefully betrayed.

(Their less obvious overlap, which they may or may not have discussed – their mothers were both active in the suffragette movement; Bessie's greatest personal stage triumph once she'd separated from Boris was a parable about a woman who dresses as a male in order to be allowed to drive – "Chantshe in America"; Florence, meanwhile, had served in the State Suffragette party and actually observed the ballot-counting the day New York voted for female enfranchisement.)

And yet, the overwhelming familial difference could be put out of mind so long as Dr. Milton and Agnes continued to go out driving. So long as he persisted in telling her she was the one.

Dr. Milton was undoubtedly handsome, his van-dyke facial hair lending him passing resemblance to those dark silent-film stars Rudolph Valentino, John Gilbert. Agnes had dazzling reddish-blonde hair upon which everyone felt compelled to comment. They hadn't crossed paths without reason. Somehow, in time, this relationship could be justified to concerned parties and thereby made public.

It could be endorsed officially like those couplings of Agnes' siblings': In January 1930, her brother Lewis Jr., now a Merchant Marine and aviator, married his beloved; in June 1930, her sister Betty did the same – in fact, Betty tied the knot with a doctor (albeit one of Irish descent...who'd die just two years later, incredibly young, of cancer).

However unreasonable to an outsider, Agnes Birdseye was possessed of hope. And of a ring: in the winter of early 1931, Agnes showed her sister Chico a ring – possibly indicative of an engagement, though neither sister spoke publicly of the object, or what it meant or who purchased it. Possibly Agnes had been instructed to keep all of those details secret.

(Maybe Dr. Milton didn't buy her the ring at all, despite his long history with Agnes. Maybe she'd purchased it herself, hoping it would prompt Dr. Milton to pose the question customarily attendant to the presentation of such expensive tokens. Except Agnes was a 30-year-old assistant. How would she have afforded it?)

Dr. Milton had other matter on his mind – primarily his summer holiday destination. His friend, an engineer at the Jewish Hospital named Philip Pines, would be spending July at a camp in the Adirondacks.

Point O' Pines – in Horicon, New York.

He was perhaps unaccustomed to camps, but how vastly different could it be from his father's villa in the Catskills?

And Agnes had her father's Connecticut farmhouse in Branchville to which she could repair for a vacation while Dr. Milton went away – an added bonus: all of that land would make excellent ground for Dr. Milton's dog, Fritz, to roam.[140]

So Dr. Milton handed Agnes his pup as he took his leave at the end of June. She no doubt saw this pet-sitting assignment as a sign of affection. He seemed to find her *useful*.

CHAPTER 8: BIRDSEYE-THOMASHEFSKY-BERNSTEIN

Agnes and Fritz.

The convergent, combustible summer of 1931.

For 10 days preceding Memorial Day weekend, it has rained across the greater Glens Falls region, a verdant and mountainous hamlet-flecked expanse, flanked by Saratoga Springs in the south and Ticonderoga in the north, veined in the middle by slanting, serene bodies of water, almost puddle-like amidst the pine-covered slopes – Lake George, Schroon Lake, Brant Lake.

The area is anxious, former timber towns dependent on the tourists who come yearly to the camps and resorts perched along their shores, as if somehow the weather won't inevitably right itself, as if the sun's late reticence was by divine decree, a punishment for all the hoteliers' unknown sins.

They needn't have worried. The last day of June brings 120-degree heat to downtown Glens Falls. It's 90 in the shade, beneath the coniferous canopy of the Eastern white pines 18 stories tall.

Back in New York City, a ticker tape parade is being thrown for Post and Gatty, daring aviators who've just circumnavigated the globe in eight days, 15 hours and 51 minutes.

But Dr. Milton Thomashefsky has abandoned those sticky (now confetti-strewn) streets, the suffocating sensation their concrete seasonally imposes, for a parcel 800 feet above sea level, on the edge of Brant Lake, in the town of Horicon.

Camp Point O' Pines.

He likely spends Friday, July 3rd like everyone else in the area, in anticipation of, if not in preparation for, the parties to be held Saturday night – the July 4th concerts, the fireworks to be launched off the wharves over the lakes.

There are 8 pm Shabbos services at Temple Beth El in Glens Falls, but he's not traveled up here for religious reasons nor suggested himself the faithful sort, on any number of levels. Maybe at 10 pm, awaiting the festivities of the next day, not quite able to turn in early, he turns on a radio, tunes in the big heavyweight championship bout on WEAF. Listens to Schmeling knock out Stribling in the final round, with just 14 seconds remaining.

CHAPTER 8: BIRDSEYE-THOMASHEFSKY-BERNSTEIN

Or perhaps he sits up in his camp bed and peruses the local paper, reviews the advice column by a psychologist for those considering matrimony.[141]

"Now that you are sure you love each other, carefully consider whether you believe you always will…

"Does the one you love come from a family you always will be glad to welcome in your home? Will he or she fit well into the customs and ideals of the family in which you grew up?…

"Conventions have their value to those with character enough to live by them. You doubtless would not choose a mate who to your knowledge had had sex experience out of wedlock. You would want, therefore, to prove to your mate the same guarantee."

* * *

It may begin with Reveille being bugled across the campus. And the actual record of this day being thin, one can only imagine certain details – until two very crucial interactions occur.

Doctor Milton blinks open his eyes on Independence Day utterly unaware its events will lead to a tormenting dependence on others. He shifts in his bed – perhaps he felt its springs in his back the entire night, the entire milieu slightly too rustic, or maybe he appreciates that thin mountain air seeping into the corners of his eyes, the sawdust smell particular to bunks now wending its way into his nostrils.

He shuffles to the sink, too drowsy to think while twisting the knob and extending his hands beneath the faucet. It coughs out frigid water, which in his somnolence, though he can feel the painful cold in his fingers already, he splashes onto his face without hesitation.

The bracing chill, running through his cheeks, is a divine pain. He's now fully open – to the day, its possibilities.

He moves to a window, or even to the grounds just beyond the stairs leading from his bunk. Perhaps in no more than a robe, he takes in the luxuriant view: vast, untroubled waters at his feet, dense, mountainside forest rising in the distance. A haze shrouding those peaks suddenly lifting.

Behind him, campers are already chowing down in the cafeteria, hurried by the exhortation of impatient counselors and a prior awareness of the day's ceaseless duties.

Dr. Milton, a guest, strolls to the chow hall unburdened by the boisterous importuning everywhere around him. Recumbent on a dining hall bench, he pokes warily with a fork at the chunky porridge set before him before yielding to his hunger and devouring the lot of it. Eggs and flapjacks, too. He's on holiday – he feels entitled to that great quantity of food and less precious than a moment earlier about its quality.

He wanders the grounds, observes. In a gazebo, campers and counselors practice "Stars and Stripes Forever," halted repeatedly by an accented instructor who divines someone playing a discordant note, to his great displeasure (and then fury). He watches maintenance men set off crackling fireworks into a blindingly sunny sky. They're impossible to make out, so Dr. Milton dons sunglasses, but still, he can't see anything but faint dotted lines like segmented tree branches. He can hear, however, the explosive booms – followed by that crackling sound like the start of a film reel only amplified by a million.

All the time, Dr. Milton has no idea what's in store for him besides the show.

But two meetings that day having been noted, we do – and here imagination is no longer required.

As the Fourth advances toward its bombastic, saltpeter-fueled, sky-brightening climax, Dr. Milton meets up with his friend Philip Pines, the engineer at the Jewish Hospital whose apartment building on Eastern Parkway is situated feet away from his own.[142]

Perhaps figuring Dr. Milton might want to meet the beautiful woman responsible for all this percussive pageantry, Pines introduces him to the comely 25-year-old camp supervisor.

Norma Jeanne Bernstein.

They first lock eyes July 4th.

Fireworks.

CHAPTER 8: BIRDSEYE-THOMASHEFSKY-BERNSTEIN

* * *

A giddy camp summer – only one experienced by ostensible adults.

He tells of his own time in Paris – when he stayed in the 16th Arrondisement, at the Hotel Majestic, on Avenue Kleber.

In the day, he studies her closely – notes the hairs of her left eyebrow, nearer the nose, tend to sway in unruly fashion.

He gazes at her "brown eyes like gold in the sun coming through the haunches" of the trees. And the "dear little wrinkle in the corner of [her] mouth when she smiles."[143]

He watches her swim in the lake and then climb out – how water remains on her lashes so that they sparkle.

They spend nights together, once Norma has finished the camp casino and other amenities. Together one evening they climb a mountain; at the top, her hair glimmers in the silver moonlight. They share a bottle of some drink and she feigns exhilaration, deliriousness, an act he finds endearing.

Of course, they talk for hours.

He hears her laugh even when he's alone – that "heh heh" to which she constantly in conversation resorts, which sounds part-spontaneous and part-sardonic, its owner, 25, herself unsure the degree to which either is intended.

But she has definite, earnest feelings on her craft.[144]

"A painter copies nature with all the exactness which he is able to command," she believes. "The work of an artist is different. He tries not to copy but to create."

Most important to her: "The character and soul of the subject must stand revealed. A 'Dorian Grey' must be done every time."

He may not discuss his own vocation, otolaryngology, in any depth – the real reason, in a family of performers, even as he fled the stage, he focused his studies on the throat – on the tenuous vocal cords upon which the actor relies. Whose injury can ruin him.

But he does mention his assistant Agnes Birdseye – not their assignations, almost certainly – but some humorous aspect of her presence in his office.

Perhaps he insists his secretary-nurse is hopelessly fond of him, always has been, but it's a crush unreciprocated. The girl is just dizzy. But Norma becomes aware of this woman, even if not as a potential rival.[145]

And yet, she perceives some deeper Dorian Gray truth to this 34-year-old doctor. She's said it already – an artist must sense such things (before setting them down).

Norma Jeanne explicitly tells Milton she can cure him – but of what ill exactly, what complex or defect, she does not specify.

The month of July elapses in a steamy blur. He must return to the city. But she should not despair – their separation will be brief – and eased by the correspondence they will keep up – in letters, phone calls.

This is only a temporary goodbye. And the geographic distance, the time apart, won't alter his view of her nor the plan they've discussed eventually to marry.[146]

Dr. Milton may very well mean every word of it, too – a lover boy reformed, prior darlings not so much forgotten as disregarded. Why not abandon all flings and move forward? Norma can see into him; her penetrating gaze can make of him an honest man. Perhaps all along, and unwittingly, he was waiting for someone whose unflinching gaze wouldn't permit the romping for which his father, his family, was notorious.

He had a love-hate relationship with Boris – he'd sided always with his cast-off mother Bessie – yet he'd caroused with his father's abandon.

Maybe a true artist, aware of the ugliness within him, that Thomashefsky lechery, was the partner his split persona required.

Norma Jeanne has no doubt she is, even if she's unaware of Milton's exact past indiscretions. She senses something off inside him but feels drawn closer to him as a result. Destined to heal the doctor.

He gives her a beefcake photo of himself in a dashing, puffy blouse. The next time she sees him he'll no longer be able to walk.

CHAPTER 8: BIRDSEYE-THOMASHEFSKY-BERNSTEIN

If Dr. Milton Thomashefsky has made too many promises in his 34-year life – conflicting vows that by their very nature cannot all be kept – he does at least keep his word with regard to correspondence. His first letter to her back in camp is stamped by his local Brooklyn post office on July 31 itself, as if it was dispatched the moment he returned home.

It's an unusual, almost Joycean dispatch – free of indentation or proper punctuation, perhaps inspired by his family's Vaudevillian scripts – in which Dr. Milton switches back and forth from a fictional conversation with the mother of a boy (seemingly named "Mrs. Rosenstein," although Milton's penmanship is fiendishly difficult to decipher) whose tonsils have just been removed and descriptions of Norma's irresistible winsomeness – impish and forward observations already cited above:

> *You can let [him] out of Bed day after to-morrow if it's sunny* <u>out</u> *her Brown eyes were like gold in the sun...No, I wouldn't let him go swimming yet – you may take him to the beach – but no swimming – when she came out of the lake, there were drops of water on her lashes...The anesthesia has made him a little dizzy – Wasn't she sweet with her simulated exhilaration...Oh, yes, he'll breathe fine through his nose now – the funny little [an onomatopoetic sound that looks like "neigh" or "whine"]* <u>she</u> *makes with her nose and tries so hard to suppress – Why, of course he'll be cured – She said she could cure* <u>me</u> *– I wonder what she meant – Yes you can take him for a ride – take him to the top of the mountains in the moonlight where there were silver lights in her hair...I don't think he'll be undersized but he surely will grow now that his tonsils are out – Oh, yes, he'll grow and grow and get tall – very tall – 12 feet maybe! How would you like to be 12 feet tall, Sonny? Well, goodbye! Be a good boy and eat some spinach and maybe someday,* <u>you'll</u> *have a dear little wrinkle in the corner of her mouth when she smiles – goodbye Mrs. Rosenstein – Hello?*

Now, on the backside of the same page, Dr. Thomashefsky learns of a patient with ethmoiditis (a type of sinusitis):

"I see – perforated into the orbit, eh? How much do the eyes protrude? I see! Are they brown? – I mean, is the case scheduled? Well, then, order it prepared and I'll be right down."

Dr. Milton is told by a colleague of a woman in room 617 plagued by back pain in this imagined hospital (no doubt patterned after the actual

Jewish Hospital in which Dr. Thomashefsky has worked, now overseen by his assistant Agnes Birdseye's father, its superintendent)

"Get her a polo belt," he writes, "size 28." He turns his attention back to Norma, to make a most personal inquiry of her measurements: "How *is* 28?"

He advises his colleague to give the patient codeine and then counsel her to forget her pain, and then, back to Norma:

"I said forget it – it's easy to forget – tell her to go right back to work, and work hard and she'll forget and she won't feel miserable, she won't have the longing and the ache."

Finally, Dr. Milton turns the breathless soliloquy on himself: "Maybe this is a good time to get busy and finish the monograph on functional testing of the acoustic and static labyrinth – what was it that made me stop it a few months ago?…oh how I love you Norma."

Milton folds and slides the letter into the envelope below on his own, addresses it himself.

But this is a busy office suite – Milton shares it with Dr. Joseph Kasnetz and Dr. Philip Liebowitz, the former a pathologist and the latter an otolaryngologist, both of whom have worked at the Jewish Hospital – and Dr. Milton believes somehow he can keep his affairs, no matter how obviously conducted, private.

His assistant Agnes will later talk of her relationship with a postal clerk, too.

Dr. Milton perhaps gives her this letter to mail, then – slips it in with all the rest of the office's outgoing papers and parcels.

But its destination is visible, and Agnes is beginning to worry.

Norma Jeanne calls Dr. Milton – but at the office,

Agnes picks up, apparently tells her the doctor can't come to the phone. Norma Jeanne, unaware she has aroused (perhaps further) the suspicion of a woman who has visited her beau's apartment and spent hours in his arms, replies she'll call back.

Agnes tells Dr. Milton later, as if she's blithely and by rote performing her clerical duty: A Miss Bernstein phoned you – *probably a patient, but –* said she'd ring again.

Agnes has begun to understand what's transpiring – she is piecing together bits of info overheard and espied. She is perhaps sensing from Dr. Milton an attitude toward her altered. However slightly.

And then sent a letter sent *from* a Norma Jeanne Bernstein arrives in the office.

Agnes either unseals the envelope secretly only to reseal it later or finds a way to read the note after Dr. Milton himself has torn open the container and reviewed its contents – but either way, Agnes peruses this latest romantic missive without permission.

Its contents outrage and terrify her, implying such treacherous behavior by the doctor whom she has loved: Milton wooed another woman at this camp furiously, as if he'd never once touched Agnes or brought her home or spoken of their future.

And the note implies this new couple has already reached an advanced stage in their courtship.

CHAPTER 8: BIRDSEYE-THOMASHEFSKY-BERNSTEIN

Agnes realizes this Norma Jeanne Bernstein paramour, being Hebrew and likely beautiful and so very far along in her wooing, will beat her out for Milton's heart.

So Agnes decides she must intervene – disrupt Norma's relationship in order to save her own. She anonymously writes a letter to Dr. Milton, a poison pen missive intended to make Norma seem dissolute, promiscuous.

Agnes begins the note "Dear Doc Mickey Thomas," and then, for the sake of verisimilitude, discusses the referral of a patient to Dr. Milton's office. Then she goes in for the kill:

"Didn't I see you out a few times with little Miss Bernstein? I passed her one night early this week by the side of road necking to heat hell (sic) with one of Dr. Shields' patients."[147]

Of course, as the note is fiction, it's unclear exactly to whom Agnes refers, but a Dr. James Skidmore Shields was at the time a dentist with ties to the Brooklyn Jewish Hospital, who lived both in that borough but also in Saratoga Springs – that is, a 50-minute car ride away from the camp Norma Jeanne ran.

Dr. Thomashefsky seems to believe every last word of the thing – and so he writes Norma again, this letter postmarked August 8th and devoid of the prior note's odd humor:

> *Sweet Norma, It's so good to have you to think about – it's become chronic – and in the past week, several acute exacerbations – one when Miss Birdseye (really!) told me a Miss Bernstein had called and would call again – probably a patient but – and again when Bill Pines made earnest mention of Norma – and again when Arthur Freund was in town – he never called to tell me how you cried when I left – to-day two letters about Norma – one written by herself and mis-directed so that it travelled to a few post-offices – and the other from a snake. I haven't the slightest idea who he is, but he writes quite peculiarly to "dear Doc Mickey Thomas."*

And after relaying Agnes' falsified note, Milton continues:

163

> *Know, Miss Bernstein, <u>little</u> Miss Bernstein, that I love you! Know, little Miss Bernstein, that I adore you! Know that I long for you! Know that all the themes in the story books have happened to me on account of you. Know that I never want to see you afraid – but I'm coming up to camp soon for a kiss! Norma, Norma! Iago's letter was a knife thrust. Can you realize the state I'm in? Isn't it funny? I can hear you "heh heh." And I want you to laugh. I just stepped aside and took [a] look at myself sitting here in the heat writing a love letter and I laughed aloud! At my age, I've gone...completely nuts! And I'm writing it all down so I'll remember it. I used to do that when I was a little boy. I can remember things better when I write them – and I <u>want</u> to remember this. If I had only written a description of my sensations the last time I felt this way – fifteen years ago – it would be more than just a rogue remembrance and so if I write "I love you! Loveliest Norma", it matters not that you will know it – but that I will remember it – and if I neglect to write of the <u>misery</u> and hopelessness that are surely coming by Tuesday or Wednesday, I shall have forever only the sweetness of it all.*

And here the note gets truly mind-boggling. Sure, it's odd that Milton believes the vague character assassination note or claims to and odder still – or perhaps in keeping with his selfishness – that he attaches more importance to his future ability to recall his summer love of 1931 than Norma's knowing how he actually feels about her.

But then Milton brings up the only person who can perhaps calm him, keep him sane, at such an imperiled point in his romance with Norma. And while he calls her only "Mrs. Z," one can't imagine him having told Norma at camp about any Mrs. Z in sufficient detail and with enough frequency that he could later omit the rest of her name besides one woman:

Mrs. Regina Zuckerberg – his father Boris' longtime mistress, the homewrecker who forced his mother from the family abode. His surrogate mother, in a sense.

Apparently, Milton had not exactly taken his biological mother's side when Boris had betrayed Bessie. In fact, Milton had formed a special bond with the woman whose affections constituted half of that treachery.

And yet, he was obviously conflicted about his attachment to his father's lover – he quite literally curses her for being so calming and helpful.

Or maybe, just maybe, he is mocking her – accusing Mrs. Zuckerberg of being so caught up in psychoanalysis and her own bullshit she'd try to talk him out of a romance truly felt (much as she broke up the very real connection his parents once had).

Or maybe it's not her at all:

> *Monday, I shall have devised with Mrs. Z – wise and understanding – my only <u>confidante</u> – and damn her, I <u>know</u> she'll restore my equanimity – how well she'll explain that this thing is impossible unless the spirit is receptive – that my reaction to yellow pajamas in a canoe on a lake on a summer's day was <u>merely</u> a substitution neurosis – a compensatory phenomenon – a whole lot of life's <u>sound sense</u> which will refute the fact that I love you – darling Norma – I love you.*

Norma Jeanne reads the letter with a modicum of confusion – how could the doctor believe me wanton and debauched? (Never mind all the boyfriends she has had in New York and Paris whom perhaps she has alluded to in her conversations with Dr. Milton but maybe not.) She writes him back in defense of her virtue – but also with the casual updates on camp life that have always marked her diary entries – with the camp affairs that might strike others as mundane but have compelled her to return again and again to the woods – which enabled her to meet Dr. Milton.

> *Mickey dear,*
>
> *I'm not laughing now and I'm utterly bewildered that any one should stoop so low. I can't believe you would give the matter serious thought. I have read about such people, but I never dreamed that any one would do such a rotten thing. There is one person I can think of who may have done it, some one who resented the fact that I completely ignored*

him.

I believe I can guess who would do such a thing, but always I have instinctively avoided that person. It was done for spitefulness on his part, and underhanded way of working. Where was the letter mailed from? Was it signed or anonymous? Oh, why worry about it? But it does seem a lousy thing to do.

I actually worked yesterday. I turned the Casino into a nightclub, causing the hit of the Summer. Mother and dad came up for a few days. Hattie left last week. I wish I could go home with the folks for a couple of weeks on Wednesday.

And that if your dear, wise friend can cure you, send me the recipe and –oh, did I remember to tell you, dear, darling Mickey, that I miss you so much?

Norma Jeanne mails the letter immediately, without any known delay – her guess about her detractor – some male admirer of hers spurned – obviously wrong.

The letter will arrive at Dr. Thomashefsky's office on Tuesday, August 11. By that point, her actual rival will have heightened the situation considerably – set in motion a chain of events that will end in the death of one of the three and the debilitation of another.

* * *

Agnes sees her note did nothing to revive the relationship she once had with her employer – the doctor seems as uninterested in her – as cold and indifferent – as ever.

She is enraged – and perhaps of the belief that, having shared her body with this man, she's also ruined.

Or maybe they are still passionately making love – only Agnes knows he's two-timing her, that he's speaking of true love in letters to Norma. Agnes understands she's just a plaything.

On Monday night, Aug. 10, 1931, a day before Norma Jeanne's reply to

CHAPTER 8: BIRDSEYE-THOMASHEFSKY-BERNSTEIN

the poison pen letter is to arrive, Agnes finds her way into Dr. Milton's apartment.

This a curious entry – the doctor will later claim he was playing cards with the very friend who introduced him to Norma – Philip Pines – until at least midnight, if not later, in his apartment. How does Agnes know when Pines will leave? And Dr. Milton's mother, Bessie, with whom he lives, is also out town. Did Agnes know this also?

And the apartment cannot be accessed surreptitiously via the fire escape (newspapers will later try it) and no employee of the building sees Agnes arrive or leave. She also has no key to the residence, Dr. Milton will later insist.

She's also tiny – just 5'2", 125 pounds – for her to overpower a man is unlikely. For her to have been in his residence already because they were in the habit of making love perhaps more so.

No matter how she achieves it, Monday night, Agnes enters Dr. Milton's apartment. In the wee hours of the morning, when she begins her procedure, he's already asleep in his bed.

She places a chloroform-sodden cloth over his mouth and nose. Perhaps during this procedure, the doctor opens his eyes – sees her face for just a millisecond – before everything goes blurry (he will at one point later claim he did).

She then removes a scalpel and begins the vengeful procedure of cutting off his penis or testicles or both.

Agnes, who is by one account studying medicine at night in the hopes of becoming a doctor herself,[148] makes a few slashes, but the act then proves too grotesque for her to continue, and overwhelmed by the blood, she bandages the still-unconscious doctor, then leaves a nonsensical note ascribing the attack to a gangster's vendetta against his brother Harry, with whom he collaborated on the lyrics for the 1919 Thomashefsky production "Parlor Floor and Basement":

"Harry: This settles an old score. A.C."

Tuesday morning, Dr. Milton wakes up, still drugged, notices his bandaged nether regions and calls a few people from his bed. The first is Philip Pines, the man who introduced him to Norma Jeanne Bernstein on July 4th and with whom he was supposedly playing cards the night before, per his later retelling.

Dr. Milton asks Pines to be his bodyguard for the next few days, until he figures out what had transpired. If he did see Agnes' face the night before, he's very clearly unsure she was his attacker – indicating she was likely there for other reasons entirely.

Dr. Milton also calls his brother, Harry to read him the note, ask him about this mobster out to avenge a past wrong, warn him a further attack may occur, this time on Harry himself, should the hoodlum realize he mistook one brother for another.

He also asks Harry to meet him at his office later in the day.

Finally, he contacts a surgeon, so his wounds can be properly treated, apparently in his home. And then he packs some belongings and moves into Pines' apartment temporarily, scared to stay in his own, for now.

That afternoon, Harry arrives at the office – only to bump right into Agnes Birdseye at reception. She begins to tell him that his brother has been slashed but then stops herself.

"He'd better tell you himself," she suddenly says. "Don't say that I said anything about it."

And then Norma Jeanne's letter – the one that begins "Dear Mickey darling" – finally arrives.

By now, Dr. Milton has assembled in his mind a fuller picture of what has transpired. He has not been as slick as he has believed – the nurse he'd teased and tempted and taken out for years has indeed found out about his love affair with Norma Jeanne, this fashionable painter who has called his office from the Adirondacks to flirt with him and gotten Agnes on the other end of the line by mistake.

Wednesday: All day the doctor rows with Agnes about her interference in his current romance, about their own past liaison, about promises supposedly made. Apparently, Pines just observes all this without interceding. But the office is turned upside down – this furious argument leaves paperwork and cabinetry scattered and askew. Glass drug bottles are broken; even a

CHAPTER 8: BIRDSEYE-THOMASHEFSKY-BERNSTEIN

light bulb is somehow shattered.

If Agnes has never really been the doctor's lover, as he will later claim, it makes very little sense that the argument should have been so heated, gone on for so long, involved so much drama. Why wouldn't Milton just call the cops, having been slashed?

In fact, the argument is so protracted Agnes calls her family in the middle of it and reaches a sister – she says something terrible has happened but nothing more.

Dr. Milton apparently dresses down Agnes:

She's a monster for having slashed him, out of her mind for being so envious, and destined always to be apart from him. They will never marry. In fact, she won't even see him anymore – she's fired from this office. Through, finished, washed up.

As a long, raucous day settles into a night that can't possible prove any more fractious, Philip Pines – the engineer-friend-bodyguard – takes leaves of the doctor's office, sometime after 6 p.m. – he wants to ready himself for dinner with Dr. Milton and he seemingly believes his friend safe, even though he'll be leaving him alone with a woman who clearly hates him.

Pines doesn't live in this building, but his own is just five minutes away on foot – if he makes haste, he should be back in 15 minutes, give or take. Why he needs to freshen up for dinner – what item of clothing he must exchange, why he needs to shower or wash his face when the doctor who has been stalking the office all day in fury doesn't — he'll never explain. He will say that Agnes hated him for having effected the doctor's introduction to Norma. Perhaps he simply wants to escape, however briefly, a room in which he has suffered his own share of verbal abuse.

Agnes, 5'2", 125 pounds, clad in an all-white white nurse's uniform, breaks down – she begs on her knees for forgiveness, mercy, acknowledges the ghastly knifing, says a postal clerk helped her draft the note attributing the slashing to a vengeful enemy of Milton's brother (a clerk the police would later search for and never find),[149] implores the doctor – who still has significant ties to the hospital her father oversees – not to tell anyone of her dastardly mistake.

But also: "If I can't have you, no one else shall."[150]

The buzzer rings to the front door of the office – which opens up onto Eastern Parkway. It is either 6:40 or 6:50 pm.[151]

Agnes perhaps believes whoever is at the door – her father, the police – will catch wind of her embarrassing admission to the mutilation attempt. She also knows Dr. Milton to be right, in more profound ways than he realizes: She *is* finished.

There is nothing Agnes can say or do in the summer of 1931 – in an age of Boris Thomashefsky lying about a reunion with his wife on a hospital bed – inviting his estranged wife Bessie back home only to keep up his extramarital affair, to give the starring role he'd promised Bessie to that mistress; of Dr. Abraham Glickstein raping Lillian Raizen and attempting to make love to her just weeks before her wedding, only for Lillian to be accused of whining and whimpering and imprisoned for life by Agnes' father's friends – that will restore the humanity and wholeness warped romances of the era requisition only of the female actors.

Dr. Milton turns to open the door.

Agnes grabs from her desk drawer with her left hand a .38 caliber revolver she acquired months earlier and stashed there for reasons unclear.[152]

She blasts one shot at Dr. Milton's back. The spiraling lead breaks through into his spine, severs it, before settling in his lung. He crumples.

Agnes then turns the weapon on herself.

She points the downward-slanting barrel at her stomach, just above and to the left of her bellybutton. Dr. Milton, lying paralyzed on the floor, hears a gun's hammer being cocked.

Agnes squeezes the trigger.

The bullet slides through her abs, tunneling between her muscle fibers until it exits her torso at the right hip, six inches below where it entered on the opposite side. The projectile then continues spiraling on its penetrative course – boring a tiny hole through a door just beside her.

Agnes has escaped real harm; like a skipped rock across a plane of water, the bullet never entered her abdominal cavity but merely scraped its surface.

Does she feel, even for a moment, the smallest sense of relief? Why has she aimed at the area of her womb?

Agnes raises the .38 caliber to the left side of her head, just above and behind her ear. If she pulls the curved, cold trigger now, the bullet will not graze her – it will tunnel into the left side of her head, through her brain, a relentless lead augur.

Dr. Milton hears the cocking of the hammer.

Agnes squeezes, setting off a destructive pinball: the bullet blazes a half-inch wide hole through her temporal lobe, ricochets against the hard surface of the parietal eminence, dive-bombing toward the base of the anterior fossa, where it fractures both eye sockets. The bullet snags in a tract of tissue near the site of entry, deformed itself from the neurological caroming that has ended almost exactly where it began.

Agnes falls down in a heap. Blood pools behind her shattered left orbital bone, making it appear as though she has been punched in the face.

Her father has been in the habit every year of sending out a Christmas card containing the legend of an archer in the time of Camelot whose accuracy was such that he was able to fire an arrow directly through a flying bird's eyes – the ostensible origin of the surname the family has carried ever since.

The resonance of that now.

Her white uniform bears the residual powder and burn marks of her firings: a hole, as if someone has stubbed out a thick cigarette, almost a half-inch in diameter, just below her left breast – smudged with particulates; similar small piles of sinister grains across her left shoulder, the revolver's dandruff.

Outside, just beyond the front door, the man who actually rang the bell was not Agnes' father but the Dr. Milton's friend and makeshift protector, Pines. He has heard all three shots and run into the residential lobby of the Turner Towers, in search of a building superintendent who might have a passkey.

Meanwhile, yet alive but well aware of his spinal severance, struggling to breathe, Dr. Milton claws his way along the floor, blood smearing beneath him, toward the gun Agnes used to attempt his murder and achieve her own.

He understands what it means for a bullet to slice a man's spinal cord in two, for it to lodge in his chest. He will be paralyzed below the waist for as long he lives.

"I wanted to finish the job," he will later say.[153]

He cracks open the revolver's chamber with his hand – if there are unused bullets in that lethal wheel, he intends to use them on himself, to succeed in his elimination where Agnes has failed.

There aren't.

Philip Pines and the superintendent burst in; the former exclaims, "My god! They got him!" – a strange use of the plural tense by a person who would know better than anyone the room had been locked with just two people inside. One of the three people still alive in the room places a call to Agnes' father.

Another call is made – to Norma Jeanne Bernstein at camp – which leaves her "weeping" and "frantically demanding to know what had happened to the man, she said, *she was to marry*."[154]

Her father, former State Assemblyman and lawyer J. Sidney Bernstein, drives her from the Adirondacks back to the city, for official police questioning.

The end of everything – the undoing of generations of industriousness – the outcome of ominous earlier dissipation, too – in a single spasmodic episode of violence.

And also, just the beginning.

II

Descendants

"Any moment might be our last. Everything is more beautiful because we're doomed. You will never be lovelier than you are now. We will never be here again."
Homer

"Some of you are doomed to be artists."
Robert Edmond Jones

Chapter 9: Smith

A look at Norma, the lone lover not present in the room and, therefore, the one most easily labeled an escapee of its horror (even if it had been, by her looming specter, ostensibly animated; even if that which occurs in our absence can haunt us all the more).

If Agnes Birdseye's crime, however singular its convergence of three fascinating New York families, was also at least in part a product of its era's imbalanced, unjust sexual relationships, of the period's unspoken social rules for what a man could do (see Dr. Glickstein and Dr. Milton Thomashefsky both) and what a woman could not in response, so, too, was Norma Jeanne's life constrained by those same social mores.

She was the one who lived longest beyond the cataclysm of 1931. And yet, she lived only as a shadow of the self she could have been. And her essence receded from her so insidiously, slowly, she didn't realize it had departed until it was too late.

Here was a woman who'd studied art in New York and Paris under the demanding teachers of the painters and illustrators we all know, if not esteem, today (ostensibly, Rockwell), who won a presidential drawing contest, who'd been featured on television at the birth of that medium, and yet she wound up so caught up in expectations of domesticity attendant to her time she entirely lost touch with her native ability to create, was left feeling unskilled and unmoored after having devoted her soul thoroughly to raising a family.

Was forced to exchange her palette for Pampers, in a sense.

But not really, because this was a slow loss of self, and like much slippery, unannounced change, it began with what seemed a continuity.

She met in 1934 a charismatic suitor (she'd always had suitors) with a kind of caveman appeal – a 6'1", 35-year-old shoe salesman named Sam Smith whose hulking features – not just his build but his prominent, Neanderthalic brows – made him seem almost a wrestler or a handyman. She called him "palooka" and they began a hot, fast courtship.

So far this was very much in her wheelhouse – as were the glittering parties Sam took her to, including one at which Albert Einstein was briefly a guest (the brilliance of which cameo was not reduced by the staid, scatological origin of the host's wealth and status; Sidney Matz was the vice-president of Ex-Lax – and the son of that laxative's founder; he'd die 12 years later in the crash of a plane he was piloting) .

In fact, not only was Norma partying per her norm but she was sketching, too – she immediately jotted down her impression of Einstein after this party encounter and then fleshed out the rendering with loose daubs, strokes, splotches of color (there's a red around Einstein's left ear that evokes almost the legendary severance of Van Gogh's; I doubt that was Norma's intention, but it prompted an intriguing comparison of disparate geniuses for me).

CHAPTER 9: SMITH

The culmination of Sam Smith and Norma Jeanne Bernstein's six-week rollicking romance was no less sudden, whimsical or artistic than their actual dating or Norma's earlier life as a seductress of foreign men on Lido Beach and as painting prodigy in Paris:

They arranged to be married in Norma's studio – and Norma gifted to Sam as a nuptial present her portrait of the model "Mimi" – which just so happens to be a fleshly pink-nippled nude (albeit one exquisitely rendered

177

and whose blue backdrop is subtly tinged with the body's pinkish-orange hues).

The highly visible presence of this gift mortified Norma's mother Ida – here a prominent rabbi was supposed to perform the ceremony and he'd have to do so in the presence of a zaftig, nearly Ingres-esque buck-naked model (no matter that she was incorporeal, composed only of lustily thick brushstrokes).

Ida, tensing up, made her unease highly apparent (despite her best efforts to conceal it) to the rabbi whose judgment she so feared.

And so the rabbi, assessing the situation, sought not to hide the painting for reasons of modesty but to put the bride's mother at ease. He withdrew his large white handkerchief, covered the face of "Mimi" – neither her breasts nor genital area but her visage alone – and said to Ida and the others therewith congregated:

"I make it a habit when I perform marriage ceremonies that I never have a nude looking at me."

There was a collective sigh, if not an outright chuckle.

CHAPTER 9: SMITH

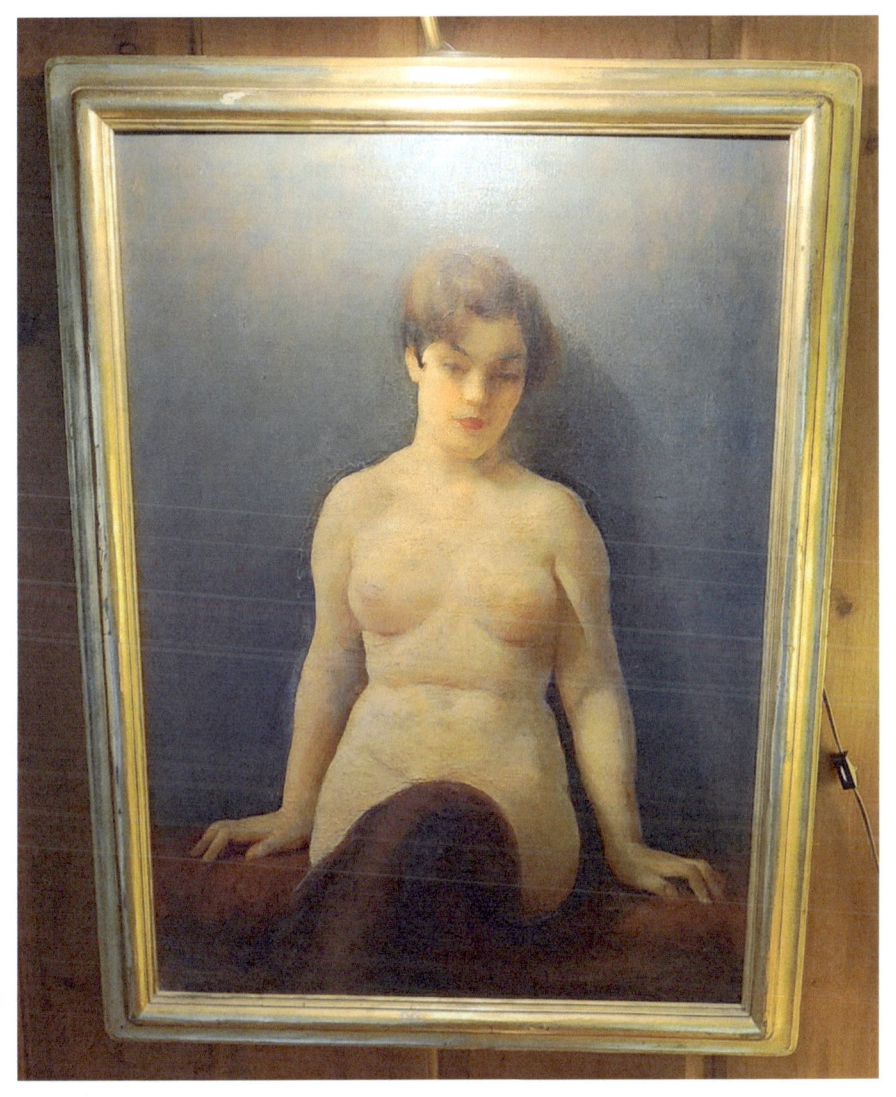

"Mimi," as she hangs today in Norma's daughter-in-law's dining room.

But neither the artistry woven into the romance nor its swift nature were the strongest ties this new development in Norma's life had to the past:

She actually brought future husband Sam during their courtship to visit Dr. Milton Thomashefsky in his lonely hotel room – to expose her current beau and potential partner for life to the man who might have been both, had circumstances turned out utterly differently.

I know this was done as a gesture of kindness on Norma's part – she and her family truly seemed to make every effort to include incapacitated Dr. Milton in their lives, and yet I can only imagine the meeting deeply painful for him, rife with the worst regret a damaged man, yearning and soulful and bitter, but unwilling to be totally candid about his bitterness, can harbor, best expressed in the final spoken lines of Hemingway's "The Sun Also Rises":

"Oh Jake," Brett said, "We could have had such a damned good time together."
"Yes," I said. "Isn't it pretty to think so?"

There's such a tremendous futility to this meeting of boyfriends past and present. One gets to leave with Norma, of his own volition, by his own bipedal power. The other is left behind – consigned to the same wheeled chair in the same suite of rooms, the same neural severance between the site of his ideas and desires and the muscles he'd otherwise use to carry them out.

The impotence effected by that paraplegic separation – it must have been psychic agony.

Doc Milton had, in his known letter to Norma, even referred to these demons (a "goblin," was his preferred term).

But there is another strange aspect to these continued meetings between Norma, her husband-to-be and Dr. Milton beyond the pain the final member of this new triangle must have felt knowing full well he was the odd man out:

The notion that Norma seems to have forgiven Dr. Milton entirely – if she ever blamed him, in the first place – for his dalliance with his secretary for years.

Surely, there was no societal talk then of inappropriate power imbalances in workplace romances, but even the DA of Brooklyn, FX Geoghan, had announced late on the night of the shootings that Doc Milton had led on and dated his assistant for the entire five years of her employment.

Even in 1931, that was considered shady behavior, and the papers were rife with accounts of the Doc parking his car with this girl to neck, of him

CHAPTER 9: SMITH

taking her to the theater, of him bringing her home.

Either Dr. Milton was such a suave talker as to have been able to convince Norma Jeanne all these stories were inaccurate rubbish or Norma Jeanne never read them at all or Norma Jeanne decided she did not care a whit for the man Dr. Milton had been prior to his meeting her.

Or she'd believed it all and found it in herself to forgive him.

My personal opinion based on her continued letter-writing and visitation of this man whom a DA had pronounced a lover boy and exploitative employer:

Norma Jeanne believed some of the stories, but as Agnes had committed an act so violent it could be termed crazy, so Norma felt confident most of Agnes' ostensible relationship with Dr. Milton was the imagined courtship of an unsound mind – of a woman hysterical.

This was a time when media narratives conduced to a disbelief in the stories of violent women supposedly spurned. Beyond the Lillian Raizen case already cited – in which a woman who was raped, after avenging her abuse, was called "whiny" by an esteemed judge – there were any number of instances when a violent woman was reduced by male newspapermen and justices into an exotic femme fatale or gold-digger or hysteric.

The day after Agnes shot Dr. Milton and herself, the New York World-Telegram ran an editorial entitled "Women in Crime." It mentioned not just the Birdseye-Thomashefsky-Bernstein affair but several other shootings involving women, concluding:

> *Possibly the unusual number of these crimes within a single month indicates a new tendency, aggravated by the Depression, toward lawless aggression or revolt on the part of members of a sex which in being emancipated yet remains dependent. Most or all of the crimes in one way or another involved money and the desire for it in more copious quantities.*

In other words: All recent women shooters were in it for the cash — no matter their ability to collect those bills in the wake of their gunfire (Agnes,

NEW YORK CITY LOVE TRIANGLE, 1931

having aimed at her own head, was somehow still cited as proof of this gold-digger/hustler theory).

Maybe Dr. Milton dated Agnes — but only very briefly, if so. Otherwise, theirs was an invented relationship on Agnes' part— her response to which fantasy was correspondingly unhinged from reality.

So, I'd venture, Norma thought — that she never fully bought the notion that her summer camp lover, Dr. Milton, had led his secretary to believe she, a petty helper, was his true partner.

Norma never admitted to herself the possibility that this was a man who'd made promises of real heft – only that his attacker was naïve and simple enough to take even a modest flirtation and blow it entirely out of proportion (and only a silly prude would mistake banter for avowal in a Gatsby-esque age of propulsive partying).

One must recall just how many suitors Norma had already swatted away.

In any event, at the age of 28, she had fallen for Sam Smith in the doctor's absence — due to Hemingway-esque infirmity – a shoe salesman seven years her senior born in Chelsea, Massachusetts, in 1899, just a few years after Boris and Bessie Thomashefsky had put on a night of Yiddish theater in that same town.

Was that anything other than a near-coincidence? Who was Sam Smith actually (besides a man standing 6'1" with brown hair and brown eyes)?

Recall J. Sidney Bernstein's attempt, in naming his children Norma Jeanne and Arthur Hendricks, to apply names of the least Jewish variety to his children who were by birth precisely that. In the name of assimilation and political climbing…yada, yada, yada.

Recall also that the Thomashefsky son who'd had real Hollywood success – not Boris or Harry but Ted –truncated his surname to "Thomas."

Well, Sam Smith was born into this era of willful heritage-incision, in essence making him a great match for Norma on those grounds alone – and no coincidence that he hailed from a site the Yiddish theater of New York had touched down in but only briefly.

One of seven children, Sam Smith, though his name would never indicate it, was actually the son of Frederick Smithkins, a peddler from the old country of tinware and clothing who later shortened his surname, and Rebecca Cheifetz. And when Sam's Heeb parents were married in 1893 – by Rabbi Hyman Shoher of the Mishkan Israel synagogue (founded in 1865) in Boston – the Boston Globe literally called the bride, Sam's mother, "one of the city's fairest Hebrew maidens."[155]

All of which is to say that, while Norma might have gifted Sam a female nude, may have thrived on coquettish provocation and impetuous decision-making, she did not quite flee the assimilated-*yid* milieu in which Thomashefskys became Thomases and Jacob Sidney Bernsteins went by "J. Sidney."

That strange space occupied by former shtetl-dwellers in a fancy new world whose greatest promise was reinvention – or at least, attenuation of Hebrewness, a thinning out of ties to tradition.

Sam Smith was of that liminal space. And though he'd spent his entire career in the footwear business – first as an inspector for A. G. Walton, a local maker of children's shoes, and later as a traveling salesman of Bata footwear from Czechoslovakia – he came from enough money to treat Norma to the lifestyle to which she was accustomed. He was of this class also.

In fact, eerily, Sam Smith was traveling in France itself in August of 1931 – the month Agnes shot Dr. Milton, the man Norma thought she was to marry. Sam Smith was in that *other* place that had imprinted itself so thoroughly on Norma's identity. On Aug. 31, as Milton's letter to Norma, the one in which he expressed how nice it would have been to see her through his morphine haze in the hospital, was postmarked in New York, Sam Smith was boarding a ship in Cherbourg, France, to return to the Big Apple. By the time he arrived back in September, the love triangle affair was no longer a news item. As if by magic, Norma had been spared an indignity in a pre-Internet, linear-news age in which only a dogged researcher – not a shoe salesman – was likely to pore over periodicals to search out a person's unspoken past.

In essence, during the great scandal of Norma's life, her future husband was conveniently absent and, better yet, was engrossed in the affairs of her adopted home.

It's as if Sam Smith had always been fated to replace Dr. Milton the month after the Doc was taken out of commission.

(Also eerie: though he sailed back to New York, Sam Smith was still living in Massachusetts in the cataclysmic year of 1931 – but not in Chelsea; his residence was on Beacon Street in Brookline, where my own wife spent the first half of her childhood.)

Sam's honeymoon with Norma was fittingly lavish and long and in keeping with their mutual prior travels on the Continent and their common, truncated, sybaritic heritage: They married June 22, 1934, and boarded the French Line's cruiser SS Champlain the very next day. Sailing with them were two aviators recently awarded the "Grand Prix of the French Academy of Sports" for their world-record distance flight from New York to Syria – as well as the flyers' plane.[156]

Sidney Matz, the Ex-Lax heir, sponsored their dinner on the second night of their journey, which consisted of caviar, consommé, filets de sole, fromages and crepes, among other dishes. Five nights later, on Friday evening, the main course was *poulet* (naturally, the meal still began with caviar – but this time it concluded with "Happy Honey-Moon Cake").

Paquebot "CHAMPLAIN"

DINNER

Tendered on board S. S. "CHAMPLAIN"

to

Mr & Mrs Sam SMITH

at the occasion of the 2nd day of their marriage

by

Mr Sidney MATZ

Sunday June 24th 1934

MENU

Caviar d'Astrakan

Consommé Croûte-au-Pot

Filets de Sole Véronique

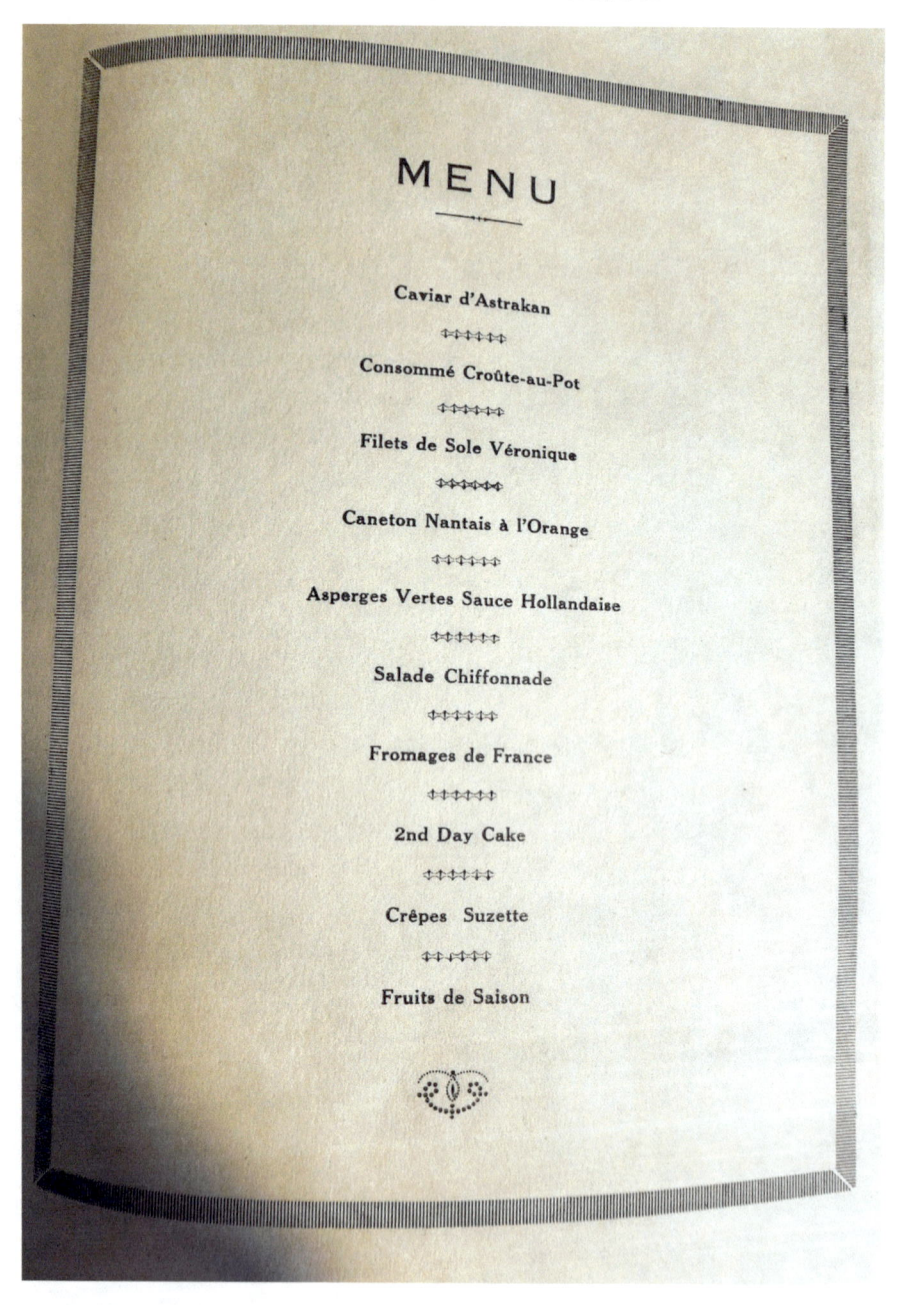

Caneton Nantais à l'Orange

Asperges Vertes Sauce Hollandaise

Salade Chiffonnade

Fromages de France

2nd Day Cake

Crêpes Suzette

Fruits de Saison

Besides France, the couple planned to travel through Italy and Switzerland (they'd had Congressman Sol Bloom attempt to finagle papers allowing them unfettered access to those countries ahead of time) – and given that one photo at least seems to have been developed in Vienna, it's likely they hit Austria, as well. And then, of course, there's England, where their attendance at Wimbledon on the day of the men's singles semifinals is well-documented by the program they kept:

One of the semis featured English champion Fred Perry, but more pertinent to this story is the presence in the other semi of Frank Shields, grandfather of Brooke and former high school doubles partner of a man named Julius Seligson...who'd also eventually live in the same building in Manhattan I do and that Norma returned to from summer camp upon learning of Agnes' shooting of her beloved in 1931. Oh, and the semifinal they attended was on *July 4* — exactly three years (to the very day) after Norma Jeanne and Dr. Milton met in camp. *Just* three years later.

NEW YORK CITY LOVE TRIANGLE, 1931

The married couple on its travels.

CHAPTER 9: SMITH

At some point during this procession (or perhaps on a subsequent romp through society – the timing is sightly unclear), the couple made the acquaintance of welterweight champ Jimmy McLarnin, who noted the swell time he'd had with the pair:

But the swell time was due to end – the real world had to intrude on the honeymoon phase, which technically ended with their return voyage on the SS Champlain, which docked in New York on Aug. 1, 1934 (although the couple returned to France for another interlude that October).

That this arrival as a married woman would forever alter the course of Norma's art career, no matter how many return trips she made to France, she almost certainly could not anticipate.

But she was quickly, on her return, pressed upon with maternal duties the implications of which for her art she could neither process nor understand in real time.

In 1936 she gave birth to a son and then in 1938 another.

Norma Jeanne, by her daughter-in-law's account to me, was highly unsuited to the maternal role she was now expected to assume. The role as it was imposed upon women in that era. Time and again, her daughter-in-law told me Norma Jeanne had been born a generation too early – that she was an artist whose fullest flourishing in that career was stifled by all that society expected of her as a caregiver.

Of course, there was some overlap: Norma did not disappear as an artist the moment her children appeared – here's a sketch she did of Peter at eight months:

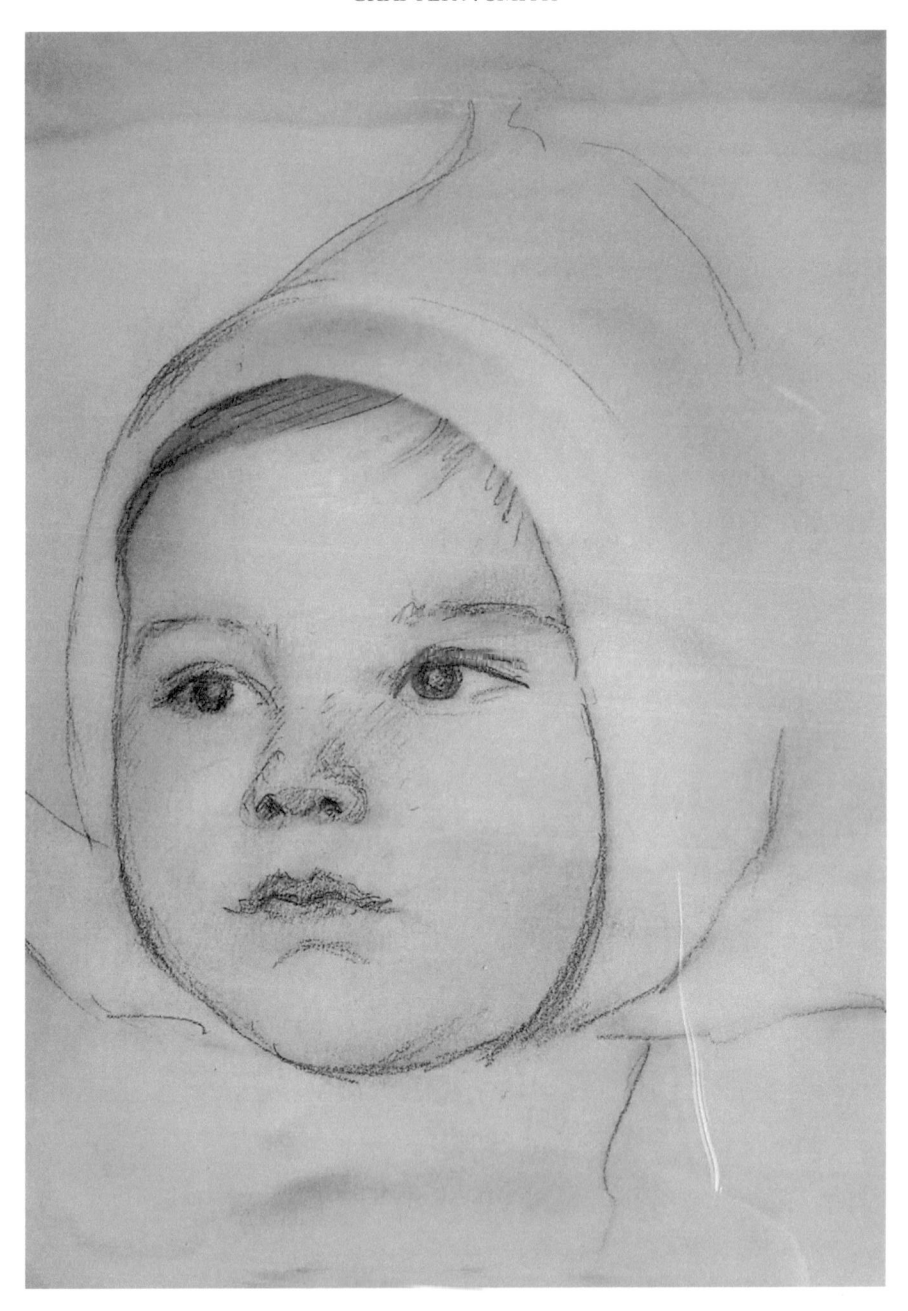

But by the same token, as her sons were born, a tiredness began to creep into her eyes that seemed so much the opposite of the dazzling figure whose glinting features had captured Dr. Milton's attention and that of countless suitors before him – a fatigue endemic to all parents in that first phase of oversight but also so counter to the elan, that bursting spirit, so essential for the production of her best work:

CHAPTER 9: SMITH

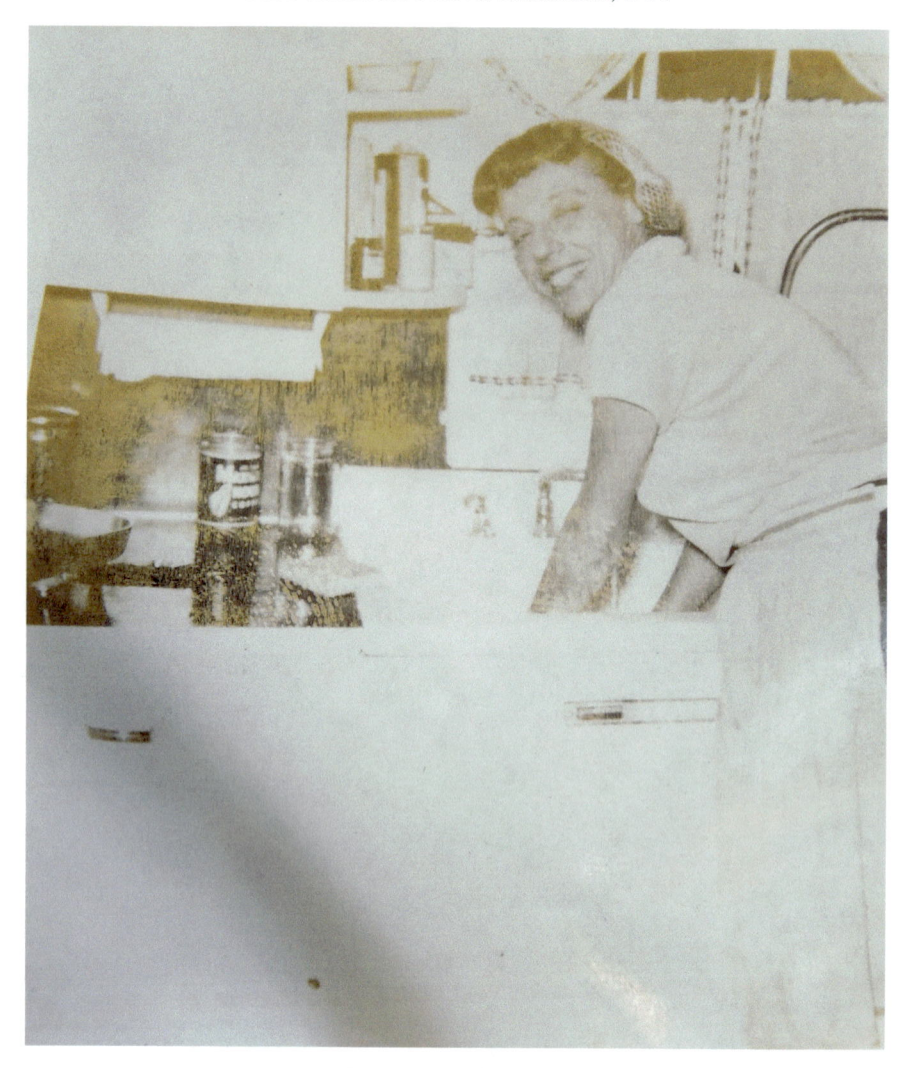

Norma doing dishes.

But Norma Jeanne's work likely could have survived parenthood alone; for starters, she obviously had the economic resources to hire a live-in nanny (in 1940, the family had a 28-year-old maid named Estelle and a 55-year-old nurse named Fanny).

Unfortunately, her journey into parenthood, family life, domesticity, was accompanied by a remove from the bustling city society that was so much a wellspring of her portraiture. And it all happened almost by chance, as if Norma Jeanne was swept along entirely by winds geopolitical and social and had no agency herself.

To whit, by 1928, Sam was working as the American sales representative (essentially, company CEO for North America) for the Czechoslovakian shoe manufacturer Bata, which was so dominant at the time, American figures publicly worried it might overtake all domestic brands and monopolize the US footwear market.[157] It had been founded at the end of the 19th century by three Czech siblings (surname Bata) in a town called Zlin that by 1932 was home to 17,000 employees (and factories featuring the latest in mechanization).

CC by SA 3.0.

In 1938, Norma accompanied Sam on a European trip that coincided with the beginning of the end of this company and Sam's representation thereof; it was August, or about a month before Hitler was to demand from appeasement-minded European powers a large swath of the Czechoslovak Republic – the so-called Sudetenland (before invading the rest of the country the following year).

Records show Sam and Norma managed to escape Hitler's warmongering – but only scarcely, in a sense. They made it aboard the SS. Ile de France, departing from Le Havre, on August 30th – reaching New York Harbor on September 5th – or just 12 days before Hitler effectively announced that if he wasn't given the Sudetenland, he'd merely take it.

But even during their visit there was tremendous unrest in Czechoslovakia as Hitler encouraged residents of the Sudetenland to take up arms against their own nation and many did. This was a time when Czechoslovak citizens hid in the forest from their own compatriots.

A close call – a holiday that very nearly overlapped, chronologically and geographically, with the second Nazi land-seizure after the annexation of Austria. (And according to Sam's Boston Globe obituary decades later, he'd make a trip in 1939 to Czechoslovakia that would overlap exactly with Hitler's invasion – although it's possible this is a mistaken account of the year-earlier trip).[158]

Either way, the effect of Hitler's expansionism was the termination of Sam's job, which was a loss of tremendous salary. Sam, as a Bata importer who traveled thrice yearly to Europe, who'd sourced the site for Bata's American factory in Maryland, had an annual income of more than $5,000 at a time when the average was $1,368.[159]

The couple and their two children, having departed New York City for the suburb of Great Neck in a new Automobile Age, was now somewhat unmoored. They were monied enough not to have enter the breadlines that had predominated a decade of Depression-era America, but they were suddenly without direction – for Norma had taken on a role of mother ostensibly incompatible with her being the breadwinner with her art. Sam being a stay-at-home father or working in part-time capacities that would allow for Norma to have her own career – these were compromise manners of co-parenting never mooted. And so if Sam had no employment, it was as if the family itself had been severed from the economy, from productive society.

For Norma, of course, the simple move to the suburbs, though she perhaps did not realize it, had severed her from the sources of her art (remember she had been quite inspired, however ill-at-ease her sense of exoticism might make the contemporary critic, by Chinatown and Harlem – not to mention the Great White Way – her Broadway subjects having included actors Ethel Waters, Richard Harrison and Tamara – all of them major stage stars). It had also created a distance between her and the Art Students League of New York, whose contest to sketch FDR had vaulted her and her work into the Oval Office, literally.

And with Hitler's move into Czechoslovakia, that dislocation was about to become far greater.

Chapter 9A: 1931

Both broken bodies were lying on the floor of a place of medicine. Two ambulances arrived.

Dr. Milton was rushed to Brooklyn's Jewish Hospital, the very same institution Agnes' father led as superintendent and where he had long worked. Agnes was pronounced dead on arrival inside her ambulance.

The police come, too, naturally. The first officer associated with the scene was Patrolman Scott, of the 80th Precinct, but soon two of the station's detectives were on the case: John O'Neill – who'd tracked to a Harlem cellar a man wanted for a fatal stabbing during a dice game earlier in the year[160] – and William J. Casey, a pal of Dodgers pitcher Dazzy Vance.[161]

Inside the deceased Agnes' purse, the police found a diamond solitaire engagement ring and a wedding band – neither of them engraved, their purchaser seemingly known to police but left unannounced.

Per one account, as Dr. Milton was carried into Jewish Hospital, Agnes' father was told in that same place his daughter was certainly dead. He collapsed.[162]

Meanwhile detectives questioned Dr. Milton: "Who did it?" they asked.

Dr. Milton weakly tried to shoo the cops away, before mouthing: "Don't bother me," according to one account.[163]

According to another, Thomashefsky kept repeating, in response to police queries: "Shot me as I was about to answer the door."[164]

Once Lewis E. Birdseye was taken to the scene of his daughter's crimes, he collapsed again.

Dr. Milton was rushed into the operating room, to be worked on by his own friend and former colleague, Dr. John Linder. Seven years earlier, Linder had made the news for saving the life of a 65-year-old named Aeta Bozinsky by extracting from her brain four shards of glass. In a further three and half years from this date, Linder and 11 other physicians who'd worked at the Jewish Hospital for a full quarter-century would be honored by Mayor Fiorello LaGuardia.[165]

In 1924, Dr. Linder had even joined with Lewis E. Birdseye to save several women in the operating room of the Jewish Hospital from a raging fire that wound up incinerating 70 feet of the fifth floor at a cost of $10,000.[166]

Now, in the case of his friend Dr. Milton Thomashefsky, Linder told papers that any procedure to rescue him would be, in the words of the Daily News, "extremely delicate and dangerous."[167]

And there was another doctor involved in Dr. Milton's care at his own former workplace — Dr. Alexander George Davidson, who'd been born in Bialystok, Russia in 1893, immigrated to New York in 1908 and in 1920 graduated from Cornell Medical College (with a $300 prize for "general efficiency in medicine"). Extremely near-sighted and therefore bespectacled, Davidson had interned at the Jewish Hospital while Dr. Milton was still on staff. Davidson would go on to lead the hospital's intern alumni association as treasurer and then president.

He'd also be the one to sign Dr. Milton's death certificate — but years later — not now.

Agnes' lifeless body was dispatched for autopsy to the city medical examiner, which received it as case 2939 at 8:01 pm Wednesday night – or an hour and fifteen minutes after she'd shot herself in the head. Agnes was also attended to by another medical man who'd been subordinate to her father and a colleague of Dr. Milton's at the Jewish Hospital – a former Navy physician named Romeo Winton Auerbach (often called R.W., he would go on to perform research on intravenous oxygen crucial to the development of the heart-and-lung machine).

This would seem a bizarre conflict of interest, one that would undermine whatever report Auerbach wound up producing – his having worked for Agnes' father and alongside her victim. What if there had been some terribly tragic reason for her having shot herself in the stomach just before killing herself anyway? What if that had been her final symbolic gesture – one hinting at pregnancy?

A newspaper with a strangely conspicuous interest in clearing Dr. Thomashefsky of having ever engaged in a tryst with Agnes claimed rapidly and falsely, within a day of the shooting, that this autopsy made clear "that reports of an affair between her and Dr. Thomashevsky (sic) must have been baseless" (the implication being the examination stated Agnes was a virgin).[168]

But the actual autopsy revealed Agnes' uterus to be "small and non-parturient," (she was not pregnant), and that she'd on the contrary been in the midst of having her period, at the time of the shootings, wearing a "sanitary-napkin with light brown blood stains."

So R.W. Auerbach wrote – and there's no reason besides his bizarre closeness to every actor in this story to doubt his work for a moment.

And wasn't everyone suddenly shown to be highly and reciprocally entangled? Wasn't that the great climax of the first half of this New York Story – these strange strings already tying together an otherwise varied, prominent cast?

The triangle was even made official late on the night of incident.

The current District Attorney of Kings County (Brooklyn) – William F.X. Geoghan — who would come under great scrutiny in the following decade for his association with two mobsters – examined the sordid scene, conferred with his underlings, and then hinted to reporters late on Wednesday night that the entire episode had been the result of a passionate love triangle.

One journalist asked the DA how he could draw such a conclusion, and Geoghan said:

"Well, five years she worked for him, and five years they went together."[169]

When Agnes' father Lewis Birdseye regained consciousness at the scene after his collapse, he protested his daughter's involvement – a major figure laid low by grief, imploring a public to believe in a relation now lost forever: "She didn't do it," he said, his voice reportedly a rasp – a groan. "I know she

CHAPTER 9A: 1931

didn't do it. She wouldn't harm a soul. Someone murdered her."

* * *

Perhaps this collision — of the progeny of families of robust New York heritage who yet possessed unique origin tales — speaks to the combustible power of the dense city's diversity itself. Which can go either way — effect Gotham's most ingenious ideas, collaborations, edifices or the riotous tearing apart, the repugnant destruction, of all three.

Our differences, when reconciled upon such interpersonal impacts, can make us so collectively great. Look upon all the Bernstein Democrats and the Birdseye Republicans built up, if not in exact unison then in take-turns electoral aggregate, during their early-20th century stewardship of New York. They transformed the low-rise city in that period from a major spot on the globe to its unrivaled, skyscraping epicenter — culturally, financially, symbolically.

J. Sidney's Tammany Hall mentor, Isaac Hopper, quite literally built Carnegie Hall with his own construction firm and supplied power to a bustling new Subway.

J. Sidney's successful run for state assemblyman in 1905 coincided with the beginning of construction of the Metropolitan Life Insurance Company Tower — the world's tallest building upon its completion in 1909.

And it's no coincidence that Lewis E. Birdseye's son — Agnes' brother, Lewis Jr. — worked as that very building's superintendent for a time (it's the place of work listed on his World War II Draft Card, for instance).

Meanwhile, the tower was eclipsed as tallest in the world by the construction of the Woolworth Building, erected from 1910-1913, the period during which Lewis Birdseye Sr. was chief assistant to the NYPD commissioner (overseeing city fractiousness or, in the more hopeful moments, its happy absence).

The Yiddish theater so built up by the Thomashefsky family gave birth first to Fanny Brice and her ilk — the former being the "Funny Girl" made famous for later generations by Barbra Streisand's portrayal thereof —

and then to Hollywood itself — Paul Muni, star of the original "Scarface," married a Thomashefsky, was rooted himself in its theater.

As was George Gershwin.

These familial, political, entertainment forces, when working in a kind of chaotic union, propelled the city ever forward by their reasoned-out-and-thus-peaceable path-crossings (and there will always be such collision — it's attendant to urban congestion and perhaps its greatest feature).

But recall also Agnes' fear that her rival Norma had a step on her in the romantic race because Norma was Milton's coreligionist. Or the ways the Tammanyites fought these internecine battles to dominate tiny little district clubs every night (perhaps a healthy exercise in democratic debate — but only to a point; how many argumentative political clubs is one too many?).

It's when fear, mistrust, disloyalty seep into the city consciousness that even our incidental impingements of each other are considered *casus belli* — when rather than letting our shared city travails serve as the basis for our very different ways of building upward, those differences serve as justification for tearing down our respective contributions .

I'm not saying that Dr. Milton didn't have revenge coming — only that a less fearful Agnes might never have considered genital slashing and revolver-firing worth it. And especially suicide — the aggrieved removing her own self though she was the party aggrieved (yes, this is a simplistic view of suicide).

Imagine if instead of that ultimately auto-eliminating move, Agnes had gotten in touch with Norma. Told her, Hey, I think, we're both being played by this Don Juan. How about we band together?

Not that reaching out across party lines is the least bit easy. But the very history of New York, with its contributions from myriad, distinct huddling masses, suggests its grand possibility.

Chapter 10: Smith

The year was 1939.

Sam Smith, married to the former Norma Jeanne Bernstein, and employed earlier by a shoe company whose Czechoslovak home base was now overrun by Nazis, needed a job.

He was friends with industrialist Armand Hammer, the lone capitalist seemingly allowed to work unimpeded in the Soviet Union, who knew of an empty factory, rendered so by the Depression, up in New England – in a town called Newmarket, New Hampshire. He suggested to Sam that the shoe man repurpose it into a footwear factory of his own.

And so he did, founding the Sam Smith Shoe Company, which was originally known in Newmarket as part of a threesome of local shoemakers (the others being Rockingham and Royce) – it was a shoemaking town. Sam hired his employees, such as bookkeeper Phyllis Stackpole, straight out of the local high school.

From the start, Sam's enterprise distinguished itself by its patriotism. Later, after America entered World War II, the company would produce Army boots, but even ahead of Pearl Harbor, Sam sensed from his time working with a Czechoslovakian company that a war was already brewing, the outcome of which would dictate the course of the entire world, even that of a small factory town in New Hampshire.

In essence, his message was that such a hamlet was in no way insulated from the tyranny overrunning Europe – and his subordinates, no matter that few had any secondary education, agreed.

In the summer of 1941, Sam promised to pay any employee who elected to join the Army a full week's salary upon his or her departure – an offer taken up first by one Steven Kleczek before he headed to boot camp in Florida.

He also enabled his employees to set aside a portion of their salaries for the purchase of postal stamps that in aggregate could be converted into USO bonds. At one point, the 250 members of his factory were purchasing jointly $120 to $125 in stamps weekly.

By the time, the US was actually an active participant in the war, the factory was already well adjusted to the sacrifices martial moments require. In 1941, employees canceled their annual holiday party and instead donated more than $230 to the American Red Cross.

And even after the US won, in April of 1947, when President Truman asked businesses to effect price-slashes to facilitate a post-war market recovery, Sam cut prices on average 18 percent, "despite the fact that leather and shoe production costs are at a peak," gaining the attention of The New York Times: [170]

"The action was described as the first adjustment in the shoe trade conforming to President Truman's request."[171]

But Sam's other major business decision of this time, though ostensibly as patriotic as his compliance with Truman's entreaty, was a feat of marketing demonstrative of just how great a priority his business now took over Norma's art:

He named a subsidiary of his company "The Yankee Shoemakers" whose output — children's footwear – he dubbed "Little Yankee Shoes."

Whether Sam was a brilliant reader of the zeitgeist or just lucky, he chose a name that struck a nerve with returning GIs who, having witnessed havoc, now wanted to raise in peace and tranquility their brood.

The ads featured ponies, see-saws, the Good Housekeeping seal of approval – in essence, all the objects and insignia attendant to the nuclear family of 1950s America – all those features that added up to a sense of suburban safety.

The slogan: "Great Shoes for Little Americans."

CHAPTER 10: SMITH

Consumers fell hard for this line of promotion (shoe sales took off), even if it contained within it the sort of unsubstantiated claims the Federal Trade Commission was created to keep in check — and did (in January of 1955, the commissioner of the FTC issued Sam's company a cease-and-desist order – the company could no longer represent "directly or by implication"

NEW YORK CITY LOVE TRIANGLE, 1931

that Little Yankee Shoes "will keep or help keep the feet strong, healthy or normal").

But it wasn't the ads' line of argument that betrayed Sam's mindset regarding Norma Jeanne's work as much as his choice of artist for them:

Norman Rockwell, who'd been trained at the Art Students' League by the same teachers who'd taught Norma Jeanne just a decade later.

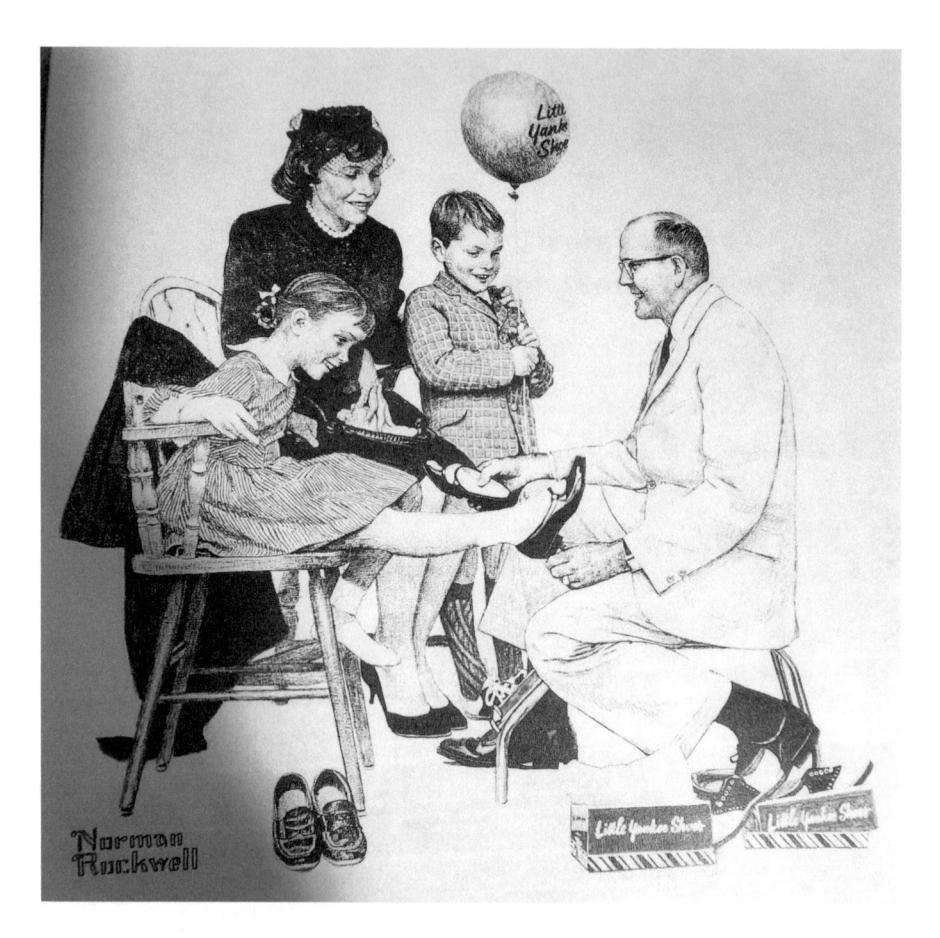

The Rockwell ad, while highly indicative of Sam's commercial success, of his flourishing in a chosen career, raises the thornier question of Norma's own work: Where the hell was it?

Why was her husband commissioning art from an artist who'd studied under the same teachers she had rather than propagating her own? What had happened to Norma Jeanne Bernstein, promising painter who'd been awarded her first one-person show at the tender age of 24?

She'd been just footsteps behind Rockwell only yesterday…

* * *

Enter "Butch" Cowell, football coach of the nearby University of New Hampshire (a school formerly known as the "New Hampshire College of Agriculture and the Mechanic Arts").

It's hard to overstate how big a figure Butch Cowell was in an era when amateur football far eclipsed the pro ranks in popularity and coverage. But suffice it to say that Butch was elected president of the American Football Coaches' Association in 1926.

And also that, in 1927, he presciently anticipated, after a recent NCAA rules change, the tremendous trouble referees on-field would have distinguishing incomplete passes from catches that are subsequently fumbled:

"If a quarterback makes a bad throw to a halfback, the ball is dead where it touches the turf," he said. "If the latter gets control of it and then drops it, it becomes a free fumble. But how severe or lax will officials be in *judging control?*"[172]

The control issue remains unresolved – and constantly debated – yet today.

NEW YORK CITY LOVE TRIANGLE, 1931

Cowell, pictured here in a three-piece suit, also served as school athletic director, and in 1935, he bought a parcel of land near the university and assembled the cabin of his dreams.

Except as the house was completed in 1938, he suddenly fell ill – he was plagued by uremia, the proximate cause of death two years earlier of one Dr. Milton Thomashefsky – an inability of the kidneys to cleanse the blood of toxins.

Cowell was forced to leave his job and spend increasing spans of time in the hospital, including a nine-day stay that ended with his Aug. 29, 1940, death. That this occurred just as Sam and Norma and their two boys arrived on the local scene, looking for shelter as Sam launched a new shoe company, was propitious for the family.

Sam, Norma and their two boys rented Cowell's house in the summer of 1940 when Cowell was an inpatient; they bought it after he passed.

Right away, Sam went to work renovating this house (whose basement featured bunks so the coach could host local athletes for training camps), turning what had been a second-floor attic into a spacious, light-filled studio for his wife.

The Smith house in Durham, including the renovated second-floor atelier.

The problem was the vista those windows featured when Sam's remodeling had been completed: trees, a flowing river somewhat visible between them.

All of which is to say: Landscape – a verdant, estuarine, rocky landscape, sure, but one by definition devoid of the bustling humanity that had sparked Norma's creativity in New York and Paris and provided her with the models for the art in which she specialized – portraiture.

Sam had had the best of intentions when creating that studio for Norma, on the second floor of a house at the very Eastern edge of the continent – but as a space for an artist whose entire passion was coaxing from city subjects the souls they often kept hidden, he might as well have marooned her on a desert island – or constructed a more literal jail, steel bars and all. For that's effectively what this remote studio was to Norma: a light-filled window onto a world she'd never volunteered to occupy and in which she found no particular magic.

She was the last of the three lovers still alive, but she'd given up the work that animated her, vivified her, almost *incidentally*. By way of a business

CHAPTER 10: SMITH

transaction and a housing alteration over which she had little control. By way of the nephrological failings of a dying football coach.

The parameters of a woman's role, 1940.

Agnes' death may have seemed the most immediate. The doctor's the most ghastly and torturous. But an artist being shorn from the source of her work, from the practice of it, from what gives her life meaning – it's a death superficially less gruesome, more metaphorical than literal – but only somewhat less painful for being so

Would it be fair to say the love triangle brought about a shared ruination of the three? Perhaps. More accurately, one could say the triangle itself reflected the era's dynamics – women were to be led astray and not to be believed; they were to be left without legal recourse when they felt wronged to the core; men were to have their swaggering way on stage and off; and decisions were to be made for and on behalf of even the most talented of women.

And we know full well Norma was aware – terrified – of the diminution of her artistic talent as she languished in that New England aerie.

In the years after her move to the second floor studio amidst the oysters and tides, she yearned for intriguing subjects. But mostly she had to settle instead for neighbors, friends and even those her family employed as domestic help – Joe, Mabel, Tony the Gardener.

Which isn't to say all her work of this period was lacking – hardly.

That last aforementioned figure, Tony, was rendered with exceptional attunement to color – the scarlets behind him so contrast with the indigo of his denim shirt and the tan impasto of his cheeks, Tony seems almost to exist as the ecru personification of autumn, a beige bridge between green summer leaves turned blazing red and iced-over, bluish, wintry roads:

NEW YORK CITY LOVE TRIANGLE, 1931

But a brief glance at Norma's depiction of "Joe" (above) reveals a portraiture lapsing into an unfortunate, if unintentional, caricature:

Norma, taking on childcare duties expected of a mother without question, was also painting less and less frequently, which unhabitual practice only compounded her fears, when she finally did take out her paints, that she was no longer bringing to her canvasses her former acumen, the keen eye that allowed her to meet FDR and landed her sketch of him in the New York Public Library's collection.

So after dispatching her younger son Peter to Philips Exeter for boarding school in 1952, Norma set about trying to regain her artistic mojo.

She studied with the landscape painter John Hatch, whose wife Maryanna was Norma's close friend and who taught at the University of New Hampshire. But Norma took an even greater leap for a woman who felt stranded and afraid, weighed down by her successes early in life and her sporadic work ever since:

She went back to school at the Art Students' League, the place most singularly responsible for her style (perhaps tied with one atelier in Paris) and took a class not in painting but in sculpture – with Nathanial Kaz, whose work would wind up in the collections of the Met, the Whitney, the Brooklyn Museum (which happens to stand across the street from the office in which Dr. Thomashefsky was shot).

After he died in 2010, Kaz's death notice in the Times began: "[He] lived and breathed art; it was the essence of his being and the power behind his great love of life."

But there were serious issues with Norma's choice of both instructors, no matter their skill or enthusiasm.

As to the latter and more renowned artist, Kaz: His was a figurative sculpture of eccentric subtraction (see his lanky, pockmarked "Don Quixote" of 1950, whose very arms and legs seem to have had entire muscles torn out). I'm not sure that qualified him to work with someone who needed to recall just how evocative her work could be when its pallet-knife paint applications were viewed in the aggregate. Norma had been a builder of character on her canvasses. An additive portraitist.

And Kaz seemingly couldn't match her for sketching technique. See the Kaz sketch below (now in the public domain) – made while the artist was still young but still bested by Norma's own pencil work of her youthful days:

CHAPTER 10: SMITH

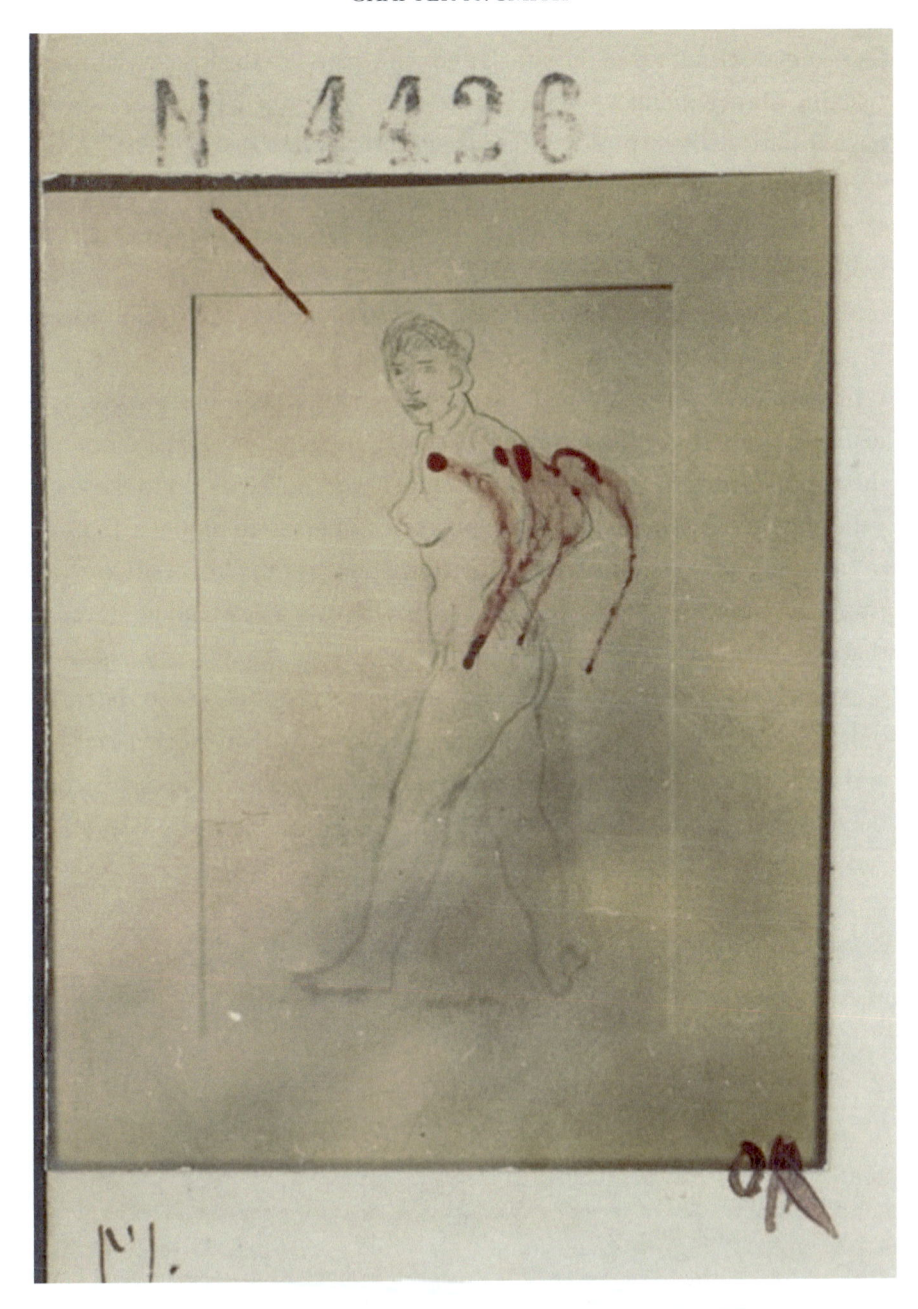

Professor Hatch, painter and professor at the University of New Hampshire, was another interesting pedagogical choice. His specialty as a painter was a kind of calmer (arguably less interesting) Winslow Homer canvas, if you like – his work captured the shoals and white tides of the local coastline in relaxing grays and blues – with little of the of roughness that rocky shores have traditionally inspired in their keenest observers.

Here was a painter who – if he believed the soul a turbid thing – never let those ideas of inner turmoil inform his work. Or at least, not in a way one would expect of a mid-century artist. The greatest tension in his work is built up in mid-century Cubist canvases that seem very late to that Picasso-Braque party of an earlier age.

In fact, that's perhaps the best way to describe Hatch: he could imitate nearly any artistic style popular in the recent past, but he made none of these modes entirely his own and certainly never looked ahead to those not yet on the scene. He was far more professor of art than pioneer. In point of fact, he'd actually taken up his teaching post at the University of New Hampshire the very same year he'd graduated from Yale – and he stayed in that post for the next 26 years.

(And if this sounds overly harsh and judgmental of both Kaz and Hatch, it's only because they've both received more recognition than Norma ever has, and while art should not be a zero sum game, consciousness and recollection inevitably are, and Norma deserves both.)

A painting Norma's daughter-in-law Marjorie owns of a John Hatch (which she much fancies, and I rather rudely consider hotel room art).

CHAPTER 10: SMITH

Another Hatch – whose placidity leaves me indifferent rather than relaxed – that hangs in Marjorie's home.

To Hatch's credit, however, he did endeavor earnestly to shake Norma from her version of Writers' Block. As Norma's daughter-in-law wrote for a lecture to a local Durham club in the 1990s: "John tried to help Norma get her self-confidence back. He set her certain tasks – to paint something other than a portrait, to limit her use of color."

One impressive result of these exercises – it caught my eye, anyway – was a still-life Norma wrought with a blue evocative of the Biblical color *t'chelet* or the lapis lazuli used in medieval manuscripts – an azure I absolutely adore in the darker form of the bottle, especially as it contrasts to the russet-bronze containers in the foreground:

But for the most part, Hatch's exercises, rather than opening up the rest of the world to Norma's artistic eye, led her nowhere but to each project's specific completion. Norma's production, say, of monochromatic tableaux did not coax her into creating a new series of portraits marked by the most minor, but telling, variations in hue. She just executed the assignments.

CHAPTER 10: SMITH

A still-life by Norma in which she restricts her use of color.

"While she continued to exhibit in most years," Norma's daughter-in-law later wrote, "there are very few indications that she painted at all after the early 1960s."

The final love triangle death – an artist going voluntarily silent, overwhelmed by all that she has done and fears she no longer can.

And yet, Norma lived until 1984 – as she was not literally deceased, how did she spend those final years in which she was too diffident even to call herself an artist let alone work as one?

Unfortunately, here, in the final chapter of Norma's life, the very luxury and privilege that first afforded her an education in the arts allowed her to slink away from them – to give herself over to easy travel and revelry. She allowed herself to be a passenger in life.

Sam and Norma and their sons spent late December 1956 into New Year's in Varadero, Cuba, partying – and in the figure of Norma you can see a woman who seems resigned to this social circuit – who perhaps once longed for more but has abandoned such enthusiasm (perhaps that's reading too much into photographs, or maybe her tired eyes tell a story deserving of that deeper exposition):

CHAPTER 10: SMITH

Really, it's Norma's sons – Peter in the center of the photo foreground and Tony to his right in the matching white dinner jacket and bow tie – who here possess the youthful energy for which a young Norma, petitioned by innumerable suitors, once was known.

Mind you, this wasn't really just a New Year's trip – after the clock struck midnight and the boys returned home to school, Norma and Sam kept plowing ahead into Latin America, as if in flight from some harsh reality back home (or winter, at the very least).

They traveled by boat and plane to Montevideo; Sao Paolo (very briefly); Rio de Janeiro; Buenos Aires; Caracas; Puerto Rico; Nassau. Norma wrote a letter to her mother Ida, still living, in which Norma sounds very much a pampered, bourgeois 1950s society matron, however painful (and possibly misogynistic) that is to say:

She complained that once she had learned a few Spanish words she was forced to move on to a country in which Portuguese was spoken; she compared Montevideo to Nice but without the beach.

"We enjoyed seeing the gauchos driving the cattle and the sheep to the slaughter houses," she wrote, adding that she'd bought some alligator purses.

"Met a couple of American couples (tourists)," she wrote, "but no one particularly interesting (except us)."

"No one should come here without knowing Spanish. It's not at all like Europe, that way."

Only in small spots do her observations obtain a grander, more romantic sweep: Of Rio, she wrote of "great rocky mountains jutting straight out of the ocean (like Capri)."

She wrote she'd spend a couple weeks in Florida so as to recover from the vacation itself. By the time she flew back to New York on British Airways, she'd been away from Durham for about two months.

Norma was in Lisbon in the spring of 1959 (or at least, that's the city from which her Pan Am flight back to America departed). There are countless other trips for which documentation is lost or exceeded my present grasp (if only Norma had not married a Smith, a nomenclatural bane in a search of historical ship and plane manifests).

And yet, despite Norma's retreat from her art; her embrace of the high life with an uncritical eye; however existentially empty its champagne dinners; however banal her sinking into a more traditional motherly role (in 1956, her son Peter sent a note home from Bowdoin featuring a photo of him holding a trumpet, requesting a pen-and-ink set and promising he'd soon send home laundry), one aspect of her being at the time of the love triangle a quarter-century prior persisted:

She was still deemed an object of great amorous appeal by notable men.

It almost seems impossible that a woman could have undergone so much change in her life only to receive notes so reminiscent of those that had led to the shootings, but in 1955. Judge Samuel Rabin, a former state assemblyman who'd end up serving as a judge on all three level of New York State's court system, wrote her a well-mannered note that nevertheless included the line: "The many evenings that I spent at Chez Bernstein, and particularly with Norma (if Sam doesn't mind my saying so), were among the most pleasant that I can recall."

CHAPTER 10: SMITH

Supreme Court of the State of New York
Justices' Chambers
Jamaica, N.Y.

SAMUEL RABIN
JUSTICE

January 18, 1955

Dear Norma:

It was a pleasure to hear from you. I am happy to know that Mother enjoyed our little telephone conversation; I know that I did. The many evenings that I spent ~~at~~ Chez Bernstein, and particularl with Norma (if Sam doesn't mind my saying so), were among the most pleasant that I can recall.

I hope that before too long I *will* have a chance to say hello to you and your family in person.

Meanwhile, warmest personal regards.

Sincerely yours,

Mrs. Sam Smith
River Bend
Durham, N.H.

Chapter 10A: 1931

August 13, 1931.

At first, Dr. Milton Thomashefsky, semi-conscious and most definitely paralyzed, refused to give his account of the prior three days to the authorities, even turning his head away from an assistant district attorney to face a wall in the hospital.

But by the day of his surgery later in the week, the lung that had been pierced by a bullet had collapsed and he'd sunken into a coma.[173]

Which meant the police and the newspaper reporters had but one person to whom they could turn for further information – the third member of what seemed to be one of the most sensational and bizarre threesomes in recent city history – one in which all members were brimming with backstory.

Norma Jeanne Bernstein's parents drove her down from the summer camp she was supervising on Thursday, August 13th, a day after the shootings, and she submitted to a brief police interview at headquarters in Brooklyn, ordered to return the following afternoon for further questioning.[174]

Also on the 13th, perhaps to confirm what the DA had said a night earlier about a love triangle, the police released to the public one letter – the note Norma Jeanne wrote Dr. Milton denying Agnes' silly, anonymous denunciation of her rival –which Norma had ended: "Oh, did I remember to tell you, dear, darling Mickey, that I miss you so much?"

J. Sidney Bernstein handed out to the media a statement in Norma Jeanne's name that, in part, read, "We were never engaged to be married and there was never any suggestion of it." And her father added, of the note in which Norma Jeanne called Dr. Milton "darling" and denied the poison pen letter accusations:

"She calls everybody 'darling.' It is just a common form of salutation with her and not a term of endearment. She is a great kidder."

Of course, he was lying.

The lawyer of great Democratic prominence hid an affair so well and so entirely that the existence of a trove of love notes — extending from before the affair and continuing well after it — was a secret to the press and to the world and, when I embarked upon this book, even to me.

And then I visited Norma's final house and was presented her keepsakes by her daughter-in-law.

In fact, Norma and Dr. Milton were *still* sending each other messages even after their earlier correspondence had resulted in Dr. Milton's horrible maiming – letters nobody would see besides those lovers until I visited Norma's daughter-in-law in 2024.

During the first or second week of Dr. Milton's hospitalization, Norma Jeanne sent him flowers and a note (the latter of which might be lost). On Friday, August 21st, with absolutely no ability to control his lower half, Dr. Milton nevertheless replied to his camp flame by hand, with a fountain pen, from the hospital.

He mistakenly addressed the envelope to Camp Point O' Pines – which Norma had long ago been forced to abandon by police request (she had to be interrogated), so that the note spent five additional days bouncing around post offices before ending up at the building in which I am now writing (a century later) on the Upper West Side of Manhattan, at the start of September 1931. In full:

> *Would have been nice to see you here thru the morphine haze of these first few days – Norma dear – But perhaps it was better judgment – as I understand that your name had been dragged into the sordid mess – so sorry sweet girl – Soon as I can I'll write you – n tell you – all about it – it's all really <u>very</u> funny dear – you'll enjoy it – "heh heh" –*

the funny little poison pen letter and all are clear now.
   Your flowers were lovely – but please – no more of <u>that</u> nonsense. – Your banged-up Mickey is thinking of you all the time – and he has so many lovely thoughts that the hell is more endurable. –
   Love to you Norma dear

To me, the note possesses a strange flippancy, a humor inapt and uncomfortable, a dryness Dr. Milton had perhaps earned through his maiming but still sounds wrong. After all, a woman was dead. It was publicly proclaimed by the district attorney he had led this dead woman on, for five full years. Or maybe tone is a difficult thing to tease out; maybe the note is entirely melancholic, the humor not actually that, as much an intentionally false, meta-act as his interaction with the mother of the boy with tonsillitis in his earlier note.

(And just maybe the DA had been wrong – maybe Agnes' rage was the consequence of mental illness – that despite what reporters and prosecutors were told, Dr. Milton had never romanced Agnes fully; Dr. Milton himself would admit that they'd gone driving and to the theater and to his apartment – but did that mean he'd really promised her the world? What if Agnes had bought herself those rings? But if she was observably crazy, if he knew he was her obsession, if hers had been a passion unrequited, why would Dr. Milton have accepted blithely her acquisition of a gun? And who takes just any girl home to their Jewish mother? Or to the theater or on pleasure drives, in this era?)

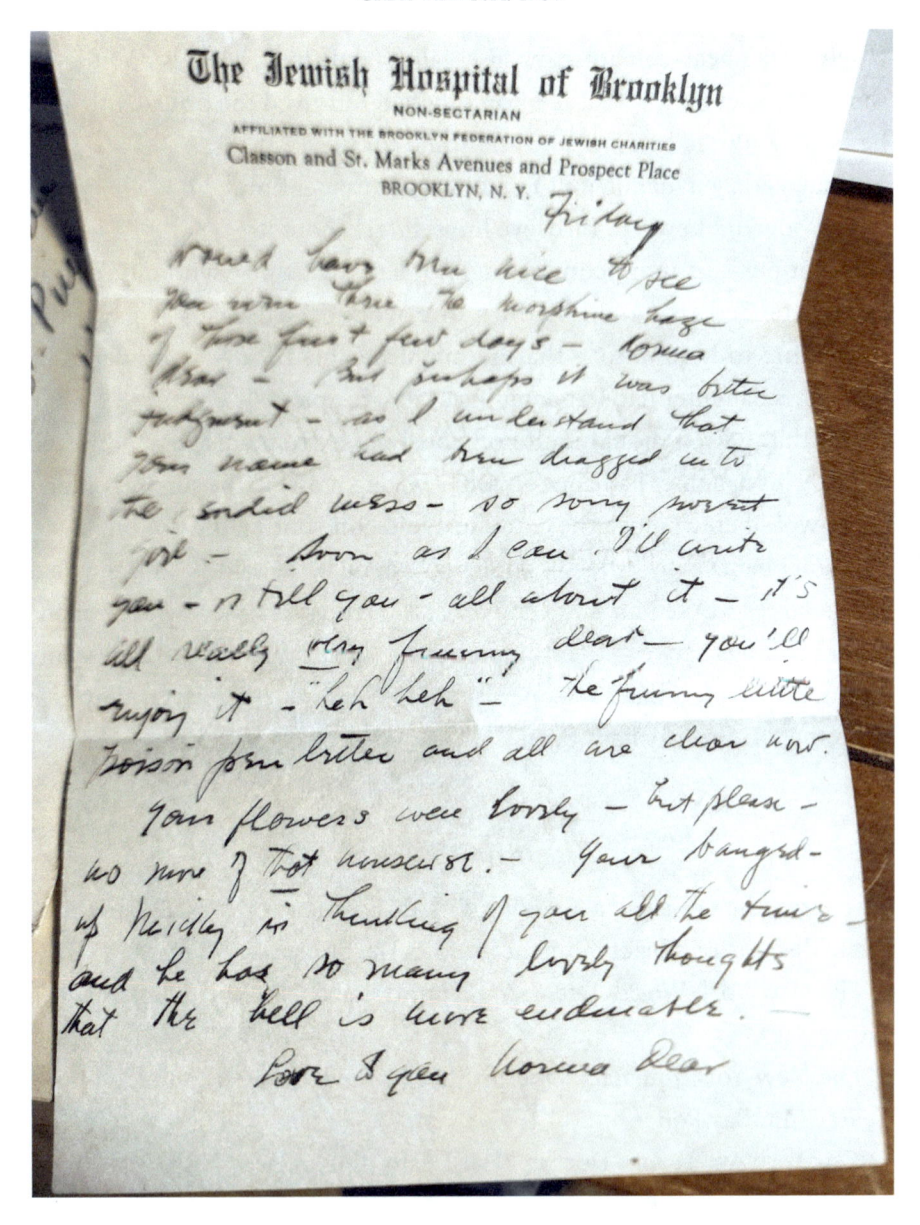

Maybe the strangest thing about this letter is how utterly devoid it is of mention at all to any Birdseye - not just to deceased Agnes but also to her father, Lewis, the man ostensibly still overseeing Dr. Milton's healthcare.

Lewis E. Birdseye, father of the would-be-killer, was yet responsible for keeping his child's victim, suffering from a collapsed lung and lapsing into barely-lucid, near-comatose malaises, alive (and already at this point, even the newspapers knew that if Thomashefsky survived the ordeal, it would be as a "paralyzed [person] and an invalid for life"[175]).

What a crazy dynamic for Dr. Milton not to mention.

And how did Lewis E. Birdseye himself feel about it?

Was it perhaps more comforting, not less, that those whom he'd long known tended to Agnes' victim's dire wounds? Perhaps it gave him something to hold onto – that he might be able to save from death he whom his daughter had left dangling at its precipice.

Not that Lewis, though quite obviously in extreme distress, admitted publicly his daughter had done anything wrong. Possibly, he simply couldn't – and would do whatever he could to avoid confronting the notion.

"I don't believe my little girl could have done it," he said.[176] "I knew that my daughter worked for Dr. Thomashefsky, but I had no knowledge of any tender feelings between them, and I don't believe now that there were any such feelings. I feel that someone else shot them both, but I haven't any idea what the motive may have been."[177]

* * *

Of course, the press had a field day with this scandal – it was all New York could discuss for a brief moment in time. Headlines:

The New York World-Telegram: "Thomashefsky Sinking, Shots Laid to Nurse"

The New York Journal: "Doctor Shot in Love Quarrel: Suicide Nurse Feared 'Jilt,' Say Police"

New York American: "Doctor, Near Death, Tells of Dead Nurse's Jealousy" and "Missive Seen as Cause for Gun Attack"

The Evening Graphic: "Doctor, Wounded as Nurse Dies, Bares Sinister Bedroom Knifing: Hint Secret Love Tangle in Rich Brooklyn Office of Stage Family's Scion"

The New York Times: "SHOOTING OF DOCTOR LAID TO JEALOUSY; Nurse Who Wounded Physician and Killed Herself Crazed by Letter, Police

Find. SHE CHLOROFORMED HIM Thomashefsky, Near Death, Says Woman Told Him it Was She Who Stabbed Him in Sleep. Confessed Attack on Doctor. Father Defends Nurse"

Daily Mirror: "Girl, Spurned by Doctor, Used Scalpel Before Gun: She Tried to Thwart New Love"

The Daily News: "Love Revenge Blamed by Doctor"

Standard Union: "Doctor, Dying, Says He Tried to Kill Himself When Shot"

And yet the media never understood – or took the time to try to – what set this triangle apart from so many others. The papers did pick up on the notable immediate forebears of the three lovers – a major actor, two prominent politicos – but not on the real consequence of their descendance.

Agnes was an innocent American of the country's most vintage stock whose father had painstakingly worked for years to restore his family to a socioeconomic level becoming of such a lineage. And yet despite her long ties to the country, Agnes seemed the character least hip to the Roaring '20s sexual ethos that had led to her ruination (in part because of her father's moral rectitude). By the same token, through her condemnable violence, she was nevertheless the best representative of the extreme measures women discarded in that era had to take to claw back at least a modicum of relevance and agency (this isn't to justify her criminality but just to contextualize it). See the Lillian Raizen case.

Meanwhile, Dr. Thomashefsky, the media failed to mention, was the lone member of his clan who'd made a conscious effort to escape its gaudy and meretricious history of vaudevillian performance and actorly promiscuity – and yet he turned out more than any other member of his generation to embody those unseemly and philandering attributes most notorious in his lionized actor father.

And then there was Norma Jeanne, whose striving father had sought to offer her an education in the finer things – piano and painting, most notably – that would permit her always to live above the muck of lurid relations between the sexes – that would elevate her via refinement, discernment. She was given an education in the arts and an access to exclusive camps as an insulation from the tawdrier side of life. And yet, as when a Greek tragic figure attempts to flee an inexorable fate, her very push into these highfalutin places is what led her into the sultry, low-down scenario that ended in gunshots.

And the artistry she worked so hard to cultivate Stateside and abroad would end up constrained, confined and ruined by the same social view of women that so narrowed Agnes' potential choices once she'd been Raizen-style wronged.

And as these larger connections were never by the press explored, the story quickly passed from their pages, as if any other bit of urban sensationalism. Today's top story soon yesterday's vaguely-recalled episode.

But this was and always had been a deeper tale (and perhaps, if explored properly, so many murders otherwise seen as mere tabloid fare would be, too).

* * *

Six days after the shootings, Lewis E. Birdseye wrote an open letter to the press in defense of his dead (and, he claimed, defamed) daughter.

"The police having marked closed the case in which my daughter was involved, may I beg that you give the same publicity to a few words from her father that you have to news from other sources.

"It seems but right for me to break silence that her friends and mine may learn the published accounts seem to be at variance with the truth. Agnes was gently reared and grew to womanhood a credit to her family, Americans since 1693.

"Small in stature, cheerful disposition, loving life, in all everything the opposite of what she is depicted in the reported statement of Dr. Thomaschefsky (sic) as to her part in the recent sad happenings. Gentlemen protect the honor of a woman so long as is possible, after which they cease to talk.

"I was among the first to enter the doctor's office after he telephoned me to 'come quickly, something terrible has happened.' He was perfectly

CHAPTER 10A: 1931

conscious, refused to tell me how he came by his wound, later giving the same refusal to the detectives and the District Attorney.

"After removal to the hospital, he came under a sinister influence, was constantly under narcotics and then there came a statement placing the onus of the whole affair on a dead girl, besmirching her character in such beastly fashion I am loath to believe he knew what he was doing.

"Unfortunately, there are no known witnesses, but there are some circumstances that indicate the doctor's story is a fanciful account. The medical examiner assures me that the one bullet that entered his body paralyzed him instantly and completely – without doubt my daughter had been shot when the doctor 'phoned (sic) me to come.

"When I entered the suite the doctor lay 15 feet from my daughter's body, in another room, perfectly conscious but unable to move. Besides my daughter's body lay a revolver, broken [open]

"The doctor's statement is that after he was shot, he picked up the revolver intending to turn it on himself, and he said his left arm was paralyzed. He broke [open] the revolver to see if there were any cartridges left.

"It requires two strong hands to break such a gun – the police tried it. The wound in her head, the fatal wound, could not have been inflicted without bending the arm in a cramped position.

"I believe there was another person present.

"Space forbids discussion as to other charges. My daughter had no nursing training.

"Everything in the girl's life and career belies the attempts to blacken her into a fiend and this is evidenced by the scores of letters and messages received since her death."[178]

Obviously, the note is a kind of hodgepodge – filled with denials, hypotheticals, character references. It advances the Birdseye legacy in America as a founding family as some small exculpatory detail. It even reads to me as lacking the courage of its convictions. Birdseye basically says as a gentleman, Dr. Milton should never have said anything publicly regarding his daughter. He later berates the doctor for his initial refusal to name his assailant or narrate what happened.

233

For perhaps those reasons and others, the press never wrote new articles exploring Birdseye's theory that the assailant of the couple was a third person, that the injured doctor could not have opened the gun to check the number of remaining bullets, that Agnes was not sufficiently trained to bandage a chloroformed victim after a scrapped mutilation (when Birdseye says space forbids discussion of the other charges, he means the nature of a daily periodical's space doesn't allow mention of something so graphic, not that he was allotted insufficient room to mention it).

The police – despite Lewis having once been on the force himself, having served as secretary to the commissioner – didn't re-open the case based on his claims.

But neither did they ever question Milton's account more thoroughly: this whole story of mutilations – it was entirely dependent on what he told them, the supposed assailant now being dead by suicide. The whole story of what had happened inside the locked office during those 15 or so minutes when Philip Pines stepped out – relayed alone by Milton (and likely to his benefit), the other occupant of the room still dead, by suicide.

In short, there was one man's word, the mysterious presence of *two rings and a gun* inside a medical office, the bizarre way Agnes shot herself in her stomach though she was planning on blowing her brains out anyway and Agnes' supposed and inexplicable entry into Dr. Milton's apartment earlier in the week – a roster of these and other small details that just never added up fully, that the police never elaborated on in sufficient measure such that its recreation of the crime read seamlessly. No, Lewis E. Birdseye was most certainly right on one point, even if all the others were the mere product of grief:

The case, when closed officially, still had holes.

Agnes' funeral was held on Friday, Aug. 14, at 8 pm in the Fairchild Chapel at 86 Lefferts Place (the chairman of Fairchild's also had a residence in Connecticut, 25 minutes away from the Birdseyes'), before just 25 mourners – family and a few friends – and a great number of floral wreaths. The Reverend Doctor Harold Olafson, associate rector of St. Paul's of Presbyterian Episcopal Church of Flatbush, presided – just 10 months before he'd give the invocation at the commencement of the graduating class of Packer College Institute – Agnes' alma mater.

Agnes was interred the next day in her family's plot in a small cemetery in Branchville, Connecticut, that is today bounded by a small pond on one side and an elementary school and baseball field on another.

As the weeks and then months passed after the shooting, Lewis E. Birdseye adjusted his life as if to account for what Agnes had almost certainly done – if not to atone for it.

First, it was reported after her demise that Agnes was in the habit of driving her own automobile, a rarity for a woman in that day (and how did she afford it?); in fact, the Daily News reported just the day after the shooting that Agnes' Ford coupe was parked outside Dr. Milton's office during the attack.[179]

Lewis, her father, in the months after her death, arranged to trade in this 1930 Ford Coupe, as well as a four-door Ford the family owned, together worth $700, to a Connecticut auto dealer for a brand new, six-cylinder Hupmobile Model S Coupe (serial number 45761) worth $995 — plus a $295 check to balance out the transaction.

Birdseye also moved his family's Brooklyn base – from its longtime home at 249 Brooklyn Avenue to 1069 Sterling Place (that house's former residents were a separated couple in the midst of a wild dispute; the husband, having failed to pay alimony and been jailed, had sent his brother-in-law to intimidate the judge in the case inside the judge's chambers).

But the exchange of external trappings that reminded Lewis of Agnes was not nearly his most consequential move after her demise – not even close.

Citing grief, Lewis had announced his resignation from the Jewish Hospital in October (effective Nov. 1).[180] He was to live out his days quietly – step aside and retire from not just from his job but life itself, in a sense.

Only he followed through on just half the move.

For New York had since 1866 been home to the St. John's Guild charity, which had in intervening years worked with the charitable arm of The New York Times to acquire ships, turn them into floating hospitals and, docking at ports along the five boroughs, offer free medical care in the summer to impoverished and immigrant children (while educating their families on public health perils and hygiene – and feeding everyone – hot meals for older children and mothers, milk for babies).

The charity ran on donations alone (especially from the Juilliard family), its motto: "To afford relief to the sick children of the poor of the city of New York without regard to creed, color or nationality."

For just a 25-cent donation in 1912, one could pay for a baby's medical trip aboard the ship. A dollar would afford the same for an entire family.

That was in 1912. But this particular healthcare initiative had proven remarkably enduring, and the Floating Hospital was still plying the water and serving the poor in 1931, at the time of Agnes Birdseye's suicide.

Somehow, between his retirement announcement and the actual date it was supposed to go into effect, Lewis E. Birdseye realized he could do nothing more righteous or redemptive or meaningful now than put off his own rest entirely to join the Floating Hospital and offer his services to these otherwise at-risk souls.

So he did. On Dec. 7, 1931, he took on the role of "general agent," or main leader, of the Guild and its floating hospital. And thereafter he spent all his time caring for, attempting to save, the neediest children in the entire metropolis, running the floating hospital from an office on the East River pier at 42nd Street.

It was a paid gig, sure – but it was a job selfless in so many other respects and one that required work of some kind 52 weeks of the year. Many in New York who knew and loved Lewis E. Birdseye, who'd worried he might become a pale sliver of a man after his daughter's demise, were incredibly heartened and encouraged by his brave stance to board the charitable ship.

No one more, perhaps, than the president of the Jewish Hospital himself, a major lawyer named Joseph J. Baker, who from his office at 37 Wall Street wrote: "I assume…that the Guild has succeeded in obtaining the benefit of your service. I am really very happy about it."

> BAKER & OBERMEIER
> COUNSELLORS AT LAW
>
> JOSEPH J. BAKER
> LEONARD J. OBERMEIER
> ALVIN S. ROSENSON
> OSCAR S. ROSNER
>
> 37 Wall Street
> New York
>
> December   1931.
>
> Mr. L. E. Birdseye,
> c/o St. John's Guild,
> 1 East 42nd Street,
> New York City.
>
> My dear Mr. Birdseye:
>
> I assume from your initials which you have preceding the words "General Agent" on the stationery of St. John's Guild, that the Guild has succeeded in obtaining the benefit of your service. I am really very happy about it and congratulate you and the Guild upon the association.
>
> With best wishes,
>
> Sincerely yours,
>
> JJB.ES

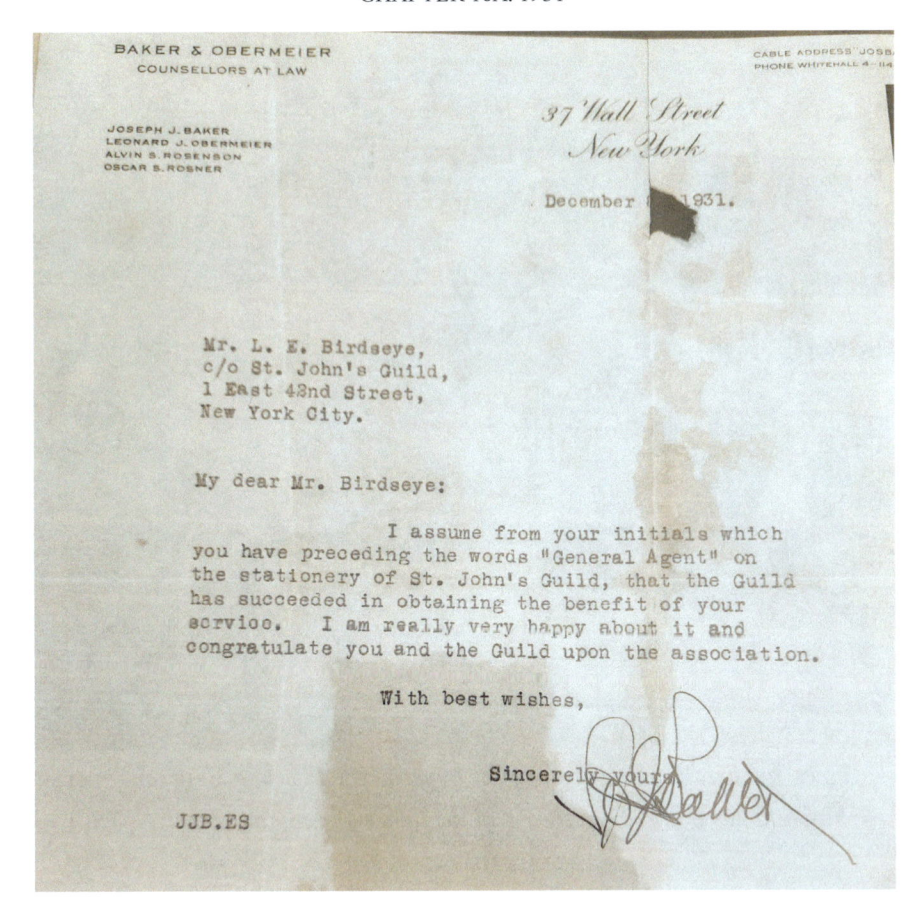

And Lewis E. Birdseye wasn't going to exclude Agnes' mother. Florence Gedney Birdseye, from whatever healing this venture might afford mourning parents – there are extant photos of her at the 1936 dedication of a new ship — aboard the Floating Hospital itself.

NEW YORK CITY LOVE TRIANGLE, 1931

Agnes' mother, Florence Gedney Birdseye, on the Floating Hospital — her husband has marked her figure, in the upper-right hand corner, "FGB."

CHAPTER 10A: 1931

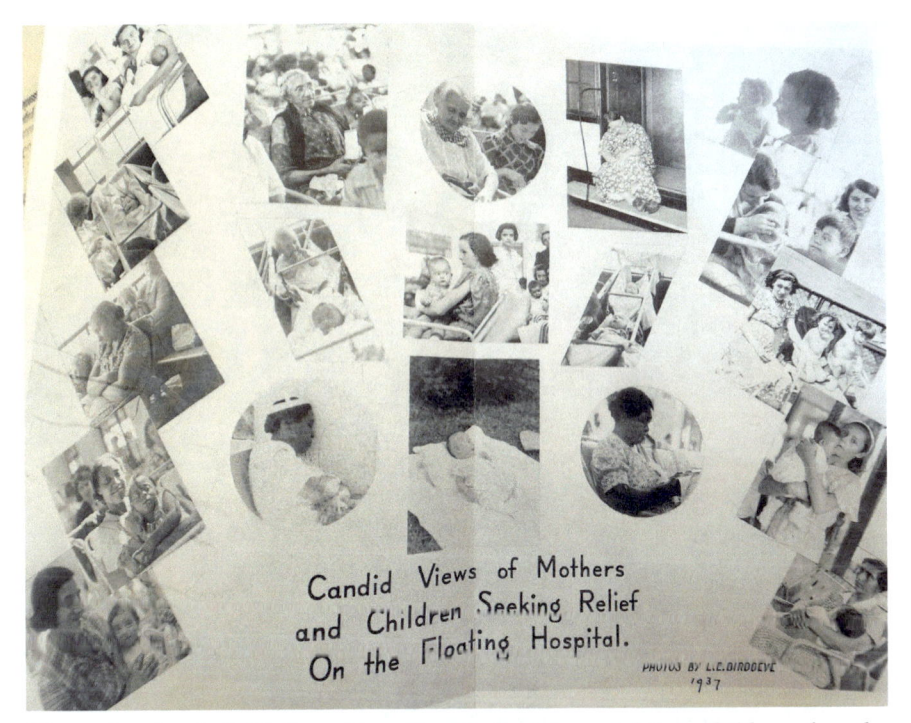

Photos that Lewis E. Birdseye himself took of mothers and their children aboard a Floating Hospital ship in 1937.

NEW YORK CITY LOVE TRIANGLE, 1931

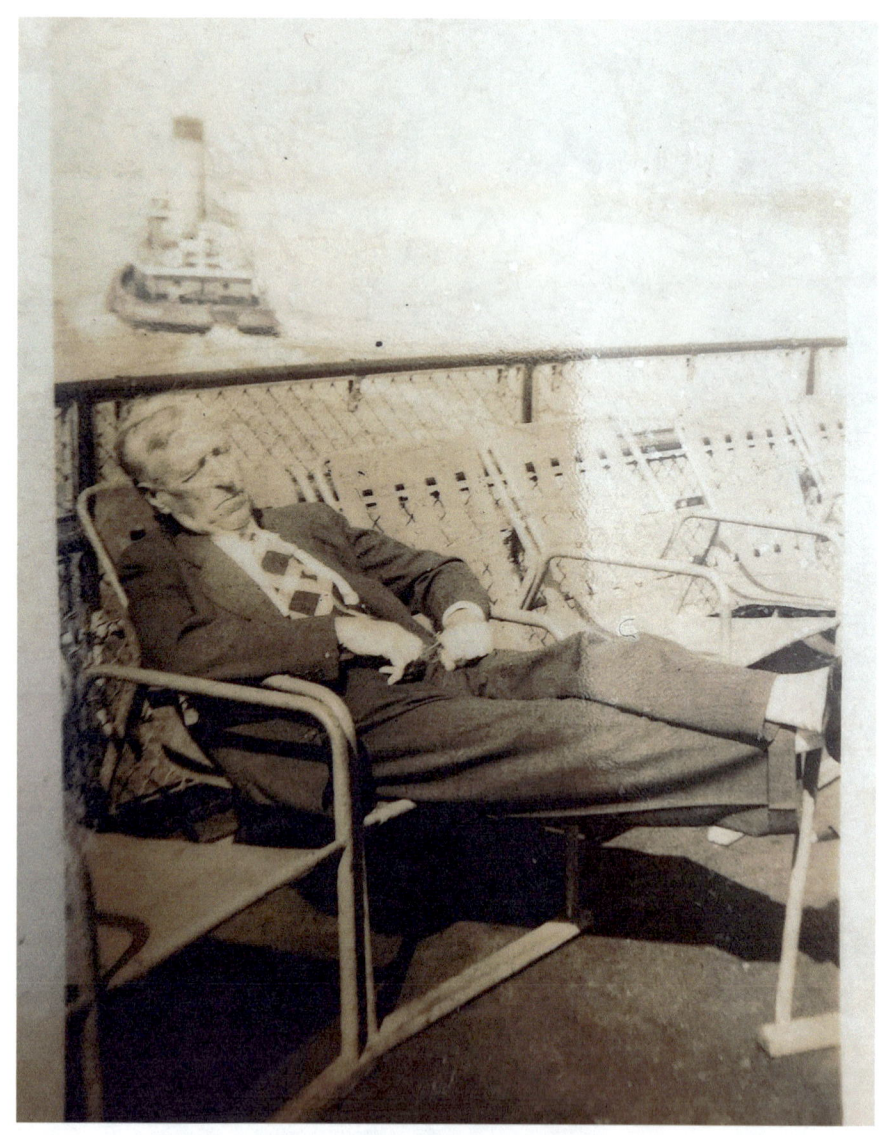

And yet, how much relief could this charitable venture provide a man grieving a daughter dead by lurid, widely-publicized suicide? Here is Lewis Birdseye ostensibly at rest on the Floating Hospital, looking not at all like a man at peace.

Chapter 11:
Thomashefsky-Bernstein-Bachelors

In 1931, as Milton spent months as a hospital inpatient, Boris kept on working, almost as if nothing had transpired. He debuted his first major production in English on Broadway on Sept. 10th – or *less than a month* after the Aug. 12 shooting.

And he wasn't the only member of the family involved in the show: his *other* son, Harry, had worked on it, adapted a Yiddish operetta about a cantor into the show, now titled "The Singing Rabbi."

Perhaps producers beyond Boris had already sunk money into the production, such that he couldn't delay it. Perhaps Boris, himself short of funds, had laid out his own dough for this run in the Selwyn Theater on 42nd Street, and he needed to recoup it soon. Or maybe the only thing that kept the Thomashefsky acting family sane following the sordid affair was the work – putting their minds to what they did best – playing make believe.

And maybe Boris was a bad father, at least to some of his children some of the time.

"The Singing Rabbi" flopped, but Boris simply returned to the Second Avenue Theater, where he staged a Yiddish show called "Der Mames Zundele" in November.

And yet the journalist Richard G. Massock reported that just before the Broadway staging of "The Singing Rabbi" in September, Boris's "heart was heavy with grief" and the usually confident actor even told a friend, "It is hard now to put myself into this – on account of Milton."[181]

On Monday, Dec. 28, 1931, Walter Winchell, in his "On Broadway" column for The Daily Mirror, wrote: "Dr. Thomashefsky, the son of the famous Yiddish actor, who was shot by his nurse last summer, is still in the B'klyn hosp, hopelessly paralyzed."

Dr. Milton Thomashefsky was released from the hospital that very week, at the turn of the new year – 1932 – Variety pronouncing him "doomed to a wheel chair for the remainder of his life" on the same page that it said New York City nightclubs were allowed by cops to stay open past their 3 am curfew on New Year's Eve.[182]

He moved into a three-room suite with his mother, the former actress Bessie, at the Half Moon Hotel on Coney Island – but more on that institution in a moment.[183]

Three years later, a theater columnist actually broke the news that Bessie would rejoin her estranged husband on-stage, after a 25-year break romantically and theatrically, to stage a "special performance, the proceeds of which [would] go to their son," called on this occasion "a helpless cripple."[184] It was the only time a reunion between the separated couple, riven earlier by Boris' unfaithfulness and ruinous financial mismanagement, was ever considered.

Meanwhile, Dr. Milton, who occasionally returned to the hospital for further treatment, spent his free time devising plays and film scripts (which he presumably dictated to an attendant or his mother).

None of the work was ever produced professionally, though Milton was reported to have worked with amateur theater troupes, some of which may have used his work for dramatic exercise.

In April of 1934, the Half Moon Hotel, the 14-story structure built less than a decade earlier on the Coney Island Boardwalk by local business bigwigs so as to turn their shore into a legitimate tourist-destination rival of Atlantic City, the structure where Dr. Milton was now living out his post-paralysis years, hosted an anniversary event for the Madison Park Hospital, an institution created just a few years earlier.

The party could have been put on by any number of those affiliated with the hospital (which employed 100 doctors and 40 nurses). But in actual fact, it was arranged by a few folks, one of whom was R.W. Auerbach – the medical examiner who'd performed the official New York City autopsy on Agnes Birdseye.[185]

Did Auerbach help steer the party to this hotel because he knew Milton lived there? Would Milton have wanted to chat with him at a party? Did they wind up crossing paths that night?[186]

That's unclear. But there was another strange aspect to the entire gala business at Milton's residence.

A year earlier, in 1933, The Half Moon Hotel had been sued by its mortgage-issuer, which had wanted to foreclose on the place – the hotel's only real revenue being its banquets business. The identity of the mortgage-issuer, the hotel's creditor? It was Title Guarantee & Trust – the president of which, Clinton DeWitt Burdick, was the most famous resident of the building at 135 Eastern Parkway, where Dr. Milton had occupied a ground floor office before he'd been shot inside it and paralyzed.

As Agnes' father plied the rivers of New York overseeing the administration of medical care to the poor, as Milton sat by a window, isolated from the world in a Coney Island motel, the Bernsteins were still on the move. Norma Jeanne's brother, Arthur, had joined her father's legal firm in 1932, an appointment announced with some small fanfare (despite the fact that Arthur, secretly gay, was nothing like the lawyer his father wanted him to be; it was a profession he undertook to please a parent alone, his family told me; he later founded a greeting a card shop with his partner, once his father was dead). And Norma – camp now ruined for her – returned to the place so connected with her art and leisure, her lone paradise beyond the woods native to the northeast: Europe – including Paris, of course. And J. Sidney moved the whole family out of the apartment building in which I would reside 100 years later and into a brand new edifice on Central Park West, between 88th and 89th.

> BERNSTEIN & PATTERSON
> 250 WEST 57TH STREET
> NEW YORK
>
> WE TAKE PLEASURE IN ANNOUNCING THAT WE HAVE THIS DAY BECOME ASSOCIATED IN THE PRACTICE OF LAW AT THE ABOVE ADDRESS.
>
> J. SIDNEY BERNSTEIN
> LESTER W. PATTERSON
> ARTHUR H. BERNSTEIN
>
> DECEMBER 1, 1932   TELEPHONE COLUMBUS 5-6330
>   5-6331

During this time, Norma was pulling away from Milton physically, from his sad corner of a sad hotel on Coney Island, her life and career on a trajectory exciting, romantic – while also making what seemed an honest effort to stay in touch with the man who'd won her heart before being so incapacitated.

In fact, it's quite astounding what the final letter from the doctor to Norma reveals – it's quite astounding it even exists, of course, and that I chanced upon it – but the contents involve the extent of her adventures abroad, her plunge into new dalliances, the range of efforts her family and his were making to keep these two would-be partners somehow connected even marginally. And the magnitude of his depression – the great efforts he was making to seek hope in cures with only the slightest chance of working.

The letter mentions Norma Jeanne's brother Arthur calling Milton and chatting about the former's legal cases. And that Milton's brother, the film producer Ted, brought flowers to a ship for Norma Jeanne as she took an ocean liner for Europe in the summer of 1932 (but the wrong ship, initially) – just a year after she'd met Dr. Milton in camp.

Basically, Norma was pulling out of New York and a proxy for the

CHAPTER 11: THOMASHEFSKY-BERNSTEIN-BACHELORS

immobile doctor was chasing after her along a pier as she waved goodbye, forever.

It's all the pain – a raging at futility – of a well-read doctor knowing he has almost no chance of recovery but he'll be more mentally disturbed if he quits submitting to small surgeries just the same.

And a gutting loneliness evident in so many words he typed and in the absence of so many you feel he wanted to. A remarkable testament to the lives being lived by the two remaining members of the triangle a year on – and the last note I found in Norma Jeanne's daughter-in-law's house – postmarked in Brooklyn on June 2, 1932 and again in Paris on June 14 – delivered to Norma via the SS Leviathan at the Hotel Reynolds, 6 Avenue du Parc-Monceau:

> *It's very good to read your letters. The birthday cable was a real surprise. I was pleased that you made friends with Olga and LULU, but you never even mention NYANYA. You poor little girl – all alone in Paris with only two or three dozen friends – and WHAT friends – famous tennis players, Russian princesses, and scientists who have new Wasserman tests. Never heard of your doctor friend – but that doesn't mean he isn't well-known. Your letter a I tear as I read. (sic)*

(Is he ripping the letter as he reads it or is he tearing up, *crying* – what to make of this line and its typo and that word that can be read two ways?)

> *Arthur called me yesterday. Seemed to be very unhappy about his murderer – appeal denied or something. Do you like pressed duck? Summer here – zzzzz zzzzzzzzzzzzzelectric fan. Eugene is married. Took a night off for his honeymoon. No thoughts. Minutes since the last sentence. Can't write to you. Nothing's important.*

What can he possibly say to this high-flying girl who's partying in Paris, who is so far away – and you notice, too, the depression seem to set in, as he writes, the moment he recalls a mutual friend's wedding – an occasion he will never have for himself now.

Oh yes. Must go to the hospital soon. Slight operation. Long chance. Principal benefit will be psychic. Will have annoying doubt forever removed from my mind. Goblin sits on shoulder in dark moments and says if maybe perhaps. Can't be happy with goblin on shoulder. So I'm going to have it removed. No danger. Simple operation. Can't die.

The stakes have become so miserable. The operation can't achieve much – the consolation is that it cannot kill him either.

Just removal of goblin under local anesthesia. Will be back at the window in two three weeks. Then plan to go somewhere else. Battle Creek maybe. No steak. Corn Flakes. Heard yesterday of fellow who began to move three days after goblinectomy. Lucky guy. Doctors made mistake. Found something more than goblin. Medical literature full of in all probability, not infrequently, of course there are cases on record, every careful observer has met with exceptions, prognosis must be guarded. Prognosis means telling what's gonna happen.

Dr. Milton is so obviously left cold by all the words he likely himself deployed in his profession — that is, when he was not the patient. Now, he finds the entire practice of medicine a cold one, the bedside manner of its practitioners lacking, their words cold and empty. Purposeless.

Had great doctor here to see me. Diagnosis: BLAHBLAHBLAH But said nobody can tell without taking a look. Must take a look. Maybe find something to fix. Without looking, lousy. Suppose get better. Goblin will always whisper might have gotten better long time ago. Suppose don't get better. Goblin at 3 A.M. hollers might have gotten better if somebody looked and fixed. So we're gonna have a look. No harm. Can't make it worse. Do you agree?

CHAPTER 11: THOMASHEFSKY-BERNSTEIN-BACHELORS

What could Norma ever write back to help quell his agony even a little? He's tormented by the thought that he must try to regain a life he knows in all probability he has already lost. He is alive. But he's all but dead.

Prize contest. Cash for best letter – 20 words – no more no less in case of a tie, duplicate prizes will be awarded. UNCLE BILL just coming out of his car with three neices (sic). His time off is spent most enjoyably by visiting and playing with his family's kids.

No idea which Bill this refers to – only that the life he describes for Bill again seems to be one outlined chiefly for the way it mirrors what Dr. Milton cannot have — enjoyment in his own children. Like Bill, he may delight only in others'.

But there's also this deeper truth about Bill, perhaps: Philip Pines, the engineer who introduced Norma Jeanne to the doctor at Camp Point O' Pines and later served as the doc's bodyguard and later yet discovered the doctor and Agnes both bleeding out on the floor of the office, seems also to have been known as William "Bill" Pines (this is the name the police took down for him; it's the way the cops refer to him in their final report). Is Doc Milton describing to Norma the familial and social life of the man who introduced them and then was so integral to the story of his maiming?

Know a girl who liked Bill but gave up after a few days of his taking her out —- to see his neices (sic). But the best guy in the world. Sends his best to you.

That very well could be the man who effected Norma's entry into the triangle sending her his regards. Wild.

Almost called you the day you sailed to ask you to change your booking. Asked my brother Teddy to get a flower for you. He's thorough. Took the flower from the florist and to make sure there would be no hitch, brought it himself to the boat———to the BREMEN. Guess he fixed it somehow.

I think Armand is out west. His Paris house sounds interesting. Too bad he is not there now. You could find out why I like him so much. Your Hotel must be nice, but Ah the Majestic—-on the third or fourth floor was my room and at three or four in the morning when I came home once, there was a scratching at my door and when I opened it there was the poor girl with the toothache who wanted a cigarette – the poor thing was barefooted and wore a black fur coat held tightly together at the neck and chest to display something pink and silk. So I gave her a cigarette. My mother thanks you for your card and wants to be remember d (sic). Here comes somebody. Dear Norma:

The letter, in that unorthodox way of ending at the start, evokes all his offbeat correspondence of better times.

There's nothing to suggest Norma didn't write Dr. Milton back or that her brother Arthur didn't continue to call him. But the photos from that summer of Norma – mainly on Lido Beach, off Venice, Italy, as the Venice Film Festival was inaugurated there – document those new affections taking the place of Dr. Milton's. Underline her great remove from the sad motel room he occupied with agony.

CHAPTER 11: THOMASHEFSKY-BERNSTEIN-BACHELORS

Norma and a man named Luigi who proclaimed himself swimming champion of Italy (I had some difficulty confirming the claim).

Norma and a handsome chap named Arcady Khasine at the Hotel Excelsior on Lido. What Norma almost certainly does not know when posing with this handsome devotee is that a man by the same name, perhaps the very same Adonis-like admirer, in cahoots with his father, Simeon Khasine, has already forged a last will and testament ascribed to a dead Russian naval figure – Admiral Alexieff – whose Eastern assets were frozen by the Soviets upon their ascendancy to power but whose Parisian bank account of 38 million francs was not. This *Arcady Khasine (if he's not one and the same as the man pictured with Norma) and his father, after contriving the false will that bequeathed to them some 20 million francs, found a vagabond notary who'd fled the Soviets and landed in France, had him testify to the spurious document's authenticity in a French civil court, and would later flee with their money to Venezuela (leaving only the notary to stand trial for the forgery in 1938, which proceeding would result in a two-year jail sentence for the miserably exploited officiant).*[187]

CHAPTER 11: THOMASHEFSKY-BERNSTEIN-BACHELORS

A man named Mario who penned a flirtatious and direct — Italian, in other words — note to Norma on the back of the next photo (what happened on that gondola ride?).

NEW YORK CITY LOVE TRIANGLE, 1931

To Norma, hoping she will remember the gondola ride, and .....

Io ti amo!

Mario

VENICE 5-6 August 1932

CHAPTER 11: THOMASHEFSKY-BERNSTEIN-BACHELORS

Norma even looked exotic, becoming, alluring in photos taken on holiday with her brother, Arthur.

Norma returned from this summer of male appreciation on the SS Conte Grande, sailing on August 26 and arriving back in New York on September 5.

She returned to a career burgeoning, flourishing, no less than her womanhood, her standing in the eyes of the continent's most comely bachelors.

In April of 1932, she once again had her work shown with the Society of Independent Artists in the Grand Central Palace – again to positive notices. A Barnard student publication mentioned her work among "some rather pleasant things to be noticed" in the exhibition.[188] And offers for her work, albeit in unusual proposals, came pouring in:

"One of the paintings (#75) caused a men's tailor to express interest in bartering, and an attorney to offer a proprietary medicine mail order business in exchange for the same. A dentist also wrote directly."[189]

If that sounds a minor collegiate mention followed by offers equally humble and meager, note Norma's inclusion in the *first ever* television broadcast on the American art scene (also, recall: the Depression had begun in earnest, and even art appreciators were loath, or simply unable, to dish out money for canvasses).

It was held on April 5, 1932, from 8:45-9:00 pm, on CBS's two broadcast stations – W2XAB and W2XE.

Norma was asked about just such transactions as were being proposed to her – art for materials useful and tangible. John Sloan, another of the featured painters, a colleague of the deceased Robert Henri and Norma's personal mentor, asked her "what she thinks about forgetting money, and painting in the hope that her art will her get her what she wants."

Her reply was both personal and political – realistic and (especially for someone who tended to shy away from Civil Rights issues) rather feminist:

> I think that Art is in itself satisfying. I know that many other artists feel the same way, but I know too, that they want and need places to live and things to eat and material with which to work. If a tailor with a few yards of cloth and his experience is willing to exchange a suit for

CHAPTER 11: THOMASHEFSKY-BERNSTEIN-BACHELORS

what my education in art and my experience with the paintbrush has produced, I think it is a splendid idea. I certainly am not going to refuse to accept a fur that I would like to wear for a painting that I enjoyed doing, and of course, I would take a trip to Europe if any steamship official should care to make me an offer for one of my paintings.

I brought this picture of "Marjorie Albertha" here tonight. Perhaps you have seen the paintings of "Beatrice" and "My Self" portrait on exhibition now at the Grand Central Palace. I do not paint like you or Mr. Gardner or Mr. Maurer, but I like the open door policy of the Society of Independent Artists which enables everyone to show his own work without having to pass any judge or jury on art. It has always pleased me that the Independents showed no sign of considering that their show is a Man's show but has encouraged everyone to paint and give the public an opportunity to see for themselves what they like.

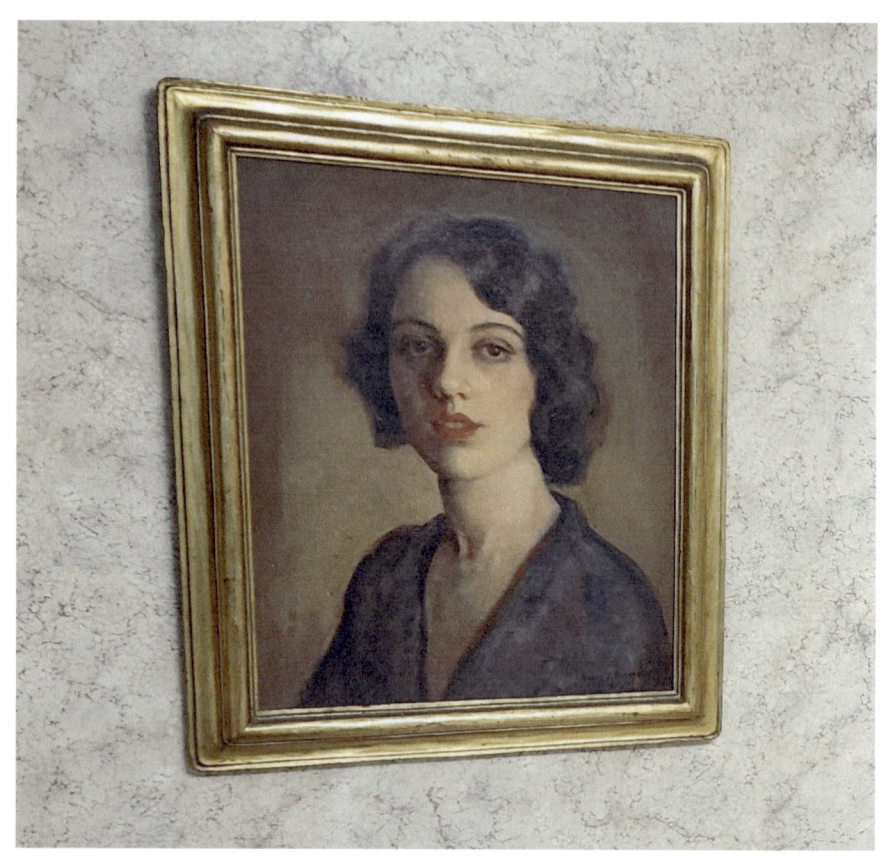

A self-portrait of Norma's featured in the 1932 Independents' show (and now hung in her daughter-in-law's domicile). A more sedate study of the artist in almost indigo-eggplant-blue and black, her open lips a look less suggestive than stiff, it lacks the yearning sultriness of her lipstick-red-and-blonde self-portrait of 1928, shown below on a flyer for a posthumous show of Norma Jeanne's art; one wonders how intentional the difference – whether it was a reflection of the artist's ideological evolution or perhaps a development of another kind; she had been through so much – she still seemed to revel in her sexiness in the real world even as she seemingly shied away from it in her work:

CHAPTER 11: THOMASHEFSKY-BERNSTEIN-BACHELORS

PORTSMOUTH ATHENAEUM
SEPT. 12-NOV. 26, 2014

NORMA BERNSTEIN SMITH
Talented Artist, Adventuresome Spirit

The Depression having altered the art market not merely in the form of transactions, it suddenly made contests – which offered prizes and fame both – a tempting avenue for the rising star.

Norma took tremendous advantage: After FDR was elected for the first time, the Art Students' League in New York challenged entrants to create the ideal portrait of the New Deal Democrat. Out of 750 entries, Norma's sketch won – earning her a trip to Washington to meet her subject, who'd then autograph the artwork, which signed piece would then hang in the main branch of the New York Public Library.

That visit occurred in December of 1933, at which time the Washington Post wrote, "Miss Bernstein...seems very young indeed for such an honor but...is already regarded as one of America's up-and-coming painters... Her technique, wherever she acquired it, is marked by versatility and imagination, the critics say."[190]

The contest was underwritten by Knight newspapers, and when it came time for Norma to meet FDR, the President actually put off a meeting with the Soviet ambassador to extend their confab (perhaps at the prodding of House of Representatives power player Sol Bloom, a family friend of the J. Sidney Bernsteins whose family hosted Norma Jeanne during her Washington stay).

CHAPTER 11: THOMASHEFSKY-BERNSTEIN-BACHELORS

Norma, her winning sketch of FDR and Congressman Sol Bloom (notice the Depression-era logo of the National Recovery Administration plastered onto windows in the background).

Norma's next contest, in its strange mash-up of Mad Men-era promotion and art-democratization, proved that for all her possible shortcomings in the realm of civil rights, she was nevertheless a truly empathic artist (or perhaps she just took a certain tack in this competition, for reasons not humanitarian, and got lucky):

In 1933, Philip Morris' ad execs had spotted a dwarf bellboy in the New Yorker Hotel whom they realized could serve as a perfect real-life stand-in for the anonymous bell-hop figure already present in their marketing of the prior 15 years – 3'11" Johnnie Roventini, whom they quickly had utter – in appearances and over the airwaves – their prized slogan:

"Call for Philip Morris!"

The tobacco powerhouse, sponsoring each Tuesday a live 8 p.m. broadcast on NBC's WEAF that commenced with the call, invited four prominent artists in 1934 to draw Johnnie – Norma included. Philip Morris would put their work on display for two weeks at the Tuesday show's venue — Radio City Music Hall, that hallowed Art Deco theater– and the public would vote for its favorite (with the winner to receive $50 in addition to the massive publicity).

Norma agreed to these terms – nearly.

For there was a small catch: Philip Morris was requesting a caricature of its already small, high-pitched bellhop figure. And Norma could not quite bring herself, for whatever reason (she later said it was Johnnie's handsomeness) to caricature a figure of proportions sadly somewhat cartoonish already.

So while her three competitors indeed submitted more exaggerated work, Norma simply drew Johnnie with the attention to inner-character she brought to bear on all her work – and of course, the public voted her version best.

The paperwork informing Norma of her win, including a photostat of the check:

CHAPTER 11: THOMASHEFSKY-BERNSTEIN-BACHELORS

PHILIP MORRIS & CO. LTD.
INCORPORATED
OFFICES AND FACTORIES
CAIRO EGYPT — LONDON 22 NEW BOND ST — HAMILTON CANADA — NEW YORK 119-5TH AVE.
IMPORTERS & MANUFACTURERS OF HIGHEST GRADES CIGARETTES

NEW YORK

27th floor, 444 Madison Ave.
New York City
May 14, 1934

Miss Norma Jeanne Bernstein
275 Central Park West
New York City

Dear Miss Bernstein:

You will be glad to hear that your drawing received the largest number of votes in the Johnnie "Call-for-Philip-Morris" caricature contest at Radio City.

Your check will be forwarded to you in the near future.

With thanks for your cooperation,

Sincerely yours,

Helene Blanchard
Publicity Director

HB:C

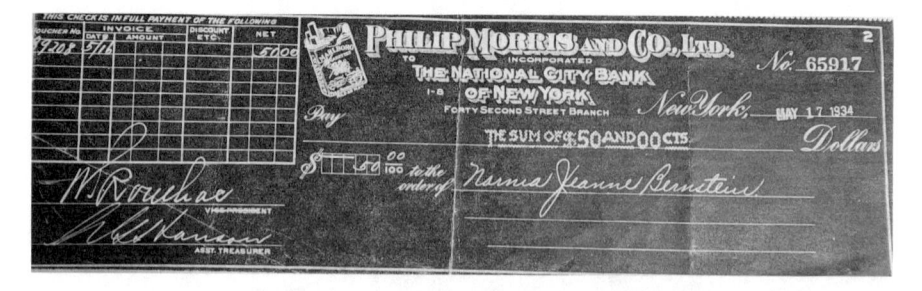

Agnes was dead, Dr. Milton was immobilized and Norma Jeanne was being feted by the most beautiful men on Lido Beach, the most powerful politician in the world and the most prestigious purveyor of the world's most addictive drug.

It's not really a fair comparison – Norma had nothing to do with the absence and withdrawal of the two other lovers with whom she'd always be linked in the great hurly-burly of life – but neither is the contrast the least bit exaggerated.

Norma Jeanne Bernstein had escaped the tawdry and violent episode of 1931 not only unscathed physically but without injury to her career or social prospects.

Seemingly.

But she was soon to marry – and fall victim to the same social mores and power dynamics that had likely contributed, at least in some small part, to Agnes' armed outburst.

Chapter 12: Elegy for a Generation

Agnes' great-niece, Elisa, having researched the case and formerly worked decades in the archives at the Boston Public Library, told me it was possible Agnes carried a ring so she and Milton could pose as a married couple when slipping into hotels for trysts; but, in Elisa's own opinion, that idea makes less sense if the engagement ring was a real diamond solitaire, as reported, and not some fake hunk; you could use a cheap stone, costume jewelry, if you needed the item just to fool the clerk at the hotel registration desk.

* * *

The autopsy ruled Agnes not pregnant and in the midst of having her period. If she knew, then, from the menstrual blood, she most certainly wasn't pregnant, why did she press the gun to her stomach almost symbolically and fire there first, before lining the gun up to her skull?

I attempted to acquire the Brooklyn DA's records of the entire episode– as the Brooklyn DA in 1931 personally visited maimed Dr. Milton at the hospital and listened to his narration of what had transpired – via the Department of Records in New York City. But apparently, they have no such Brooklyn DA records prior to 1940 (and the NYC cops told me their records for this sort of thing don't go further back than 1955 — which meant I had no chance of tracking down the diamond engagement ring from the crime scene either).

It's impossible to know exactly when, if ever, Lewis E. Birdseye became convinced of his daughter's guilt. He may have never believed the very things he wrote in his open letter to the press but felt compelled to write them anyway. To defend his daughter even though he knew her culpable, for what else is a father to do when the police have closed a case, such that her entire life seems to have been adjudged?

In his case, the answer was to give to others aboard a ship offering pro bono healthcare for a full-decade – working unceasingly until his own body gave out:

Lewis E. Birdseye suffered a fatal heart attack the day before Christmas, 1942, a couple of months after he turned 69. Which is to say: he worked years past the national retirement age on the floating hospital.

The next day, the Times ran a sizeable obituary that never once mentioned Agnes' scandal. Instead, it recalled a man who "was known widely among the poor of the city," the headline tabbing Lewis "A Social Worker" who's "Served Charity 11 Years."[191]

This was his legacy. Lewis E. Birdseye Sr.: 1873-1942.

And yet, once again, the story proves itself less simple – knottier and more enigmatic – than such a reductive and redemptive obit for Agnes' father would have us believe.

For three years before he passed away, Lewis E. Birdseye – stern Republican, father of a murder-minded and suicidal daughter, whose progeny's jealous and violent rage had gripped the city and made the front page of every paper – made a most improbable and unexpected decision as he came to grips with that tragedy (or perhaps a very fitting choice):

Lewis served as a celebrity guest detective on a CBS criminal mystery radio program whose conceit was that invited panelists could guess the killer before the hero (mystery writer Ellery Queen).

It was the July 30, 1939, episode of "The Adventures of Ellery Queen" – *entitled "Bad Boy"* – and all four of its guest panelists – its "armchair detectives" – worked in the field of child welfare. While the tape of the broadcast does not survive – and so Lewis' sleuthing has been lost – the episode's plot does: it involved a mysterious townhouse on Washington Square and a woman poisoned by arsenic in her rabbit stew.

CHAPTER 12: ELEGY FOR A GENERATION

It's impossible not to imagine that – whatever Lewis' initial reasons for accepting the invitation to the show – he was not also considering his own daughter's case as he struggled on live radio to understand what had happened to a poisoned woman left for dead by the denizens of her own brownstone in the heart of New York City.

Impossible not to wonder whether, given Agnes' clear culpability in the shooting of Dr. Milton and herself, Lewis was not working through a fictional case whose perpetrator was unknown in part for a catharsis:

Finally a chance to solve a case whose prime mover, whose tragically guilty party, wasn't unimpeachably his own kin.

An inquiry whose answer, for once, would not break his heart.

* * *

On Oct. 3, 1938, Jacob Sidney Bernstein – lawyer and Democratic insider both – finally reached the geographic pinnacle to which those professional paths inevitably led: 44 Union Square, or the headquarters at that time of Tammany Hall.

There, fellow political pooh-bahs were deciding on a slate of lawyers to run in the November election to fill two judicial spots in the First District, which spanned Manhattan and the Bronx, soon-to-be-vacated, on Dec. 31 – those of Judges William Herman Black and Richard P. Lydon.

Back then, election to the New York Supreme Court (oddly, the lowest level court in the state, New York being the only state to call its trial-level jurisprudence "supreme") granted the winner a 14-year-term, but Judge Black was bowing out of the job only two years into his second stint. His romantic life had not escaped media attention in 1931 – the year of Agnes and Norma and Dr. Milton – when his wife, a woman 34 years his junior from New Orleans, already the recipient of $400 per month in alimony from the judge by virtue of a private agreement, sought a divorce from him in Reno.[192]

J. Sidney Bernstein was put on the ballot that night in Tammany Hall, and he thereafter went about securing the backing of those clubs and organizations then affiliated with the Democratic machine and essential to the success of its candidates. He receiving the support, for instance, of the so-called Non-Partisan Textile Apparel Industries Committee – basically, a *schmatta*-PAC with division heads for Blouses and Corsets, Underwear and Millinery – which ran an ad in Women's Wear Daily that read:

"Our industries require on the Bench a man of the character, integrity and ability of J. Sidney Bernstein, whose familiarity with business problems and knowledge of the law will insure safe and sane justice."

Of course, the ad elided over J. Sidney's familiarity with the darker side of the law – with the vigilantism of spurned lovers and the helplessness of associated victims. What did the Garment District know of his daughter's tabloid brush with love and destruction?

Maybe a better question: To what degree was J. Sidney still climbing the political ladder as if that incident had never occurred? Was he benumbed by the awfulness or, with an exceptional motivation, unaffected by it entirely?

He won – regardless.

J. Sidney, along with the other nominated Democrat, were sworn in as judges on Nov. 8, 1938, with at least 426, 291 reported votes — the Daily News had covered only 1,709 of 1,821 districts by the following day, Nov. 9 – which was Kristallnacht across Germany and Austria.[193]

But J. Sidney celebrated stateside, naturally (in all fairness, the obligation of American Jews to their European counterparts at this time is an issue highly complicated, not one to be addressed casually or in dismissive fashion).

The Metropolitan Vigilant Club – some local Tammany association whose name evokes a gangster in a tux – threw J. Sidney a party on the occasion at Jack Dempsey's Restaurant just a block north of Madison Square Garden, on Dec. 21. It's possible this was the start of J. Sidney's relationship with the eponymous retired boxing champion, who'd later attend the justice's funeral.

CHAPTER 12: ELEGY FOR A GENERATION

Metropolitan Vigilant Club

Testimonial Dinner

to

Hon. J. Sidney Bernstein

by the Members of the Metropolitan Vigilant Club

at Dempsey's Restaurant

50th Street & 8th Avenue

on Wednesday, December 21st, 1938

at 7 P. M.

The actual invite. And then, there is something about J. Sidney's penguin-like face during his swearing-in, fair or not, that gives the impression he'd never blinked, no matter the tragedy around him, in his pursuit of the judicial position he finally attained:

NEW YORK CITY LOVE TRIANGLE, 1931

As a judge, J. Sidney made a decision whose historic implications he'd never learn: He declared a divorced couple married.

At the time, courts in Morelos, Mexico, essentially operated a mail-order divorce business, by which an unhappy spouse from any foreign country – though most were from the States – could obtain a dissolution of marriage (of shaky legality) merely by sending in an application – no one had to show up nor did either party have to be informed about the proceeding. In fact, Morelos courts had rules regarding secrecy that often made it difficult for a person to find out *whether* he or she was being divorced.

In November 1942, the consul posted to NY by Ecuador – Sixto Durán-Ballén – obtained just such a mail-order divorce from a court in this Mexican state; when his wife, Maria, petitioned Bernstein to annul the document in New York Supreme Court, Maria having been thrown out of federal court, Bernstein ruled that states have jurisdiction over marital matters of foreign diplomats and, further, that this particular divorce wasn't binding as the parties had not been physically present to it; J. Sidney declared Sixto and Maria legally married (still).[194][195]

As the diplomat and his wife were still separated and at odds with one another, the judge cannot be said to have saved the relationship exactly. And yet, technically, that's precisely what he did. Moreover, the judge had no idea what the issue of that preserved union would go on to achieve decades hence: the couple's eldest child, a son also named Sixto, first having served as mayor of the capital Quito, became become Ecuador's president in 1992, serving until 1996.

It's a mind-boggling legacy – enforced togetherness – for a judge whose name had made the press a decade earlier for the spectacularly violent way in which his daughter's romantic liaison had been shorn.

Obviously, J. Sidney would never see Sixto become mayor or president – in fact, he only served about five years of the 14 his election had granted him on the bench, suffering a fatal heart attack on Dec 9, 1943, at the age of 66. His funeral was held in Riverside Chapel, at Amsterdam Avenue and 76th (or 10 blocks south and a few more east of the address to which he and Norma repaired from summer camp during the love-triangle scandal).

But his was a long life, a rich one, in which he'd gotten to spend the kind of moments with his family and friends, before and after the love triangle shootings that united their families, of which a broken Lewis E. Birdseye could only dream (while fitfully napping on his charitable ship).

NEW YORK CITY LOVE TRIANGLE, 1931

J. Sidney with his fishing and drinking buddies and family (above and below). And one last Bernstein family shot.

CHAPTER 12: ELEGY FOR A GENERATION

NEW YORK CITY LOVE TRIANGLE, 1931

CHAPTER 12: ELEGY FOR A GENERATION

How young and fresh Arthur and Norma look...

NEW YORK CITY LOVE TRIANGLE, 1931

***

An account of the demise of the great Yiddish actor Boris Thomashefsky:

There had once been at the corner of Houston and Second Avenues a manufacturer called LH Mace – maker of everything from refrigerators and "woodenware" to prams and playthings (a billing slip from which, with a photo of its building, appears below).

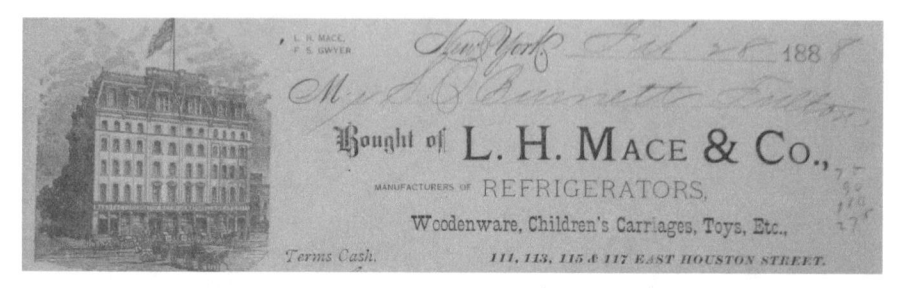

Bought of L. H. MACE & CO.,
MANUFACTURERS OF REFRIGERATORS,
Woodenware, Children's Carriages, Toys, Etc.,
Terms Cash. 111, 113, 115 & 117 EAST HOUSTON STREET.

Boris, whose troupe long worked out of the People's Theatre on the Bowery, yearned to occupy a space on Second Avenue, the more prestigious of the two Lower East Side Rialtos.

This came to pass with a glorious grand opening – albeit on a rainy night – of the 2000-seat National Theatre on Sept. 24, 1912. It was an eight-story structure, with a roof garden to boot, built on the site of the LH Mace factory – a plot 100 x 65 feet – at a reported cost of $1 million. Boris' troupe had rented it from its developer for 21 years at an average cost of $72,000 per year.[196][197]

(It wasn't really a Second Avenue theater, in that Second Avenue officially terminates at Houston and this new venue, being on the south side of the intersection, was technically the first building at the northern tip of Chrystie, but never mind).

CHAPTER 12: ELEGY FOR A GENERATION

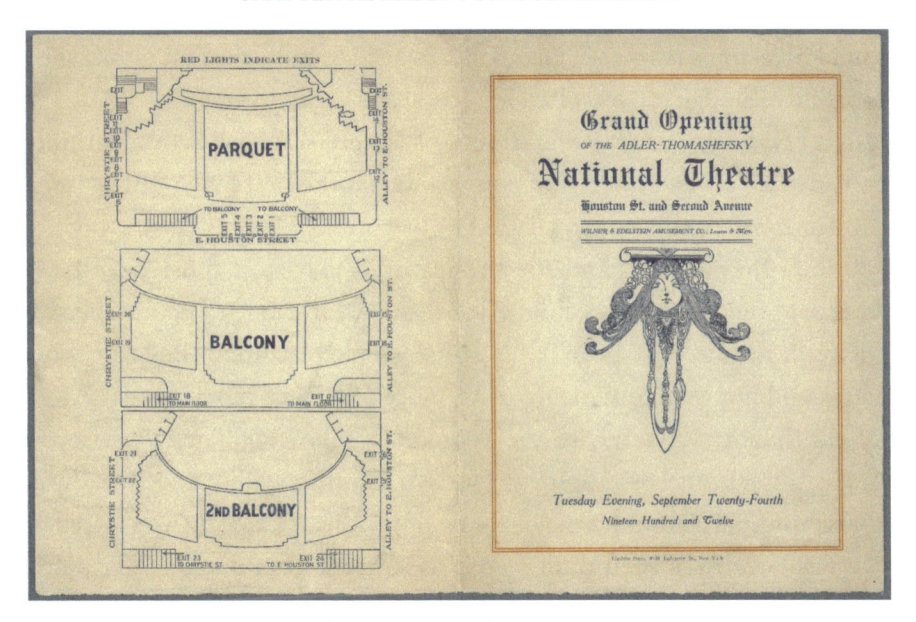

The opening night program.

In 1924, Boris was no longer quite as welcome in New York as he had been in his earlier days and was a year removed from having lied on a hospital bed to his estranged wife Bessie about abandoning his mistress to return to her, so he took his acting troupe – including his mistress Mrs. Zuckerberg and her daughter, Pauline – to South America for a tour of the Jewish theaters of the Southern Hemisphere.

Of course, Boris, then 58, paid everyone's fare (from whatever funds the troupe had raised and likely his own pocket, too). In fact, the manifest of the troupe's October ship home, the SS Western World, which traveled Rio de Janeiro to New York, shows that Regina Zuckerberg and her daughter Pauline had their passage paid by their "manager" – "B. Tommaso."

Elsewhere in the manifest, Boris is indeed listed (just below the entry for his son Harry) as "Barnoto Tomasso."

Why he chose to go by this pseudonym (perhaps merely for humor?) is unknown – it's not like his affair was a secret any longer or that the Yiddish actor would ever pass for a native Brazilian.

Back in New York, in 1930, the Times, most venerable of the papers, found occasion as this so-called Barnoto aged to report on his diminished capability (though it overstated his actual age by four years).

In a review of "Eretz Israel" (Land of Israel) – "whose action is thinly threaded on a rivalry between a husband and the first love of his wife" – the Times said of the audience:

"When they had a hand for the featured player, it must have been from sentimental motives chiefly, for the 68-year-old Mr. Thomashefsky, whatever he may have been in his prime, seemed last night sluggish in his attack and not very convincing in his more oratorical moments."[198]

Less than a year later, in the September following Agnes Birdseye's August attack on her employer Dr. Milton, the syndicated Broadway columnist Louis Sobol – a major figure of the theatrical scene – referred to Boris not even as an actor but merely as father to the infamously crippled otolaryngologist:

"Broadway itself is not particularly excited at the forthcoming invasion of the English-speaking theater by the veteran, Boris Thomashefsky, for almost half a century an outstanding figure on the Yiddish stage. Broadway, of course, knows Boris as the father of Dr. Milton Thomashefsky, the lad who lies in hospital now, hovering between life and death, as the result of a nasty love tangle."[199]

By the next year, Boris was back performing in Baltimore – but without Bessie, 45 years after he lured her into his orbit from her home there, over her father's protestations.

Now, the local paper called the performance "the fiftieth anniversary of his career as an actor," but if that's what Boris' late Baltimore show really was – as opposed to a financial and artistic necessity of an actor on the way down – it would have included all those from his past who'd helped him along the way. A true reunion of a show. Instead, the production featured Mrs. Zuckerberg playing his wife.[200]

By 1937, Boris was back performing in Paterson, New Jersey – his first appearance there in more than a quarter-century – "at the Eastside High School auditorium."[201] Though he was just 71, the paper that covered the event nevertheless referred to him as 75. Boris sat on stage and told stories

CHAPTER 12: ELEGY FOR A GENERATION

about other great impresarios of the Yiddish theater – Mogulesko, Kessler, Adler – each of whom had at one point been considered his contemporary or rival or partner.

Is there a lonelier performance than that – sitting in a high school gym relaying to those several generations your junior the lives of friends you've lost?

There was some nobility, however melancholic, in his bearing witness to an era increasingly bygone, yes.

At this time, Boris was living with his son Harry – the man who'd chosen to stay in his father's theatrical sphere even after his mother had been forsaken, unlike Dr. Milton – at 10 Monroe Street, in Knickerbocker Village, a mass of 12 brick buildings between the Manhattan and Brooklyn Bridges that constituted the first federally-funded housing project in the city's history.[202][203]

Boris's last regular gig was singing and acting alongside Mrs. Zuckerberg in a three-show-per-night cabaret – the floor act of a dingy wine cellar – beneath the Second Avenue elevated train.[204]

In November 1938, Boris filed for bankruptcy, stating his debts at $9,965 and his assets only those copyrights he held on his plays (some which had been cribbed and rearranged from others' plays, to begin with).[205]

(Harry, too, would not escape the consequences of his choices, of his decision to remain in his father's world; by 1940, in deference to longer-term entertainment trends, he'd moved out to LA and was living in lodging for aspiring motion picture people, including someone with a credit as a technical director on a Barbara Stanwyck picture of 1936 – but he'd not gotten any industry work in 65 weeks; by 1950, he had quit show business and gone to work in PR.)

And finally, the great man faded out entirely, with far less of a bang than a whimper, no matter that the proximate cause of death was cardiovascular – as he'd been ebbing away for years:

On July 9, 1939, Boris suffered a heart attack and was rushed to Beth Israel Hospital, where he died, age 73. His bier was open to the public for a few days, from the Sunday of his passing to the Tuesday of his funeral at

Gramercy Park Memorial Chapel on Second Avenue (in the heart of the Yiddish theater district).

Upon visiting this casket, Regina Zuckerberg, eyeing the man who'd spotted her talent in London 21 years earlier and, conveying her to this strange sphere of America, had utterly redirected her life-path (and broken up her first marriage), collapsed.[206]

The funeral, falling on July 11, coincided with the two year anniversary of the passing of George Gershwin from a brain tumor; Gershwin had acted as a supernumerary in a Thomashefsky play when he was just a boy and later Boris even petitioned a teenage Gershwin to write music for his operettas (this offer was declined).[207]

Only 600 attendees could fit inside the chapel once the ceremony commenced (it was delayed on account of Boris' son – Harry and Milton's brother and Michael Tilson's father – Ted experiencing a flight delay out of LA, where he was a film executive who'd found success in a world that would deny Harry entry soon), but the entire ceremony was broadcast over loudspeakers up and down Second Avenue – from Houston to 10th Street – on which 30,000 people silently stood and listened.

Another notable attendee inside was Lucy Finkel – one of the two daughters of Emma Thomashefsky, Boris' sister, who'd been shot in the back by her spurned husband 33 years earlier while on a walk with her lover.

The service was led by two cantors – including renowned chazzan Moishe Oysher – a male choir and three major composers of the Yiddish theater. A dozen speakers delivered eulogies, including the eminent editor of The Forward newspaper, Abraham Cahan.[208]

The public waiting outside then walked behind the coffin as it emerged from the sanctuary, to convey it on a valedictory round of the neighborhood, the whole assemblage pausing in front of each famous Yiddish theater, as If to let the deceased recall all the inspired raucousness he'd kicked off within those now-quiet halls.

"The vast throng included patriarchs and pushcart peddlers, housewives and shopgirls, businessmen and clerks," the Daily News wrote.[209]

That mixture of high-and-low nicely reflected the critical consensus about Boris' very acting – it was heartfelt and genuinely moving at points and utterly over-the-top and unintentionally farcical at others. Sometimes incredibly warm and sincere and other times crass, commercial and cold.

Wrote Yiddish playwright Leon Kobrin:

There are two Thomashefskys, just as in life, so it is upon the stage...The first one is of an artistic nature that can be overtaken at times with a spirit that is childlike and easily moved... Moreover, he says, he will not be reduced to play in vulgar roles. And he is believed when he says this, because he himself believes what he is saying.

> *But this very same Thomashefsky, the Thomashefsky of the good inclination...would later be stifled and buried...And most importantly, the culprit was that he himself was coarse. He wanted to play, especially in his later years, in his own plays. But his own plays never gave him the opportunity for his good inclination to show itself. And Thomashefsky's bad inclination always ruled with its ugly tones upon tones. And in this manner the coarse Thomashefsky choked the artistic Thomashefsky. The first Thomashefsky always destroyed that which the other had built up.*[210]

In Boris' defense, how many artists haven't had their better natures – on stage and off – at times overshadowed by sheer ego, human folly, just a handful of decisions painfully regrettable?

A reminiscence of Boris run in the Wisconsin Jewish Chronicle after his passing said "it was quite common for him to lose ten thousand smackers at the card table in a single night."[211]

Another summation of Boris, although also one not entirely fair: He never stopped working – not when he'd broken his wife's heart (repeatedly) and not when the son who oversaw his emergency medical care was himself hospitalized with a potentially fatal bullet to the spine.

Boris Thomashefsky stayed true to that maxim about the show going on –until the curtains came down on his own – or as the stage instruction of one of his plays would read:

Forehang!

After Moishe Oysher had chanted the prayer service and the Lower East Side folk had carried the man before all the stages on which he'd once swaggered, the coffin was loaded into a hearse and a 100-car caravan made its way to a cemetery in Flushing, Queens, to a section reserved for Yiddish actors.

Just two weeks before, Boris had acted one final time – staging a version of "The Green Millionaire" on Coney Island – or in the exact spot of the city where his paralyzed son had been forced for years to sit idly by the window, wondering about the life he could have lived if only he'd made a few decisions differently, if only a woman aggrieved hadn't attempted her revenge.[212]

Boris acted in that same spot of the city – a perfect example of the pathetic irony of his life's final decade: All he wanted was to seize upon the common man's feelings with highly emotive drama, comedy, intrigue – and yet he'd never realized his own life's tale, the melodramatic story of his son's lothario lifestyle and consequent crippling, were he to share it, possessed all the pathos a stage project would ever need.

(Or maybe he knew just how near-mythical his sister and son's shared fate was, but he feared letting his private life bleed into his public work – a fear utterly counter to the creation of good art, even if the restraint and embarrassment are understandable.)

The man who fashioned himself the great storyteller of his people overlooked the epic narratives of his own house.

Chapter 12A: 1931

Let's redefine cataclysm – let's extend our understanding of the moment of impact so that moment is seen as relative to the length of our lives – or even better, measure it against the longevity of all those whose work built us up and all those to whom we strive to leave a legacy.

In that larger picture, are whole swaths of our lives not able to be viewed in miniature? Is even a half-decade not a flash-in-the-pan?

And so a moment like Agnes' shooting of Dr. Milton neither began with her actions that day in her office nor ended with them. Yes, only she perished precisely on Aug. 12, 1931 – but why should a 24-hour period be the outer limitation of what we consider immediate when we look at all that went into Dr. Milton being just feet from her, at Agnes being so enraged with her circumstances and his part in them, with the looming presence of her rival Norma Jeanne?

A bullet struck Dr. Milton first, and from the instant he was scythed crosswise by its perilous course, he began his descent into death, a solemn sinking no medicine of that era (or even ours, perhaps) could forestall.

As the bullet lodged in a lung, its collapse was the most immediate consequence of its course after his paralysis, but Dr. Milton was plagued by countless secondary health issues once he could breathe again and besides his being confined to a chair and unable to walk.

On May 14, 1936, not even five years after Agnes shot him, Dr. Milton died at 9:30 pm on a Thursday night in his room at the Half Moon Hotel on Coney Island, from the proximate cause of uremia – the inability of his kidneys to cleanse the blood of toxic waste – and the contributing factor of chronic nephritis – a recurrent inflammation of those kidneys.

There's something slightly fitting, however inappropriate a metaphor upon someone's death, about this medical impetus: of course, the doctor died because he could not rid himself of that hideous 1931 scandal that had poisoned him heart and soul.

Yes, his was a demise entirely about the inability to filter out and move beyond that ugliness, a toxic force he may have himself initiated and which had thereafter sought his ruin.

He was 38 years, 11 months and 14 days old – that is, 16 days shy of his 39th birthday.

The location of this death was also incredibly apt – while no longer standing, the Half Moon Hotel occupied 3021 West 29th Street in Brooklyn – an address just feet from the Boardwalk and the water – from a beachy escape from the urban ordeal and ordure – but one almost fenced in by that very Boardwalk. In fact, today, the street peters out just feet away from where Dr. Milton died, its hardtop giving way to a trash-strewn, overgrown grass patch, atop which stands a rather pathetic, simple sign: "End."

No less poetic, if slightly more abstruse and historical: Less than a month after Dr. Milton died at the Half Moon, the hotel hosted the local committee pushing to make Father's Day a national holiday (which was chaired by Dudley Field Malone, who'd argued alongside Darrow for the teacher of evolution in the Scopes monkey trial, famously saying, "There is never a duel with the truth. The truth always wins and we are not afraid of it").

Dr. Milton would predecease this rather serious effort to reward fathers for their efforts, much as he'd been by his paralysis prevented ever from becoming one…with either Agnes or Norma.

And so there is this karmic thread picked up by Norma having her first child, with Sam Smith, in 1936, in essentially the same moment her former lover vanished from the world.

The funeral for Dr. Milton Thomashefsky picked up the thread of Agnes Birdseye's family's work. The service was held back at the Jewish Hospital where Dr. Milton had once served as otolaryngologist before his long tenure as a patient, and in fact, upon his passing, that institution's members expressed their condolence in a dizzying array of configurations:

The hospital's Alumni Society, its Board of Directors, its Training School for Nurses, its president (and others) all paid for separate death notices in the local paper.[213]

But the actual funeral service wasn't just held in any room in the hospital but in Leon Louria Memorial Hall – an auditorium in which Agnes' father Lewis E. Birdseye had sat in December of 1928, less than a decade earlier, to celebrate the renovation and expansion of the hospital, a project Lewis had closely overseen and of which he was immensely proud.

In fact, Birdseye had saved the handout pamphlet from that occasion, which his great-granddaughter presented to me in her Boston-area house nearly 100 years later:

The New Jewish Hospital
of Brooklyn

December 1928

A BOOKLET OF INFORMATION

CHAPTER 12A: 1931

Foreword

THE Jewish Hospital consists of six buildings, three of which have just been completed. These are the New Main Hospital, The Residence Hall for Nurses and The Employees Building.

With a capacity of over 650 beds, this will be the third largest Non-Municipal General Hospital in Greater New York.

The following is a guide to some of the main points of interest.

Page Three

Hell, Birdseye had even saved a cartoon (made by an unknown observer of this dynamic) poking slight fun at his hard-ass oversight of the 1928 Jewish Hospital construction:

NEW YORK CITY LOVE TRIANGLE, 1931

Now, Dr. Milton Thomashefsky, whom Lewis E. Birdseye's daughter had killed with the gun shot that slowly took the doctor's life over the course of almost five years (an agonizingly protracted single moment, say), was being mourned, on the Sunday morning following his Thursday night death, in the same room where Birdseye's hospital construction had once been feted. The same Leon Louria Memorial Hall, which was on the occasion of Dr. Milton's funeral packed to overflowing: "More than 1,000 persons were present...Additional hundreds filled the street, unable to enter."[214]

Whether Norma Jeanne and her new husband Sam Smith were in that teeming crowd is unclear, although circumstances would indicate they likely weren't. At the most superficial level, Norma Jeanne might have been counseled to stay away by her imposing Democrat father, whose party was observing a separate day of mourning that very same Sunday, as the

CHAPTER 12A: 1931

Governor of New York, Democrat Herbert H. Lehman, held a service in Manhattan's Temple Emanu-El, on Fifth Avenue, for the sudden passing of his brother (Arthur, a former partner of Lehman Brothers). There was a strange split that Sunday – a certain segment of New York society gravitated toward one Jewish funeral and another segment made its way to another.

But more practically, Norma Jeanne had just given birth — to Michael Anthony, AKA "Tony," on January 26th — bringing a life into the world in apparent replacement of one about to expire.

Chapter 13: Inheritance

There are perhaps freak acts of violence whose roots are pointless to trace and whose aftereffects, while terribly sad, don't possess a sort of multi-generational echo. Random slashings on a Subway platform – a bullet wound received via inadvertent crossfire (although then again, if looked into with enough care, perhaps those stories, too, possess uncanny extensions into the world of art and politics) .

And then, there's this case, an aspect of which Elisa Birdseye, grand-niece of Agnes and a retired librarian and an orchestral viola player, relays to me the very first time we ever speak (though it feels like the 100th).

> *Basically, in my career as a librarian, I went from seeing stuff occasionally on microfilm to, as the internet came into being, every now and then, I would just Google 'Birdseye" and see what would come up. And that's how I found out at some point that Michael Tilson Thomas (the famous conductor, most notably of the New World Symphony and the San Francisco Symphony) was a descendant of the Thomashefsky family (he's Dr. Milton's nephew). And there's a tiny bit of weird synchronicity in that I'm also, I'm primarily a classical musician. My librarian stuff, that was my day job just because you can't support yourself as a musician. And I was playing regularly with a woman who was a keyboard player for the Boston Symphony, and Michael Tilson Thomas was the assistant conductor. And we just got onto a discussion about suicide. And I just found that whole story really fascinating, and the story of Agnes, and it's like, how can you kill*

yourself? Why would you kill yourself?

So it was always intriguing. I read a lot about suicide. I was very sympathetic, and the woman I was talking to had had a suicide in her family, and we were chatting. She said, You seem to know a lot about this. Is there a suicide in your family? I said, Well, yeah, a rather sensational one, unfortunately. And I described it. She said, Isn't that funny? That sounds like exactly the same story that Michael Tilson Thomas tells about his family. And it was like one of those, I don't know if you've read "Roots," but he describes going to Africa and hearing the story that he had always heard in his family on the other side of the ocean about when the guy went out to cut wood for a drum, and then he never was seen again. And Alex Haley had heard his relative went out to cut wood for a drum, and he was kidnapped and taken to America. And so it was one of those moments like, Oh my God, that's the other half of the story.

Elisa wrote to Tilson Thomas. She told him she was neither looking to stalk him nor dig up that which he wanted buried. She merely wanted to apologize – on behalf of the entire Birdseye family – for what Agnes had done to Dr. Milton.

Elisa was not casting blame, per se, on her own antecedent nor absolving Tilson Thomas'. She just wrote, "On behalf of my family, I apologize for the thing that happened." Because she felt she needed to – there was a degree of closure all her years as a librarian/researcher had made necessary. She'd read the clippings. She knew how Dr. Milton had spent his final years.

Michael Tilson Thomas, world-famous conductor, wrote back: We should talk, he said. We should meet and talk about this incident that has haunted *both our families.*

Elisa was thrilled. To apologize in person – to commiserate over this romance gone so horribly awry face-to-face – would provide her a measure of relief she deeply needed, no matter that she was a couple generations removed from the woman who'd pulled the trigger. (And not that Elisa knew it, but all three families passed down the story like a kind of perverse heirloom – it was as present to her contemporaries in the other families as it was to her, even if she was more graphically informed due to her library research; heck, even this great conductor was expressing surpassing gladness at the prospect of being able to discuss it with her, as if she was one of the very few people on Earth who could understand how the story had long made him feel).

Only the meeting never occurred.

Right after Tilson Thomas' letter arrived, Elisa's marriage fell apart, and she failed to pursue the lead during a bad divorce.

That separation concluded, she was then hesitant to reach out again to Tilson Thomas after a long period of silence – almost as if she'd betrayed her lone chance, as though it would be unfair to bring up again what Agnes had done to Dr. Milton, to seek again a confab on that gruesome topic.

And then, while Elisa was considering whether to reach out a second time, racked by internal debate, Tilson Thomas fell ill with brain cancer, which closed the matter for her – "I thought, oh, he has way bigger fish to fry than worrying about this," she told me.

Except then, in September of 2024, as I am writing this book, Tilson Thomas, 79, emerges from more than three years into his cancer treatment to lead the New York Philharmonic in Mahler's Fifth Symphony on opening night.

"Concerned eyes are always on him," the Times writes. And "there have been more taut and blazing Fifths. But this one had searching, saturnine weight; it left an appropriately disorienting impact."[215]

There is something to that; sometimes a violent thing can be contextualized with a million details (likely too many, my apologies) but never fully understood or explained. And that's okay – its very heft and expanse discombobulating all those who review it, it has nevertheless in its confounding way been conveyed, propagated and thusly preserved.

The saddest thing about a tabloid scandal aren't its details – it's the way the incident is so quickly replaced on the front pages by another and thereafter forgotten (so easily, carelessly). Even if the explanation falters, I still believe that preservation has its own value.

CHAPTER 13: INHERITANCE

* * *

Just after Tilson Thomas takes the New York stage, I take the Subway not far from his Lincoln Center podium on the Upper West Side to the Brooklyn site of the 1931 shootings – the lobby of the Turner Towers on Eastern Parkway, opposite the Brooklyn Museum.

It's funny how the nature of a Subway ride so colors what one encounters on the trip. All the mosaics and masonry of the Brooklyn Museum station have an uncanny, almost unsettling quality. I am peering, almost scared, at an animalistic man (perhaps a person half-bestial), with a predilection for wanton, vicious carnage, and a woman, for reasons unknown, by this circumstance, chastened, regretful – in fact, the female recalls for me a woebegone man Norma once painted that her relatives found amidst her other work after her passing and have never been able to date or identify (there's a similarity not just in the downward gaze but in the pursed lips):

NEW YORK CITY LOVE TRIANGLE, 1931

CHAPTER 13: INHERITANCE

I approached the building's east wing, site of Dr. Milton's suite once upon a time, already aware, thanks to heavy research, that so far as the exterior goes, little has changed over the last century, despite the office's early brush with calamitous publicity. The most noticeable (and perhaps only) difference in the exterior of the office is that the doctors' nameplates have been pried off the walls on either side of the entrance – but a residue remains that indicates exactly where they once hung.

Observe interns of the Jewish Hospital remove Dr. Milton's crippled body from this wing in 1931 and the same doorway in 2024 (the stone, the transom, the fencing – it's so familiar):

NEW YORK
EVENING GRAPHIC
2¢   FOUR STAR CITY EDITION
Vol. 7, No. 2126.   NEW YORK, THURSDAY, AUGUST 13, 1931

MYSTERY BED KNIFING BARED IN DOCTOR-NURSE TRAGEDY
—STORY ON PAGE 3

WEIRD ATTACK upon Dr. Milton Thomashefsky, prominent Brooklyn physician, has mystified Brooklyn authorities investigating slaying of his blond office nurse, Agnes Birdseye, and wounding of the physician in mystery shooting affair in his professional residence, 135 Eastern Parkway, Brooklyn. Picture shows internes from Jewish Memorial Hospital carrying wounded doctor from his apartment on ambulance stretcher to hurry him to hospital. Questioning by police and representatives of district attorney's office disclosed, they say, that Dr. Thomashefsky revealed that he had been mutilated after being chloroformed in his mother's apartment on Tuesday night. His assailant left cryptic note which physician said he is unable to explain.

CHAPTER 13: INHERITANCE

What I didn't anticipate was the poetic justice awaiting me on the other side of this medical suite door: a slight staircase and then three more doors – one to my left, one directly ahead of me and one to my right.

A century after a scandal of three families, a Monty Hall selection of three doors confronts me as I try to conclude a story that almost defies such cutting off. It could never have been any other way.

I figure out from a map featured in the Daily News after Agnes' shooting that Dr. Milton Thomashefsky's office was situated behind the door to my left. I twist and tug its knob to no effect — it is locked (a doorman later tells me the space was occupied by a physical therapist who went out of business during the pandemic).

The door directly ahead of me is also bolted shut.

So I enter the office of the internal medicine doctor through the door to my right – for two reasons, really: if any had been preserved for a century, this office might share general architectural features with the Thomashefsky office closed off to me.

For instance, perhaps its herringbone wooden flooring, which I duly photograph, is original (a receptionist says it might be, though she isn't sure):

But there is another reason native to the design of this eastern building wing.

The offices behind all three doors – so far as I can tell from the Daily News diagram of 1931 — should feature long hallways that exit onto the

CHAPTER 13: INHERITANCE

Turner Tower's grand main lobby (of dark quarried stone and art-deco ceiling ornamentation). These slender corridors were in some sense the only connective tissue by which a luxurious, 15-story residence was once attached to a scene of convulsive horror.

They would also have been, in some alternate version of events, the only routes a doctor, wary of impending violence, could have taken to escape his place of work without raising the suspicion of the employee sitting at reception, the assistant with a gun tucked away in her desk.

So for the sake of enacting that alternate history, and also because I am trespassing, I walk hurriedly down the hallway of the internist's office I've entered, push through the exit door, reached the drop-boxes for blood and urine tests just outside it, and find myself at the edge of a stone lobby etched out of history — a dark, rectilinear lounge unchanged from the illustration in building advertisements 97 years earlier[216]:

NEW YORK CITY LOVE TRIANGLE, 1931

CHAPTER 13: INHERITANCE

ENTRANCE AND LOBBY OF TURNER TOWERS

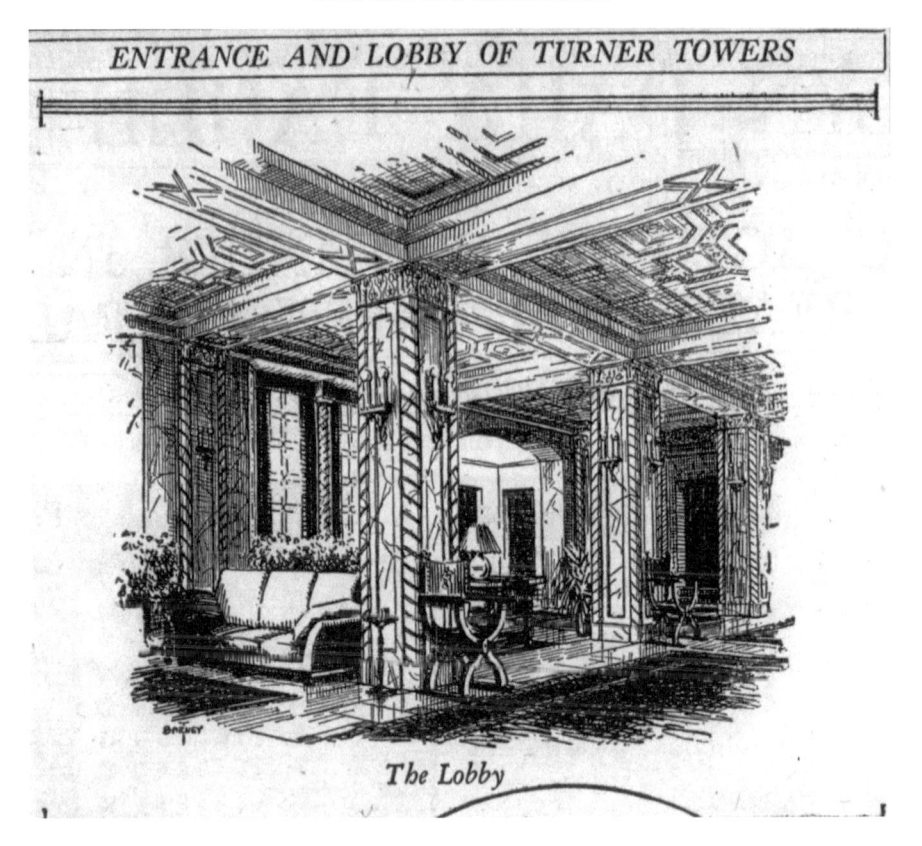

The Lobby

This incredible similarity astounds me. Such a length of time has passed between the drawing's publication and my own entrance into the building's antechamber – and I realize part of the appeal of this story from the first was the opportunity it presented to uncover just how much of this city I love has remained from a century ago.

How much has not slipped like yesterday's tabloid news but remained — resolute, monumental in its endurance?

We are obsessed with time all of us — not least because as biological beings, we are no Benjamin Buttons — we age linearly and with no real recourse — certainly no capacity to stand up and simply *persist*. I recall Norma's portrait of Sam in his younger days, hung beside the fireplace in Norma's former studio, and her portrait of him decades later, hung in a bedroom in the house.

And I think of the way all of us look at old photo albums, involuntarily seeking out those features in our loved ones and ourselves that have been altered by time and those that have more gracefully eked out something closer to sameness. At our delight and wonder in seeing features replicated across generations.

Because of course — generations — the chromosomal proposition to propagate, to keep the line going — is the way we've been by DNA — by the coding of nucleotides — programmed to defeat our individual wanings — to overcome (until extinction of the species) time itself.

That's what a writer sees in a love scandal of 1931 in the year 2024, too — an excavation of past clippings the animation of which will yield a new telling of the tale and defeat time through that other primeval, but not biological, tried-and-true method:

Storytelling around the fire.

CHAPTER 13: INHERITANCE

NEW YORK CITY LOVE TRIANGLE, 1931

All this digging — what is it actually like?

August 2024. I fly from Newark, New Jersey, to Manchester, New Hampshire, on a modest Bombardier capable of holding 70 passengers.

I land a half-hour early on an 80-degree day whose not infrequent breezes, caressing my cheeks, seemed to scatter away any tension.

To be specific, it's August 11, 2024 – just another summer Sunday, only one that's a day shy of the 93rd anniversary of the Agnes's shooting of Dr.

CHAPTER 13: INHERITANCE

Milton.

Marjorie Smith, Norma Jeanne's daughter-in-law and an 83-year-old New Hampshire state representative, pulls up in her newish Subaru station wagon.

We barely turn to each other as she pulls away – as it is, our faces are awkwardly close for a pair of folks who've never before met.

She has silvery-white hair in a short, layered bob, ruddy, rounded cheeks and slight crinkling around the mouth and eyes that somehow contributes to a seriousness of mien – a no-nonsense vibe.

Back in the airport before I'd boarded, I'd read a few clippings on her, including her 1966 marriage announcement in the New York Times, which featured her photo (she had an on-point beehive and was wearing pearls) but also mentioned her master's from Syracuse's Maxwell Graduate School of Citizenship and Public Affairs.

I ask about that moment in time, the genesis of her political involvement.

She takes issue with the term "political" for her work; she considers it "governmental."

Okay.

She tells me that in the early '60s she had to choose between jobs in a state capital (New York's) and the nation's and so she consulted her former teacher at Syracuse and mentor, the future senator Daniel Patrick Moynihan.

We head East, along our half-hour route, a whooshing highway hum an ever-present backing track.

Moynihan told her, rightly, she didn't want to be in Albany – take the federal position, and so she did.

"I was at the Department of Commerce, and I was working for something called the Area Redevelopment Administration, focusing on West Virginia. Because Jack Kennedy was quite shocked when he saw the poverty in Appalachia. He really had not expected it. Why? *I don't know.*"

She sounds almost offended that she's been asked the question, even though she posed it herself. We continue in the initial direction of Pawtuckaway State Park, moving somewhat parallel to the border south of us between New Hampshire and Massachusetts.

She speaks with a certain steamrolling purpose, a forcefulness, even while telling a discursive, winding story.

"Pat (Moynihan) called me one day to say United Mine Workers operated all the hospitals in Appalachia – West Virginia, Kentucky, particularly. And there were fewer and fewer union members, and they said they couldn't afford to keep the hospitals going. The Board of Missions of the Presbyterian Church said they would purchase and operate the hospitals, but they needed some federal money.

"Pat called me, and he and I wrote, basically out of whole cloth, the economic justification for this. And we then had to present it…to the undersecretary of commerce. And so there was a meeting called, and I was there and Pat was there, the undersecretary of commerce was there, and it was scheduled for a particular time.

"And there was just a lot of small talk going on. And I turned to Pat, quietly said, 'He's waiting for somebody to come from my agency.' Pat said, 'You are here.' I said, 'I know. He's waiting for a man to come and to start the meeting.' And Pat said, 'Don't be ridiculous.' And we chatted for a bit more. And then I said, 'Pat, I'm right.' And Pat went and whispered in this gentleman's ear, and the undersecretary said, 'Oh, I think we're ready to begin now.' The gentleman was a man whose name was Franklin D. Roosevelt Jr.

"I then became his special assistant. And when he (FDR Jr.) was subsequently appointed as the first chair of the Equal Employment Opportunity Commission, I was the first staff member."

I wonder whether her narrative style is a consequence of her years in public service – she has been a state representative in New Hampshire for every year but two since 1996.

Did you experience "that sort of uplifting feel of the Kennedy Camelot era? I ask. "Did you feel, like, 'Oh, my gosh – we're going to achieve great breakthroughs?'"

"That's why I went to Washington," she says. "I went to Washington because I believed him when he said, 'Ask not what your country can do

CHAPTER 13: INHERITANCE

for you, but what you could do for your country.' I mean, I couldn't vote for him. I wasn't old enough to vote for him."

I eye the sizable infotainment screen between us. Her satellite radio preset channels include "Seriously Sinatra," "40s Junction," "MLB Radio" and "NPR."

Where were you when he was shot? I ask.

She was on the last day of a trip with the Appalachian commission, she replies – in a lunch meeting in western Maryland hosted by then-Congressman, and future Senator, Charles McCurdy Mathias Jr. (whom she calls "Mac Mathias").

"He came in, he told Franklin, the meeting was ended, and we got in the car and we sped.

"And very soon a county police officer came alongside the car – obviously, to stop it. We were going so fast. As it happens, Franklin looked very much like his father, and the police officer took one look, realized what was happening, got in front of us."

That officer wound up escorting the car with FDR Jr. and Marjorie Smith, my present-day driver, all the way to the White House, past innumerable highway checkpoints staffed with further patrolmen, all of whom deferred to this makeshift caravan bound for a White House whose occupants, those both alive and dead, were still in Dallas.

All the same, FDR Jr. felt he just had to enter the building, once home to his father, until a moment earlier the official residence of two good friends. As it happens, he had been closer to Jackie than to Jack. She who survived.

"I did not go in. Franklin did."

"All your further work, I guess, was during the LBJ administration in terms of the Equal Employment Opportunity Commission," I say.

It's a throwaway line because I can't think of something meaningful.

Of course, the answer is yes. But also, the answer she gives is this: There was a young lawyer in the Civil Rights division of the Justice Department, who'd soon work on LBJ's most significant pieces of legislation: the Civil Rights Act of 1964 and the Voting Rights Act of '65.

The man lived on Capitol Hill, and his aunt knew Marjorie, who lived in Georgetown. Aunt Ethel passed Marjorie's name along to him. What followed was a blind date. And then that marriage announcement in the Times.

The lawyer was Peter Smith – the second son of Norma Jeanne Bernstein Smith.

And now, Marjorie Diane Kester Smith is pulling into a gravel driveway of jagged white stone and (somewhat fewer) pink and beige hunks – all of it splotched, nearer the garage, with piles of brown, twiggy strands like whole-wheat spaghetti.

A big wooden house at the bend of a tidal river, whose backyard leads to a dock where oysters are cultivated — the house that was Norma's own, her manse and prison both, until she and Sam both passed away in 1984.

Outside are plastic chaise longues overlooking the river, which takes people along on canoes and floats but can't even control its own flow — is subject to oceanic whim (to what degree was any one of our protagonists proactive, to what degree were they swayed and swirled by eddies of a history so much larger than their decision-making? Unanswerable questions of free will.).

It is stifling in the second-floor studio where Norma once painted – the only circulation provided by two thin fans duct-taped to an open window's screen. But I am so focused for four days on documenting the mountain of papers before me I honestly don't notice the innumerable rivulets of sweat running down my back (at least not until I feel the moisture in aggregate back in the hotel room I've rented down the road).

I do take time here and there to pepper Marjorie with questions about Norma Jeanne:

How, if Norma had always been so worshipped by men that she knew all their tricks, had she failed to see (or care) that the doctor she was falling for was simultaneously betraying a woman back in Brooklyn? And if she couldn't have picked up on his duplicity in real time, once the newspapers reported it, The New York Times included, why did Norma never once hold it against him? Why did she bring her husband, Sam, to visit a man whom the newspapers had shown rather definitively to be shady and unctuous if

CHAPTER 13: INHERITANCE

not also promiscuous and scheming?

Did Norma Jeanne believe the media rife with lies?

Did Norma Jeanne ever consider once Milton had reaped what he'd sowed — that he deserved some punishment, even if not a sentence as severe and agonizing as the actual one?

And we know Norma Jeanne kept Milton's letters for the rest of her lifetime. She didn't abandon him even after the fact of his having had a dalliance with his own employee for five years was pronounced by none other than the Brooklyn district attorney.

But Marjorie won't dare speculate. She tells me only what she knows of Norma's life and art. The two never discussed these more difficult queries, and Marjorie won't guess at the answers (no matter how educated her guesses might be). She's unwilling to psychologize her mother-in-law, to assess Norma's mindset amidst her chaotic *affaire de coeur*.

It frustrates me terribly until I realize it's a stance Norma herself might have taken — or the doctor or Agnes. There is such tremendous mental churn, such turbulence, attendant to emotion in extremis — to feelings of love, abandonment, betrayal.

Solid, upstanding citizens have stuck by evil spouses from time immemorial. Good citizens have taken up arms and committed ghastly acts of violence that they themselves later describe as being out of their own characters. Men have long wooed one woman too many.

If I had posed to them any similar questions — hey, Agnes, why did you first bring a gun into that office if you wanted to stay the doctor's premier love, if you had already gone through the trouble of writing a whole note casting aspersions on Norma's character in order to retain that place? — I am not sure any of the three could have given an answer any clearer — less confounding — than Marjorie's silence.

***

After my second day of work, having just read a good deal of the diary Norma Jeanne kept while studying in Paris in 1927, I feel an urge to experience all the natural beauty this property enfolds – all of the sights whose summer charm could never have served as Norma's inspiration – she just wasn't that kind of painter — but can't be ignored over the entire length of my visit, no matter how much paperwork there remains to do.

    I head downstairs to the kitchen, intending to open its glass door onto the yard. I will head across the grass and down the staircase toward the dock and the oysters being cultivated next to it and the tidal river flushing that cage of growing oysters (which are apparently liable to eat one another, Marjorie tells me). But before I leave I notice again the paperback Marjorie has been reading during my stay — and appreciating a great deal — Wallace Stegner's 1971 novel "Angle of Repose" – which sits on the kitchen table, just ahead of the door to the backyard. Maybe her present literary fixation is only coincidental in its themes and premise – but I realize Stegner's book is all about a wheelchair-bound writer struggling to tell the history of his forebears.

CHAPTER 13: INHERITANCE

The writer's boundedness, his pursuit of a past that he for some reason believes worthy of exposition in the present– this has so many echoes of my dredging up of the story of Norma, of Dr. Milton being shot in a fury for ostensible infidelity, thereafter being confined to a chair. And yet Marjorie, while praising the book to me, has not once reflected on that connection nor have I. Have we both missed something so obviously before us?

I open the door, next to a brick chimney whose whitish wear and mythological Greek mask adornment feel apposite to this story (it looks to me a god crying out in pain). I trample across the grass, mottled by brown patches during a summer of scorching heat, to the water.

NEW YORK CITY LOVE TRIANGLE, 1931

CHAPTER 13: INHERITANCE

NEW YORK CITY LOVE TRIANGLE, 1931

CHAPTER 13: INHERITANCE

I walk to the edge of the dock, which juts out into the crook of the river like a needle jabbed into an elbow vein; almost immediately I feel a strong sun on my cheeks – it was after five o'clock, in my mind a mellow hour, conducive to such a jaunt, but the sun was of a different opinion and rather strong-willed.

My cheeks soon begin to burn. A small pontoon boat filled with six men and women, a beer cooler prominently wedged into its interior, comes into my vision from the east. As it nears, I wave at its passengers, only I'm squinting because of the sun, and the wave is rather meekly executed, unenthusiastic, and they eye me like I don't belong there — like I'm an outsider on that dock.

I wonder whether Norma Jeanne felt herself such an outsider.

She was a founding member of the New Hampshire Art Association, a network of local talent, in the 1950s. But only posthumously, twice, in 2003 and 2014, did her work receive its due retrospective in galleries here.

One of the lessons of the three-family scandal apparent from this distant vantage upon the water: A generation can invest oh-so-much in its offspring; in reality, however, its an investment in the dynamic city in which that child will grow and live. You are building up, more than a family legacy, the beast that is modern urban life. Or if the river takes your child far away — that's where your energies and monies and resources will ultimately be expended, wasted, passed on, reinvested.

And also, yes, this story of three families ended in suicide, attempted murder, a stymied artistic career — but there is something to be said for the vibrancy of all that action. For one lesson being: there are brilliant communities whose side-by-side existences could be much enriched by actual (non-violent, healthy) interaction, even confrontation. We are so alone in a crowd in New York. And yet the person next to you on the subway might be the lone doctor in a famous acting clan. A young woman who has studied painting in Paris. The girl whose family has fallen on hard times is the direct relation of those who fought to free the colonies from the British, whose cousin invented frozen foods.

We will probably fuck it up — humans have never been great at going beyond their own without unintentional and unfortunate consequence (again, see "Romeo and Juliet"). But if the task is not ours entirely to complete, to make a success, neither is it one we can abandon entirely.

I hope. It sounds so naive and history has proven these forays so dangerously unrewarding.

Another river story: Agnes Birdseye's nephew (and Lewis E. Birdseye Sr.'s grandson and Elisa Birdseye's father), Lewis E. Birdseye III, decades after Agnes shot herself but contemporaneous to Norma's residence here on the Oyster River, worked as a professional river guide on a tributary of the Tugaloo River – which separates Georgia and South Carolina.

This despite LEB III – as his family calls him – having earlier earned a PhD from Columbia and having always possessed the artistic inclination to create – to write (he eventually penned five works of fiction, which "are remarkably good, according to me," he told me on the phone).

There is something to be said also for New York being unable to contain these families after the explosive event, for them seeking waterways out of town. The city is a pressurized chamber.

NEW YORK CITY LOVE TRIANGLE, 1931

* * *

Sam and Norma both passed away in 1984 – the former at the age of 84, the latter at 78.

But that shared expiration year actually obfuscates an extraordinary sequence of events.

Truly — what happened in 1984 had shades of that "Titanic" jewel recovery triggering recollection of an entire, steamy affair upon the inevitably doomed vessel — except that moment was filmic, invented, a plot device.

The following is entirely true and, like every event that preceded it and potentially even caused it, is all the more remarkable for being so:

Sam, having died in March of '84, he predeceased Norma by a few months – she died in September. But oh, what a powerful half-year separated their departures from this world — what tremendous meaning did that sequence actually command.

Those six months made all the difference – for it was only after Norma was buried that her son Peter and his wife (my later host) Marjorie sorted through her prized possessions, which of course, to perhaps everyone's surprise, included letters from Dr. Milton, as well as his portrait – objects Norma had saved for more than 50 years — maybe without ever telling her husband Sam (certainly Marjorie didn't know).

And so Sam died perhaps never knowing that his wife had never let go of Dr. Milton's notes, his photo, the residue of a romance dashed by a moment of mad violence (and initiated by a man maybe a reprobate).

If Norma had died first, however — in that alternate world where the sequence is reversed, Sam would likely have witnessed the excavation of her desk drawers after her passing; he would have made the discovery that Norma had never ceased treasuring these objects of affection sent to her by an erstwhile lover (who may have been an irredeemable playboy prior to his crippling *whom Sam himself had visited and comforted nevertheless*).

Imagine if the order had been reversed – if Sam had found out just before his own death that for a half-century his wife had still kept a place, in some

CHAPTER 13: INHERITANCE

corner of her heart, for another man entirely — and one so notorious for treachery himself.

What a twist that might have been. Would he have felt betrayed in the same manner that Agnes once had 53 years earlier?

That it could have gone either way – that the sequence of their deaths obviated such difficult deliberation, perhaps even heartbreak, but only by a measure of months – makes fate seems so weighty and yet so capricious.

Perhaps if things had gone differently 53 *years* earlier, Norma Jeanne Bernstein would have married an otolaryngologist, would have become an artist present in every major New York museum. She never would have met Sam at all.

It feels like that life was so very close to her — and other unlived-but-easily-imagined lives to Agnes, to Milton: Futures all within their grasps, all destined to slip away — like the receding ribbon of a child's fluttering balloon.

* * *

Recall that in 1912, Boris Thomashefsky opened up the theater of his dreams – the National, at Houston and 2nd Avenue. Recall that it opened with a variety show to great acclaim on September 24th. But of course, that was just opening night – a show had to go on the very next day.

On which occasion Boris staged a play he called "Di Yidishe Kroyn" or "The Jewish Crown" – a comedy in four acts. Only the well-regarded playwright Nahum Rakow, seeking an injunction in civil court, charged that "The Jewish Crown" was no comedy at all, at least not by origin – the entire production was based on a tragedy he'd submitted to Boris he'd called "God of Mercy." All Boris had done was taken his themes and shown their more comical aspects.

To quote one newspaper article, Boris had "made so many changes in it that it is now part comedy."[217]

The redemptive upshot of this court case: the annotated bibliography of Yiddish plays in the US Library of Congress now credits the theme of this whole show to Rakow.

And yet – though it seems perverse to give Boris the final word here or anywhere – the great theatrical showman had something of a point (though it was not particularly novel and can be found from Shakespeare to "Melinda and Melinda") when he felt free of compunction to portray what another saw as pathos as laughable bathos instead: Life is neither intrinsically amusing nor doleful – it's all a matter of perspective.

Perhaps Sam would have found out Norma had harbored a small, secret love for a half-century and found it more romantic than duplicitous.

Perhaps, for reasons we'll never know, Norma Jeanne was better served by her waterside life than any possible continued existence in the rough-and-tumble art world of New York (one doesn't imagine so, but who knows? It's not like artists tend to die happy).

I suppose the only stories that can't sincerely be portrayed as either comic or tragic are those cut off – ended – before they've ever really had a chance to develop.

The ones touched by that boundless rage humans have shown the capacity to harbor from time immemorial — the exact source and internal development of which we grope at — gape at — but continually fail to grasp, to truly understand.

Acknowledgments

I could not have written this book without Elisa Birdseye and her welcoming me in Boston with open arms and beautiful, dusty old family albums — and her family (LEB III and IV, of course).

No less indispensable was Marjorie Smith and her own opening up of the Bernstein family home, painting studio and archives to me.

That you'd share such personal material is a gesture transcendent — one that allowed me to reach back across decades, generations, era.

And these welcomes of a strange writer into such private familial worlds — it's a gesture I didn't and won't ever take lightly. I thank you sincerely, I love you for the hope involved in opening up these creaky volumes to a meager writer — the hope he can perhaps make of it something that shortchanges no one, that teases out and arrays the dignity of all the real-life characters — progenitors, descendants.

I just pray I did so — that in trying to tell the interwoven story of all your kith and kin I did not shortchange even a single member. They all deserve to have their bits of this tale told with the same dignity you afforded my efforts to write about them.

Nor could I have penned a word without the support of the shareholders and staff members of the coop in which I live, the centennial celebration for which building was the genesis of this tome's research and writing.

A special shoutout to my neighbor, and my inside connection at New York City's most gorgeous public archive, Barbara Mass. How you have collected such wonderful, copious connections I'll never quite know — but I'll always be thankful for the relationship our neighborly proximity initiated (which our interactions have only served to grow and to sustain).

Additional building shoutouts for the warmth and appreciation afforded me by Kurt and Jami (aka, the firm of Floyd and Flehinger), Jackie Gardener, Katelin Burns, Ed Park and all other shareholders who have been far kinder to me after I saturated the lobby with the signs than etiquette dictated they must. To Ed Park, a small literary reflection: thanks for the care you've always taken in your own work, which is affecting and energizing.

To Elana Hashman for the Yiddish translation work, to YIVO and to the Yiddish Book Center and to the Dorot collection at the NYPL for their brilliant repositories of vivid theatrical mementos. For the preservation of a Yiddish world we should not let simply pass into history.

Family is everything — my rock Claire, my mother and father, Fern and Lou, my brother, Jon (and his special person as well). Uncle Barry, Aunt Sara, Cousins Rachel, Alex, Tess, Russell. To the Shaynes, bookish and beautiful humans all. Where in the heck would I be without them? They wrote this as much as I did.

To Kailey for all the WhatsApp chats (commiserative, inspiring) and to Jenna and Ben for the warmth and scones (however glutinous).

Claire, you're a more voracious, keener reader than I'll ever be - I've lucked out in that regard. You may not know it from all my reactions, but what you take from the work you absorb, that which finds its way into your measured responses to my musings and jottings, I so appreciate your sharing. I try to get it all down — all of your extrapolations and hermeneutics — all the critiques whose emotionality I may pretend to detest coldly. You're the real deal even as an editor, forget partner (though you're that, too, and so much more).

And gratitude of the most heartfelt kind to Claire's highly-accepting, adoring family, who combine intellect and emotion more perfectly than they'll ever realize — to her siblings and parents and niece and nephews; it's rather enriching to have frequent discussions with an art historian and a judge; a professor and a political operator; with those in the world of healthcare in other countries; here's to Eva, Mel, Julia, Eitan, Levi, Jonah, Margaret, Reb — and Alie, my Celtics insider.

ACKNOWLEDGMENTS

Eitan D. Hersh — public intellectual, personal therapist. Arigatou, sensei.

Eva and Mel — thanks for the cultural discussions that are the ferment of such work.

Julia — you hold yourself to the sort of standards one inevitably feels compelled to try to hold himself to, as well, even he is a far weaker chef than you imagine he might able to become.

Thank you, Jamie-Lee Josselyn, for the guest speaker invitations. And though I am an unworthy teacher, I feel so honored to be asked and so enriched each year by the experience, by the quiet brilliance of your pupils, and by our deeper heart-to-heart discussions afterward. Thank you for being authentically you, JLJ — for your solicitude in our conversations, for the candor we share in those moments, for these chances to connect with Generations Z and Alpha. All of it's invaluable...

Paul Hendrickson — even in those moments when we haven't been in constant touch, I've sensed your support. You'll always mean more to me than I can put into words. I've known that since I read "Seminary." That truth has never changed.

To Eliot Kaplan and the Nora crew for their backing my journalistic efforts. And to Carlo Rotella and Gerald Early and Gordon Marino and Jon Wertheim for the mentorship.

JW — you're as sharp as the 2008 Wimbledon finalists. Or near enough for me to say so without being wildly hyperbolic. And you're a mensch.

To Jim Lampley and Larry Merchant (you're kinda like Merchant and Ivory) for a journalistic tutelage I could have never from others received. And for the warmth and friendship.

To Greg Domino, Chris DeBlasio, Russell Peltz, Lou DiBella and Michael Woods (plus Abe Gonzalez and countless others) for their tremendous faith in me on wild Saturday nights (along sweaty rows of writers besides 20' x 20' rings).

To Joy Amin for being a great friend and kind supporter of all my moves (as

I am of his), and everyone in the greater fragcomm who supported my last nonfiction effort so avidly. I had no idea that book would work or that I'd be happily received into a community somewhat guarded and protective of its own. I'm so grateful to have been accepted. And while I don't party as a general rule, I still can't get over how much fun I had alongside you all in Milan once upon a time.

To the incomparable (and damn funny) Dan Naughton — and Max Forti, Eugene, Persolaise, Sebastian Jara, JJ Colbourne, Marcial the Blender, John Marcello, Richard Goller, Aaron Terrence Hughes, Elena (The Plum Girl), Iva Mirisna, Kafkaesque, Daniel Barros, Nixon Dias, Marc Robitaille, Jane Daly and countless others equally deserving of praise — for lending my voice a hard-won platform.

To Harry Fremont, who has shown me a graciousness in life (and a hospitality) I wonder how I ever came to receive (but am grateful for, in return).

And Vince Kuczinski, for the familial treatment at (and invite to) that near-final deGrom game (10Ks!) at Citi Field (you threw out a helluva first pitch, too).

Thanks, Laurice Rahme, for your attendance at a book reading and the general support that incident exemplifies well.

To Luca Turin for the oil-house lookups and consistent backing and belief in my endeavors.

To my fellow Japanophile Matt Meleg for his shared reflections on life. To Sarah McCartney for being such a thoughtful and down-to-earth interlocutor. To the explorations of @wearescentient and @saynotoambrxn.

To the great olfactive innovators who gave me a chance to see a different side of the fragrance world: Alex Wiltschko, Jon Hennek, Rohinton Mehta.

To Josefina Scaro and Ben Becher, talented actors whose sincere art always encourages the production of my own.

To Jon Rosen (and Ashlyn, of course) — for the amity, the thoughtfulness. You're a tremendous writer and a fearless fight photographer.

ACKNOWLEDGMENTS

To Darius Gambino for his legal expertise, tolerance of my hissy fits, and general virtue in a world that can seem sadly vicious. To Miles Cooley for the very same (go Niners).

To the "DCU: Deep Crime Unit" team for bringing to life an idea whose conception was met by a wonderful and moving execution. Well done. I look forward to our future Japanese collaborations.

To Barz, Adam, Joe and to Brad — you remain in my heart such that I feel as close to you as I always have (and, hopefully, always will).

To Orly and Elisha, Jon Greenstein and Avi, to Maia (and to Anya), to Rebecca (and all partners not mentioned here — welcome, Danny): Let's always be the buddies we always have been. That endurance is itself a remarkable, vitalizing thing, and I believe in us, even if I'm not the best at staying in touch.

To Jon and Greg Aubrey (and your loved ones): You are and always will be family to me (and my own kin).

To the JCC Mid-Westchester for serving as yet another bastion of goodwill and encouragement — for the additional community you've provided this long-time city-suburban hybrid person (a local who wasn't anymore but now is again).

To the Bourdons, Kathy and the ingenious and giving Pierre, for their unwavering support and artistic input in years past (and to Monsieurs Rasquinet and Herault for the same at other).

To Nathalie Feisthauer for the love and insight and shared commiseration — and the reflections on world events large and small.

Thanks to Shyamala Maisondieu for having inspired so much for so long.

And to Thierry Wasser for being, above a business partner, a true friend — a great person with whom to stroll through Central Park.

To Sonia Constant, for the constancy of her efforts on my behalf in past years.

To Judith Gross for the pride she shows in who she is.

To Christophe Laudamiel for the constancy of his own efforts to bring about real industry change. And to Saskia Wilson-Brown for the creativity of her own such efforts, for her entire institute (and for that Cuban meal).

To Ugo Charron, for sparking within me a funky fire with his cosmic concerts in this great city.

To continent-hopping Alex Lee for his great global perspective on his business.

To Roxanne Fitzpatrick, for a warmth that immediately made it feel we were old buddies from college or something like that. You're an all-star.

To Bart Schmidt, for treating me like one of his own cigar-smoking buddies from even before we'd met in person.

To Cecile Zarokian, for the olfactory inducements to come up with new combinations of words.

To Francesca Bianchi for the inspiration provided by her own, animalic, instinctive, provocative work.

To Beach Geeza for being just the guy that brand name implies.

Thank you, Sharon and Harold Aspis, for being such generous and devoted readers and punctilious, thoughtful editors.

And to Miriam and Judah for being friends worthy of lifetime retention, no matter the retainer fee (kidding about that second part — thanks to the latter for listening to my long-winded summations of legal cases). And to Theo and Chloe, naturally.

Notes

INTRODUCTION

1   New York Daily News, "Body Taken from Ocean Identified," May 19, 1942.

CHAPTER 1: BIRDSEYE

2   Hart, Samuel, "Encyclopedia of Connecticut Biography," The American Historical Society, New York, 1919, page 121.

3   "Perfidy," Ben Hecht, Gefen Publishing House, Jerusalem, 1999, page 250.

4   The New York Times, "Mayor Drops Police Heads," Oct. 21, 1910, page 1.

5   Brooklyn Eagle, "James C. Cropsey Named," April 30, 1897, page 1.

6   The New York Times, " C.J. Driscoll, 56, Ex-City Official; Deputy Police Commissioner and Weight Bureau Head Under Gaynor Dies," March 25, 1939, Obituaries page 15.

7   Brooklyn Eagle, "City Finds New Live Wire in J.C. Cropsey," Nov. 6, 1910, page 1.

8   Buffalo Evening News, "People Jump from the Windows for Life," March 17, 1899, page 1.

9   The Standard Union, Oct. 12, 1911, page 1.

10 Brooklyn Daily Eagle, "Cropsey Saves $20,000 A Year for Taxpayers," Dec. 23, 1911, page 1.

11 The Brooklyn Citizen, "High Class Men Wanted for Future Grand Juries," Aug. 9, 1914, page 13.

12 For reasons that escape the author, the musical "Thoroughly Modern Millie" attempts to treat white slavery comedically, though nothing about the racialist term or act is the least bit so; if there's humor in the notion that some forms of sex trafficking, for preying on a certain color of person, are worse than others, I can't quite find it.

13 Brooklyn Daily Times, "A Just Judgment," Oct. 21, 1914, page 6.

14 Brooklyn Eagle/Junior Eagle, "The Rev. C.H. Webb Leaves. Troop 62 Has New S.M." Oct. 17, 1915.

15 Brooklyn Eagle/Junior Eagle, "Troop 76 at Camp Midwout," Sept. 3, 1916.

16 Brooklyn Daily Eagle, "Queens County Medical Society Will Co-operate with Scout Camp Plans," June 3, 1923, page 4E.

17 Brooklyn Eagle, "Scouts Study Trees," Nov. 14, 1915, "Our Puzzle Page."

18 Brooklyn Daily Times, "Scouts Spread Xmas Cheers," Dec. 21, 1915, page 9.
19 Daily Standard Union: Brooklyn, "Troop 62, Boy Scouts, Appears in Minstrel Show," May 2, 1916, page 3
20 The Standard Union (Brooklyn), June 19, 1922, page 3.
21 The Chat, "Midwood School Commencement," June 26, 1915.
22 The Chat, "Kings Highway," Nov. 4, 1916.
23 Hartford Courant, "Farmington," July 11, 1916, page 18.
24 Nickerson, Marjorie, "A Long Way Forward," Packer Magazine, Page 131.

CHAPTER 2: THOMASHEFSKY

25 Radensky, Paul. 2010. Chernobil Hasidic Dynasty. YIVO Encyclopedia of Jews in Eastern Europe. https://yivoencyclopedia.org/article.aspx/Chernobil_Hasidic_Dynasty (accessed September 2, 2024).
26 Thomashefsky, Bessie, "Mayn Lebens Geshikhte," National Yiddish Book Center, Amherst (originally, the Warheit Publishing Company, New York, 1916).
27 Michael Tilson Thomas, grandson of Boris and Bessie, in his stage show "The Thomashefskys," says the healer actual wrote individual letters Brukhe/Bessie was having the most difficulty saying smoothly onto crackers, which he then dissolved into milk and had the girl drink that.
28 Thomashefsky, Boris, "Mayn Lebens-Geshikhte," National Yiddish Book Center, Amherst (originally, Trio Press, New York, 1937), page 38.
29 Per Michael Tilson Thomas' stage show on his grandparents, "The Thomashefskys."
30 Buffalo Express, "A Brutal Attack," Feb. 10, 1881, page 3.
31 The New York Times, "A New Jewish Synagogue," Aug. 6, 1876, page 9.
32 The Catholic University of America has Rossa's personal papers, including the account book from his hotel.
33 The following account of Thomashefsky's first production is drawn mainly from Zalman Zylbercweig's "Leksikon Fun Yidishin Teater."
34 Ibid. which itself draws on Thomashefsky, Boris, "Mayn Lebens-Geshikhte," National Yiddish Book Center, Amherst (originally, Trio Press, New York, 1937).
35 Ibid.
36 https://www.germanmarylanders.org/timeline-1/concordia-house; Dolby, George, "Charles Dickens as I Knew Him; The Story of the Reading Tours in Great Britain and America, 1866-1870," New York: Scribner's, 1912, page 219.
37 Thomashefsky, Bessie, "Mayn Lebens Geshikhte," National Yiddish Book Center, Amherst (originally, the Warheit Publishing Company, New York, 1916).
38 Thomashefsky, Bessie, "Mayn Lebens Geshikhte," National Yiddish Book Center, Amherst (originally, the Warheit Publishing Company, New York, 1916).

NOTES

39 Boston Globe, Feb. 5, 1888, page 10.

40 "Shulamis" would be revived in Manhattan in 1982, to mark the centennial of Yiddish theater in America, 100 years since Thomashefsky's first production; the Times' review concluded "it is a must, even with its imperfections, for those with any feeling for this theater, which expressed the aspirations of a public that years back had few other outlets to express their hopes." New York Times, "Operetta: 'Shulamith' by Goldfaden," Oct. 28, 1982, Section C, Page 15

CHAPTER 3: BERNSTEIN

41 Marjorie Smith told me of the connection between Armand Hammer and Sam Smith, Norma's husband, and how when the latter was searching for a new enterprise after the shoe company he worked for in Czechoslovakia suddenly fell under Nazi rule, Hammer found Sam an empty factory in Newmarket in which Sam could produce his own shoes.

42 THE STAR OF 'ROBERTA' POSES FOR HER PORTRAIT: Tamara Drasin, often know simply as "Tamara" sits for a portrait by Norma Jeanne Bernstein which will be hung in the lobby of the New Amsterdam Theater. Date: 1/4/1931 Times Wide World Photos.

43 Simonson, Robert, "ASK PLAYBILL.COM: A Question About Eugene O'Neill's Birthplace, in a Broadway Hotel," Playbill, July 23, 2012: https://playbill.com/article/ask-playbillcom-a-question-about-eugene-oneills-birthplace-in-a-broadway-hotel-com 195890

44 New York Tribune, "Transactions in Realty," May. 17, 1906, page 10.

45 Brooklyn Eagle, "Hopper Gets a $5,000 Job," Jan. 25, 1904, page 1.

46 Lo Cascio, Marco, Carnegie Hall Archives, Isaac Hopper Collection, 2017, page 6.

47 The New York Times, "Lewis A. Abrams, 91, A Retired Justice," April 30, 1963, page 35.

48 Ibid.

49 The Age, "J. Finley Wilson to Broadcast on April 3," April 5, 1930, page 6.

50 New York Herald, "Samuel Mark Left $100,000," Dec. 7, 1922, page 13; The New York Times, "Marx—Samuel," Dec. 1, 1922, page 17.

51 Daily News, "Love Notes to Hindu Noble Spoil Jilted Stars Suit for $150,000," April 24, 1930, page 4.

52 The Gazette, "Hadjiriakos Is Suing Greek in US," June 30, 1925, page 9.

53 The New York Times, "Death Rate So Low He Boosts Rent," Aug. 28, 1921, Section 2, page 1.

54 Daily News, "Love in Ashes, Hot Notes Burn Jeweler in $50,000 Balm Action," Dec. 26, 1930, page 3.

55 The New York Times, "Warfield Warmly Greeted as Shylock," Dec. 22, 1922, Amusements, page 13.

56 Yonkers Statesman, "All Yonkers Communities in the News," June 19, 1923, page 4.

57 Medical Women's Journal, Nov. 1947.

58 Brooklyn Standard Union, "Art Notes," May 17, 1922, page 13.
59 Middletown Times Herald, "Daughter to Victoria Is Dead," June 10, 1923, page 1.
60 Brooklyn Eagle, "Art Notes," Feb. 6, 1921, page 35.
61 Linea, "Solid of Form and Fluid in Movement," by Jerry Weiss, Feb. 9, 2022; Art Students League of New York: https://asllinea.org/george-brdigman-student-drawing/
62 Linea, "The Prismatic Palette: Frank Vincent DuMond and His Students," by Tanya Pohrt, June 9, 2022; Art Students League of New York: https://asllinea.org/prismatic-palette/
63 Per Norma's own statement re: her greatest mentor in The Washington Post, Dec. 21, 1933.
64 The Vaudeville News and New York Star, Jan. 8, 1927, page 2.
65 Springfield Daily Republican, Jan. 5, 1922, page 3.
66 The Berkshire Eagle, "Picks Names for Two Camps at Pontoosuc," Jan. 13, 1922, page 8.

CHAPTER 4: THOMASHEFSKY

67 The Forward, "Stage Killing," Oct. 13, 2006.
68 Newark Evening Star, "Paralyzed for 7 Years, Actress Again to Dance," Dec. 7, 1911, page 1.
69 The Forward, "Stage Killing," Oct. 13, 2006.
70 Newark Evening Star, "Paralyzed for 7 Years, Actress Again to Dance," Dec. 7, 1911, page 1.
71 Newark Evening Star, "Paralyzed for 7 Years, Actress Again to Dance," Dec. 7, 1911, page 1.
72 Daily News, "Friends Mourn for Emma Finkel," April 4, 1929, page 39.

CHAPTER 5: BIRDSEYE

73 Brooklyn Daily Times, "Law Guardians on Long Hike," Nov. 24, 1919, page 3.
74 Brooklyn Daily Times, "Law Guardians on Long Hike," Nov. 24, 1919, page 3.
75 The Boston Globe, "'Opium King' Sentenced," July 4, 1913, page 13.
76 The New York Times, "President Pardons Glickstein," June 17, 1915, page 12.
77 Brooklyn Eagle, "3 Hurt in Auto Upset," Nov. 19, 1915, page 16.
78 Brooklyn Daily Times, "Held for Recklessness," Nov. 27, 1916, page 7.
79 Brooklyn Eagle, "Doctor Was Intoxicated," March 10, 1917.
80 Daily News, "When Justice Triumphed," March 16, 1924, pages 24-25.
81 Daily News, "When Justice Triumphed," March 16, 1924, pages 24-25.
82 Daily News, "When Justice Triumphed," March 16, 1924, pages 24-25.
83 Brooklyn Times Union, "Waiter Grilled in Raizen Case," Dec. 21, 1921, page 3.

NOTES

84 Daily News, "When Justice Triumphed," March 16, 1924, pages 24-25.

CHAPTER 6: THOMASHEFSKY

85 Zalmen Zylbercweig, "Leksikon Fun Yidishin Teater": https://www.museumoffamilyhistory.com/yt/lex/T/thomashefsky-boris.htm

86 The Philadelphia Times, "The Jewish Theatre," Jan. 20, 1889, page 5.

87 Commentary, Blumenson, S.L. "The Golden Age of Thomashefsky; At the Tables Down at Schreiber's," April 1952.

88 Thomashefsky, Bessie, "Mayn Lebens Geshikhte," National Yiddish Book Center, Amherst (originally, the Warheit Publishing Company, New York, 1916).

89 Thomashefsky, Bessie, "Mayn Lebens Geshikhte," National Yiddish Book Center, Amherst (originally, the Warheit Publishing Company, New York, 1916).

90 Thomashefsky, Bessie, "Mayn Lebens Geshikhte," National Yiddish Book Center, Amherst (originally, the Warheit Publishing Company, New York, 1916).

91 Sandrow, Nahma, "Vagabond Stars," Syracuse University Press, New York: 1996, Page 81.

92 Howe, Irving, "World of Our Fathers," New York: Harcourt Brace Jovanovich, 1976, page 470.

93 Sandrow, Nahma, "Vagabond Stars," Syracuse University Press, New York: 1996, Pages 81-82.

94 Forverts, Oct. 19, 1946

95 Forverts, Oct. 19, 1946

96 Commentary, Blumenson, S.L. "The Golden Age of Thomashefsky; At the Tables Down at Schreiber's," April 1952.

97 Per Zalmen Zylbercweig's "Leksikon Fun Yidishn Teater."

98 According to Boris and Bessie's grandson Michael Tilson Thomas's show about them.

99 New York Tribune, "No 'Paradise' for Son of Oscar," April 14, 1908, page 7.

100 Brooklyn Eagle, "Thomashefskys Still Apart, Though Yiddish Tetrazzini's Husband Settles His Suit," Aug. 25, 1923, page 1.

101 Kansas City Times, "A Diva for the East Side," March 16, 1908.

102 American Israelite (Cincinnati), May 21, 1908, page 6.

103 Chicago Tribune, "Notes of Current Amusements," May 28, 1908, Page 10.

104 Brooklyn Eagle, "Thomashefskys Still Apart, Though Yiddish Tetrazzini's Husband Settles His Suit," Aug. 25, 1923, page 1.

105 New York Herald Tribune, "Jealousy Led Nurse to Shoot Doctor and Self," Aug. 14, 1931.

106 Brooklyn Daily Times, "Thomashefsky Asks Retrial; Says He Had No Day in Court," April 17, 1919, page 4.

107 Brooklyn Daily Times, "Thomashefsky Asks Retrial; Says He Had No Day in Court," April 17, 1919, page 4.

108 Brooklyn Eagle, "Seek Thomashefsky," Jan. 30, 1923, page 6.

109 Brooklyn Eagle, "Thomashefskys Still Apart, Though Yiddish Tetrazzini's Husband Settles His Suit," Aug. 25, 1923, page 1.

CHAPTER 7: BERNSTEIN

110 The Boston Globe, "Queen Marie to Pass Birthday in America," Oct. 16, 1926, page 5.

111 The Boston Globe, "Queen Marie to Pass Birthday in America," Oct. 16, 1926, page 5.

112 Oregon Daily Journal, "Berlins Sorry They Did Not Wed on Ocean," Jan. 15, 1926, page 2.

113 All the following personal accounts come from the diary Norma kept in the year 1927.

114 Paper City, "Masterful Existential Sculptor Is Finally Getting His Public Due," Dec. 20, 2022: https://www.papercitymag.com/arts/giacometti-art-exhibition-mfah-houstonshowcases-sculpture/

115 Staedel Museum biography: https://sammlung.staedelmuseum.de/en/person/leger-fern and

116 The York Dispatch, "Many Models Jobless," Aug. 18, 1928, page 16.

117 Women's Art Journal, "Mela Muter: A Poet of Forgotten Things," Urszula Lazowski, Vol. 22, No. 1 (Spring - Summer, 2001), pages 21-26.

118

119 Wohl, Robert, "La revolution ou la mort: Raymond Lefebvre and the Formation of the French Communist Party," Cambridge University Press, published online Dec. 18, 2008.

120 Museo CarmenThyssen Andorra, "An amazing story of Filippo Colarossi," April 9, 2022: https://museucarmenthyssenandorra.ad/en/an-amazing-story-of-filippo-colarossi/

121 https://jolyonfenwick.com/product/oiseau-noir-c-1940/

122 I read a great deal of Norma's two diaries. However, the page on which this anecdote appears is one I did not personally view while in her daughter-in-law's house. However, Marjorie herself once gave a lecture to a local group of intellectuals called the Tuesday Club, in the written remarks for which she quoted verbatim from the entry in question (and of course, Marjorie owns the diaries and can peruse any of their pages at her leisure). This report is my source.

CHAPTER 8: BIRDSEYE-THOMASHEFSKY-BERNSTEIN

123 Brooklyn Standard Union, "Scoutmaster Class Opens at Academy," March 15, 1922, page 10.

124 Brooklyn Daily Times, "District Attorney Dodd Confers," April 2, 1924, page 10. A note: the paper here displays Lewis Birdseye talking to DA Dodd in the photo but mistakenly labels him "E.V. Littauer."

NOTES

125 Brooklyn Standard Union, "Court Is Lenient to Hospital Thief," Dec. 24, 1923, page 12.

126 Brooklyn Standard Union, "Dr. Harris Upholds Vivisection Work," Feb. 23, 1927, page 5.

127 Brooklyn Eagle, "Hospital Kennel Changed, Humane Society Says," Feb. 21, 1927, page 20.

128 Brooklyn Eagle, "Child Patients in Court as Witnesses for Doctor Charged with Dog Cruelty," March 8, 1927, page 1.

129 Brooklyn Daily Times, "Jewish Hospital to Observe 25th Anniversary," Jan. 1, 1928, page 8B/64.

130 Brooklyn Daily Times, "Agar Beats Sherwin in Temple Handball," Dec. 13, 1929, page 17.

131 Times Union, "Ehrlich Advances in Handball Play," Jan. 7, 1930, page 27.

132 The New York Times, "Forbes Watson, Writer, 80, Dead," June 1, 1960, page 39.

133 The Arts, Volume 16, written by Forbes Watson.

134 The New York Sun, "Independents Make Art Howl," Feb. 28, 1930.

135 Brooklyn Daily Times, "Hospital to Issue $300,000 in Bonds," Feb. 27, 1931.

136 Brooklyn Times Union, "Jewish Hospital to Issue Bonds for Greater Service," Feb. 27, 1931, page 11.

137 Daily News, "Nurse Shoots Doctor, Kills Herself," Aug. 13, 1931, page 6. See also the New York Times coverage, which seems to paraphrase poorly the district attorney's statement about Milton and Agnes having dated for five years: "He said the two had been working together in close association for five years." "Nurse Is Shot Dead; Physician Wounded," Aug. 13, 1931.

138 The Cincinnati Post, "Nurse Slain; Physician Shot," Aug. 13, 1931, page 13.

139 New York Herald Tribune, "Jealousy Led Nurse to Shoot Doctor and Self," Aug. 14, 1931.

140 Agnes' possession of Fritz during this period and the photo of her and the dog were both supplied by her grand-niece, Elisa, who told me the Fritz story has long been passed down in the family.

141 The Post-Star, "'Safety First' Advice Given by Psychologist on Planning to Marry," July 3, 1931, page 12.

142 Milton was at 255 Eastern Parkway, Pines at 277. Just a single building separates those two, despite the large numerical gap.

143 All quotes and even those observations without such marks derive from the letters Dr. Thomashefsky sent Norma after he departed the camp.

144 The following quote is from a newspaper article Nov. 30, 1930, in the midst of the success of her first solo exhibit.

145 We know Milton mentions Agnes in camp because when he writes Norma a letter later, in August, he refers to Agnes, as if Norma's quite familiar with this silly assistant already.

146 New York Evening Journal, "Doctor Shot in Love Quarrel," Aug. 13, 1931.

147 Possibly, Agnes wrote "high hell" correctly and Dr. Milton made the mistake himself – for we only have his transcription of Agnes' note to go on and not the original.

148 New York Herald Tribune, "Jealousy Led Nurse to Shoot Doctor and Self," Aug. 14, 1931.

149 Per the New York Evening Journal, a William Randolph Hearst paper from which I have but a scrap without the full article.

150 The New York Sun, "Love Drove Girl to Shoot Doctor," Aug. 13, 1931.

151 The medical examiner pegged the time at 6:40 while the police reported the incident as occurring 10 minutes later.

152 Those details about the shootings that follow come mostly from the police and autopsy reports filed immediately after the incident and accessed by me in the archives some 93 years later.

153 The Standard Union, "Doctor, Dying, Says He Tried to Kill Himself When Shot," Aug. 14, 1931, page 2.

154 New York Evening Journal, "Doctor Shot in Love Quarrel," Aug. 13, 1931.

CHAPTER 9: SMITH

155 The Boston Globe, Oct. 25, 1893, page 8.

156 Brooklyn Times Union, "Rossi and Codos Honored by France," June 1, 1934, page 3.

157 The Binghamton Press, Oct. 27, 1937, page 16.

158 The Boston Globe, "Sam Smith, 84," March 23, 1984.

159 US National Archives: "Brother, Can You Spare a Dime? The 1940 Census: Employment and Income," by Diane Petro, Spring 2012, Vol. 44, No. 1: https://www.archives.gov/publications/prologue/2012/spring/1940.html#:~:text=The%2016th%20decennial%20census%20of,5.2%20percent%20in%20the%201920s.

CHAPTER 9A: 1931

160 The Standard Union, "'Knifer' Barnes Finds Justice Can Move Fast,' May 15, 1931, page 4.

161 Brooklyn Daily Times, "Casey Sees Game As Guest of Vance," Oct. 6, 1928, page 37.

162 Daily News, "Nurse Shoots Doctor, Kills Herself," Aug. 13, 1931, page 6.

163 Daily News, "Nurse Shoots Doctor, Kills Herself," Aug. 13, 1931, page 6.

164 Evening Graphic, "Doctor, Wounded As Nurse Dies, Bares Sinister Bedroom Knifing," Aug. 13, 1931, page 3.

165 Jewish Daily Bulletin, "12 of Hospital Staff Get Service Awards," Feb. 27, 1935, page 3.

166 Brooklyn Daily Times, "Hospital Fire Imperils 335; Damage Slight," Sept. 28, 1924, page 1.

167 Daily News, "Nurse Shoots Doctor, Kills Herself," Aug. 13, 1931, page 6.

NOTES

168 The New York Sun, "Love Drove Girl to Shoot Doctor," Aug. 13, 1931.

169 Evening Graphic, "Doctor, Wounded As Nurse Dies, Bares Sinister Bedroom Knifing," Aug. 13, 1931, page 3.

CHAPTER 10: SMITH

170 The New York Times, "Price Cut Marks Children's Shoes," April 9, 1947.

171 The New York Times, "Price Cut Marks Children's Shoes," April 9, 1947.

172 The Barre Daily Times, "More Work for Officials," Sept. 24, 1927, page 2.

CHAPTER 10A: 1931

173 Brooklyn Daily Times, "Doctor Near Death, Shot by Girl Nurse Ending Life for Love," Aug. 13, 1931, page 1.

174 The Standard Union, "Doctor's Friend Comes Home to Clear Gaps in Tragedy," Aug. 14, 1931, page 1.

175 Brooklyn Daily Eagle, Aug. 13, 1931, Page 1.

176 New York Daily News, Aug. 15, 1931, page 258.

177 The Standard Union (Brooklyn), Aug. 13, 1931, page 4.

178 Times Union (Brooklyn), "Birdseye Denies Girl Shot Doctor," Aug. 18, 1931.

179 Daily News, "Nurse Shoots Doctor, Kills Herself," Aug. 13, 1931, page 6.

180 The Brooklyn Daily Eagle, "Birdseye Retires; Grieved for Daughter," Oct. 30, 1931, page 3.

CHAPTER 11: THOMASHEFSKY-BERNSTEIN-BACHELORS

181 Alton Evening Telegraph, "About New York: Hearts and Lights," Sept. 17, 1931, page 4.

182 Variety, "News from the Dailies," Jan. 5, 1932, page 44.

183 The New York Times, "Victim of Shooting Dies After 5 Years," May 15, 1936.

184 Times Herald (Washington, D.C.), "The Voice of Broadway: Fragments!," Nov. 7, 1934.

185 Times Union, "Madison Hospital to Have New Wing," April 23, 1934, page 16.

186 Brooklyn Daily Eagle, ""69 Graduates at College Hospital," June 2, 1917, page 15.

187 Detective, "L'HÉRITAGE DE L'AMIRAL," Aug. 19, 1937, page 12; Detective, "LE FAUX TESTAMENT de l'Amiral Alexeiff," Nov. 24, 1938, page 7; The New York Times, "Fortune Left by Russian Is Paid Out 'by Mistake,'" Aug. 13, 1937, page 15.

188 Barnard Bulletin, "The Society of Independent Artists," April 8, 1932, page 1.

189 "Tuesday's Club" presentation given by Norma Jeanne's daughter-in-law and New Hampshire state Representative Marjorie Smith based on extensive research.

190 Washington Post, "Young Woman Who Painted 'Ideal Roosevelt' Goes to White House to Meet the President," Dec. 21, 1933.

CHAPTER 12: ELEGY FOR A GENERATION

191 The New York Times, "L.E. Birdseye Dies; A Social Worker," Dec. 25, 1942.

192 The New York Times, "Sues Justice Black for Divorce in Reno," April 23, 1931, page 4.

193 "Lehman Wins; City Vote Beats Dewey," New York Daily News, Nov. 9, 1938, page 1.

194 Pittsburgh Sun-Telegraph, "Mexico's $1,000,000 Mail-Order Divorce Mill – Closed," July 25, 1943.

195 New York Daily News, "Foreign Diplomats Win Divorce Relief," April 2, 1943.

196 New-York Tribune, "Realty Notes," Nov. 20, 1912, page 16.

197 The New York Times, "New Yiddish Theatre Opens," Sept. 25, page 8.

198 The New York Times, "Boris Thomashefsky Is Welcomed Back," Nov. 27, 1930.

199 Star Tribune, "The Voice of Broadway: An East Sider Comes to Broadway!" Sept. 8, 1931, page 8.

200 The Baltimore Sun, "Boris Thomashefsky," Feb. 22, 1932, page 9.

201 The Morning Call (Paterson), "Lodzer Young Men Sponsor Program at High School," Dec. 18, 1937, page 22.

202 https://congressforjewishculture.org/people/4164/Thomashefsky-Boris-Borekh-Arn-Tomashevsky-1866-July-9-1939

203 Daily News, "Boris Thomashefsky, Yiddish Actor, Dies," July 10, 1939, page 11.

204 Brooklyn Eagle, "Thomashefsky, Yiddish Actor, Dies," July 10, 1939, page 11.

205 Brooklyn Eagle, "Thomashefsky, Yiddish Actor, Dies," July 10, 1939, page 11.

206 Daily News, "30,000 Mourners at Thomashefsky Rites," July 12, 1939, page 34.

207 According to Boris' grand-nephew Michael Tilson Thomas.

208 The New York Times, "30,000 Pay Tribute to Thomashefsky," July 12, 1939.

209 Daily News, "30,000 Mourners at Thomashefsky Rites," July 12, 1939, page 34.

210 https://www.museumoffamilyhistory.com/yt/lex/T/thomashefsky-boris.htm

211 The Wisconsin Jewish Chronicle, "Reminiscences," July 21, 1939, page 6.

212 Daily News, "Boris Thomashefsky, Yiddish Actor, Dies," July 10, 1939, page 11.

CHAPTER 12A: 1931

213 Brooklyn Eagle, May 16, 1936, page 11.

214 Brooklyn Daily Eagle, "Dr. Thomashefsky Burial Marked by Impressive Rites," May 18, 1936, page 13.

CHAPTER 13: INHERITANCE

215 The New York Times, "Michael Tilson Thomas Returns to New York, and Mahler," Sept. 13, 2024, page

216 Brooklyn Daily Eagle, "Entrance and Lobby of Turner Towers," Aug. 28, 1927, page 2D (but these sketches were part of an ad and the property of Samuel Turner's development company).

217 Cleveland Plain Dealer, "Asks Comedy Restrained," Sept. 27, 1912, page 1.

About the Author

Gabe Oppenheim has previously authored "The Ghost Perfumer," an inside look at the workings of the fragrance industry (and a small expose of one particular charlatan of that business), as well as "Boxing in Philadelphia," an account of fighters, past and present, of that gritty city.

He lives in a Manhattan building designed by architect Rosario Candela that just turned 100 — an occasion that prompted the research whose ultimate fruit is this entirely true tale, involving at least one family who lived in the very same building once upon a time.

He still owns too much perfume.

Made in United States
Cleveland, OH
12 January 2025